The Open University

AA100
The Arts Past and Present

Book 3
Cultural Encounters

Edited by Richard Danson Brown

This publication forms part of the Open University course AA100 *The Arts Past and Present*. Details of this and other Open University courses can be obtained from the Student Registration and Enquiry Service, The Open University, PO Box 197, Milton Keynes, MK7 6BJ, United Kingdom: tel. +44 (0)870 333 4340, email general-enquiries@open.ac.uk

Alternatively, you may visit the Open University website at http://www.open.ac.uk where you can learn more about the wide range of courses and packs offered at all levels by The Open University.

To purchase a selection of Open University course materials visit http://www.ouw.co.uk, or contact Open University Worldwide, Michael Young Building, Walton Hall, Milton Keynes, MK7 6AA, United Kingdom for a brochure. Tel. +44 (0)1908 858785; fax +44 (0)1908 858787; email ouwenq@open.ac.uk

The Open University
Walton Hall, Milton Keynes
MK7 6AA

First published 2008

Edited and designed by The Open University.

Typeset in India by Alden Prepress Services, Chennai.

Printed in Europe by The Alden Group, Oxfordshire.

ISBN 9780749217020

1.1

The paper used for this book is FSC-certified and totally chlorine-free. FSC (the Forest Stewardship Council) is an international network to promote responsible management of the world's forests.

Contents

Unknown artist, trophy head (portrait of a defeated enemy), Benin, Nigeria, early sixteenth century, bronze, 21 x 13.5 x 15 cm. Musée du Louvre, Paris, 73.1997.14.1.
Photo: © RMN/Jean-Gilles Berizzi.

INTRODUCTION

Richard Danson Brown

You're now halfway through *The Arts Past and Present*. In the first half of the course, you learned essential skills for the study of Arts subjects from books focused on the themes of *Reputation* and *Tradition and Dissent*. You have progressed from looking at the reputations of famous individuals to consider the broader question of the significance of ideas of tradition to a range of topics. As well as learning about these subjects, you've also begun to think about how to structure your ideas systematically, how to plan essays, and how to develop skills of critical analysis and reflection.

In this book, we begin with an approach to studying the Arts in which two or more subjects are brought together to address a single topic. Chapters 1 and 2 focus on the sculptures of Benin, in which Art Historians and Historians have joined forces to consider the art produced in that West African country, and the fascinating story of how some of these works came to be housed in the British Museum. These chapters are an example of interdisciplinary study, where we use perspectives and information derived from different subjects to illuminate a shared topic.

In fact, you've already experienced aspects of this sort of work: the first chapter of the course exemplifies the interdisciplinary basis of Classical Studies, as historical, literary and art historical perspectives are used to examine Cleopatra's reputation; the study of English Christianity in Book 2 considers perspectives from the disciplines of Religious Studies and Art History. The Benin chapters, like the sections on 'The Seaside' you will encounter in Book 4, involve an enquiry into the same subject from a range of disciplinary perspectives. Interdisciplinary study enables us to gain a more detailed, and so more nuanced, sense of the topic under consideration. By studying the Benin sculptures in the light of the history of that country's colonisation, you get both a view of the works themselves and a sense of the ways in which they have been used, interpreted and displayed.

Book 3 is concerned with *Cultural Encounters*. 'Culture' is a notoriously tricky term to define: you might like to check in a dictionary to see the wide range of meanings the term can have. In this book, we're interested in two sorts of culture, the first of which is to examine artworks such as statues, short stories and plays, alongside different kinds of cultural records such as medical texts. The second sense of culture we consider is the expression of the ideas and identities of groups of people. *Cultural Encounters* signals our focus on the ways in which cultures interact, overlap and are transformed by these encounters.

You've already done some work in this area: in Book 2, Chapter 6, we saw how Dmitri Shostakovich used traditional Jewish Klezmer music as a means to express his dissent from the Stalinist regime. Shostakovich was a Russian composer steeped in the Classical tradition, deriving chiefly from the Western European art music of the eighteenth and nineteenth centuries; yet he incorporated melodies and motifs from the rather different tradition of Jewish folk music in works such as the Piano Trio No. 2. The result was a transformation of both the classical and the folk traditions, as Shostakovich blended these disparate ingredients into a new form.

In this book you will see similar examples of artists using motifs, ideas and texts from other cultures. These include Picasso's engagement with African carvings (Chapter 2), and Seamus Heaney's translation of Sophocles' ancient Greek play *Antigone* (Chapter 6). In our study of short stories (Chapter 4), we see the ways in which prose fiction from different continents mediates exchanges between people from different places, classes and perspectives. It's important to stress that these cultural encounters are usually two-way processes of dynamic exchange: medical culture in the Islamic world (discussed in Chapter 5) absorbed Greek medical ideas, which were themselves subtly revised by being translated into a different cultural and linguistic environment.

As the last example suggests, the cultural encounters that interest us are not only artistic ones. Along with medical history, we investigate the bloody encounters between the people of Benin and the British empire at the end of the nineteenth century, and the contemporary issue of how we square liberal ideas of fairness and equality with modern societies. This book addresses questions that are pertinent both to the changing world we live in and to all Arts subjects: what is the relationship between cultural artefacts and colonial history? What happens when objects and texts are translated or transplanted from one culture to another? In summary, Book 3 invites you to consider cultural encounters on a range of levels in what our short story anthology calls *A World of Difference*.

In studying such a theme, we deal with difficult and sometimes distressing materials. The chapters on Benin analyse images of human sacrifice (which are often more revelatory about the preconceptions of colonists than they are about what actually happened in Benin) and racist assertions from an earlier century of the supposed superiority of white Europeans to black Africans. Chapter 3 on 'Cultural Encounters and Cultural Exemptions' explores the philosophical tension between competing and sometimes antithetical models of social good. You may find some of this material disturbing, but an important part of your learning is that you should be able to discuss difficult subjects by using appropriate evidence and forms of argument. You might say that if these things didn't matter to us, then there would be little interest in discussing them at all. We live in an increasingly complex world, where different cultures are continuously overlapping and, at times, conflicting. Our hope is that by studying this material, you will gain an enhanced sense of the complex historical backgrounds to our contemporary world and be able to debate these issues with greater confidence.

1 THE ART OF BENIN: CHANGING RELATIONS BETWEEN EUROPE AND AFRICA I

Kim Woods and Robin Mackie

MATERIALS YOU WILL NEED

- Illustration Book

AIMS

Chapters 1 and 2 will:

- introduce you to the art of Benin, a kingdom in West Africa which was home to a unique tradition of sculpture
- explore the ways that Europeans encountered this art both in the early modern period and in the late nineteenth and twentieth centuries
- discuss how the context in which art is encountered shapes how it is understood
- give you some understanding of the ways that the meaning of artistic objects can undergo translation as they move from one context to another
- consider why the ownership and location of Benin's art remains a controversial issue today
- demonstrate how the two disciplines of Art History and History can both contribute to our understanding of artworks.

INTRODUCTION

In this chapter and the next you will study the cultural encounters between Europe and Benin from the fifteenth to the twentieth century. These encounters take different forms, from the trade in objects in the fifteenth and sixteenth centuries, to the imperial confrontations of the late nineteenth century and the engagement with ideas about art in the twentieth century. You will be asked to think about how such encounters were shaped by contemporary understandings of Benin culture.

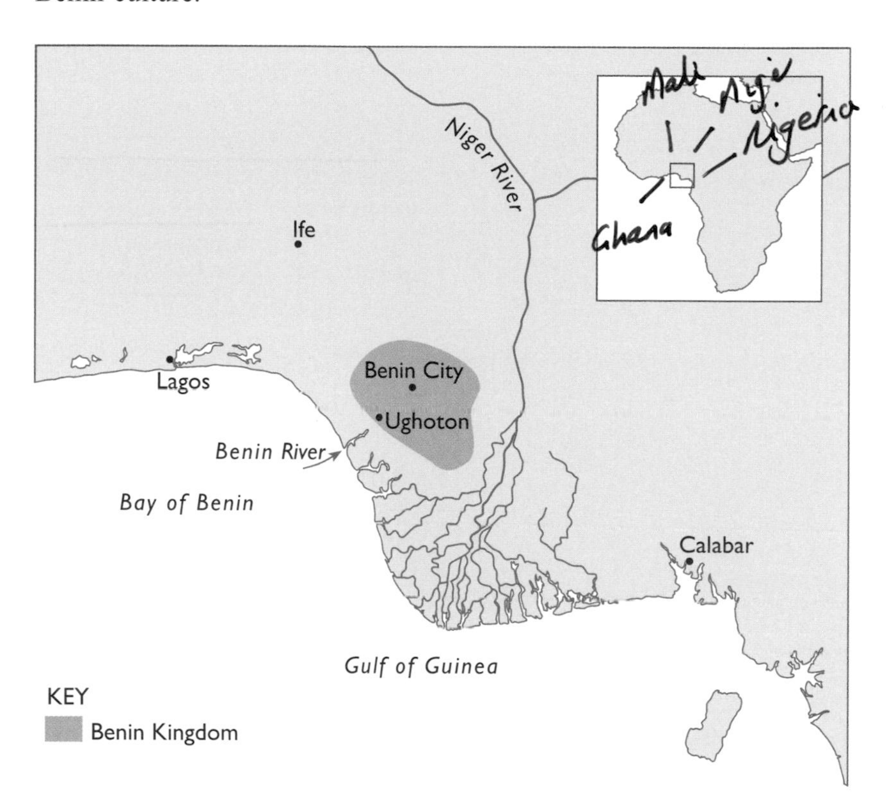

Figure 1.1 Map of the kingdom of Benin.

The powerful West African kingdom of Benin was near the River Niger in what is now Nigeria (see Figure 1.1). It is not to be confused with the present-day republic of Benin, which is 300 miles (480 km) further west. Europeans first became aware of the existence of Benin through Portuguese traders in the fifteenth century. As you will see in Section 1.1, the accounts left behind indicate that the first contacts between Europeans and the people of Benin were based on the exchange of goods, which included ivory carvings.

Direct European contact with Benin was limited during the era of the slave trade (approximately 1650–1850) and little more was learned about the kingdom until British imperial forces conquered it in 1897.

Section 1.2 explores this conquest, and shows how it led to the looting of the artworks of Benin by the British expeditionary force. Chapter 2, Section 2.1, describes how these artworks were transported to Europe, where they were displayed in museums and subject to the scrutiny of scholars and scientists who wondered how people considered to be 'primitive' could produce such sophisticated works of art. The second section of Chapter 2 goes on to show how the 'Benin bronzes' came to constitute an anomaly in the otherwise widespread influence of African 'primitive' art on the modern western avant-garde.

The encounter between British and Benin culture continues. Migration and globalisation have made people more aware of the way that their different histories are interlinked. In this spirit the British Museum now displays its treasures, including the Benin artworks, as an archive of global, intertwined histories kept in trust for all mankind. On the other hand, some African leaders and scholars argue that the looted Benin objects fulfil a different function in Nigeria from that represented in European museums and galleries. In Benin, history has traditionally been recorded through the arts – through songs, art objects and ceremonies – rather than written down. As such, works of art constitute a crucial repository for representing the past and, it is argued, they should be returned to Benin. These continuing debates show how history itself involves a dialogue between ideas about the past and political concerns of the present. At the end of these two chapters, you will be directed to the DVD ROM which will allow you to see some of the works of art produced in Benin in the context of a major exhibition at the Musée du quai Branly in Paris. This will also be an opportunity to hear some different voices in the debate on the significance of Benin art today.

Understanding the cultural encounters of the past and the changing attitudes they reflected and inspired requires you to look closely at the art of Benin and at the specific context of each encounter – the time and place in which European culture and Benin culture came together. We hope these two chapters will help you to understand these processes, which are essential to the disciplines of Art History and History.

1.1 THE ART OF BENIN

Kim Woods

In this section, we will be investigating the making of works of art in brass in the kingdom of Benin in the fifteenth and early sixteenth centuries.

Activity This brass head of a Queen probably dates from the early sixteenth century and was made in Benin (Plate 3.1.1). Examine it carefully. If you have expectations of African art, does this conform to them? Choose three or four words to characterise this sculpture.

Discussion 'Surprising', 'sophisticated' and 'skilled' are the words I chose to characterise this sculpture. It is a 'surprising' sculpture because of its very early date and because it is so unlike the sorts of African art that I am familiar with and which so influenced western artists from the beginning of the twentieth century, such as carved wooden masks (see Section 2.2). I described the head as 'skilled' because, as we shall see, the process of casting brass is technically difficult, and this is quite a complicated piece. It is a 'sophisticated' work partly in a technical sense, notably in the decorative detail of the headdress, and partly because to me the head projects a particular royal image, just as an official photograph of a ruler might do today.

Almost certainly a representation of Queen Idia, the Queen Mother, this sculpture dates from the reign of her son, **Oba** (or King) Esigie, who ruled Benin from *c.*1504 until *c.*1550. Oba Esigie is said to have ordered a representation of his mother in recognition of her services as an advisor and warrior. Her tall pointed headdress and the four scarification marks (deliberate, decorative scarring) above each eyebrow mark her out as female – men in Benin had only three marks above each eyebrow. The lattice work decorating her headdress is of simulated coral beads, and a long fringe of coral beads hangs from the bottom of the headdress, almost like hair. Coral beads are again the material imitated in the necklace, which completely covers the figure's neck. Coral, like brass, was one of the materials appropriated by the royal dynasty in Benin. It is supposed to have been Oba Ewuare, the ruler who built up the kingdom of Benin in the fifteenth century, who began the custom of the ruler wearing coral beads. Hence, the coral beads so obvious in this brass head are an attribute of royalty.

Although in one sense very lifelike, this brass head is idealised. This means that rather than following the uneven contours of a real human face, the shape of the head as a whole is a series of elegant concave and convex curves, the ears are a decorative pattern rather than a real part of the human body, and the regular youthful features betray flattery in what was supposed to be a woman old enough to be the mother of a king. In other words, it is not a portrait. The eyes of the figure are slightly downcast, an attitude probably determined by the gender of the sculpture, for, despite Queen Idia's evident status, the rulers of Benin were resolutely male. The inferior status of women in society is confirmed by the fact that although men could not be sold into slavery outside Benin, women could.

By contrast the eyes in a brass head of an Oba (Plate 3.1.2), again dating from the early sixteenth century, gaze straight ahead at the viewer. Although similar to the sculpture of Queen Idia in its regular features, youthful appearance and smoothly curving forms, and although again decked with royal coral beads imitated in brass, by its outward gaze this head conveys great authority, appropriate for a ruler. It differs from the sculpture of the Queen Mother in having a hole in the top of its head. In later times, intricately carved ivory tusks were inserted into the hole in the top of heads like these, but whether this was the practice at the time this head was made is less certain. Tusks were one of several valuable commodities traded in West Africa. Like brass and coral, ivory was a material associated with royalty, and one tusk from every elephant hunted in Benin was appropriated in tax by the Obas.

In Western Europe, gold has been the metal traditionally regarded as most precious. As European explorers found to their excitement, gold was relatively commonplace on the so-called 'Gold Coast' of West Africa. It was copper, and its alloys bronze and brass, which were most highly prized in Benin and many other West African societies, perhaps for their rarity and lustrous aesthetic qualities (Herbert, 1973).

In these chapters, we sometimes refer to the Benin bronzes. *Bear in mind that, in this context, 'bronze' is a convention used for referring to the artworks rather than a scientific description of their composition. You will see that the sculptures are often referred to in this way in the Readings.*

From at least the fifteenth century until the present day, Benin has been renowned for its production of brass sculpture. Although often called the 'Benin bronzes', these sculptures were not made of bronze but of brass. Bronze is an alloy of copper and tin and sometimes lead; brass is an alloy of copper and zinc. It is extremely difficult to tell the two apart without scientific analysis. In western culture, bronze tends to have a higher status: athletes win bronze rather than brass medals. Nevertheless, scientific analysis has revealed that some very high-status works of sculpture in the western tradition are made not of bronze, but of brass. Among these is one of the most famous works of the fifteenth century in Europe, the second set of doors made *c.*1430–52 by the early fifteenth-century Florentine sculptor Ghiberti (1378–1455) for the Baptistery in Florence (Plate 3.1.3; Krautheimer 1970, Docs. 18, 19, pp. 367–68).

Brass and bronze sculptures were made using the so-called 'lost wax' method of casting. A full-scale model of the sculpture is made in wax over a clay core. The wax image is then coated with the same materials used to make the core. When this outer coating is hard, the wax is melted out through vents, leaving a cavity between the core and the outer coating corresponding to the lost wax image. Pegs are needed to keep the core and outer layer in the correct relationship with each other. This cavity is then filled with molten bronze or brass, which takes on the form of the original wax image. Once the metal has cooled, the outer coating is removed and the surface of the cast can be smoothed and refined using a variety of files and chisels. Although stylistically different from western bronze sculpture, Benin brasses were made in a very similar way.

Zinc, one of the alloys used in the casting process, was relatively readily available in West Africa, but copper was not. There is no consensus about where Benin obtained its copper before the arrival of Europeans. In the fourteenth century there was a legendary copper mine further north in what is now the modern state of Niger (Mauny, 1962) and further deposits to the south within Congo and Angola. Since Benin was not on the caravan routes across the Sahara, it seems unlikely that Europe was the main source of metal supply before the

Portuguese reached the kingdom of Benin. Equally it is clear that Benin craftsmen did not learn how to cast from Western Europeans.

Casting was also a speciality in neighbouring Ife to the west of Benin. The zinc content of many of the Ife sculptures is lower than in Benin, and a few are even made out of pure copper. According to Benin oral history, the second Benin dynasty began at the end of the twelfth century when a new ruler was sought from Ife because of a dispute within Benin. During the following century, Oba Oguola is reputed to have sent to Ife for craftsmen to introduce casting into Benin, though this is now disputed (Inneh, 2007). Brass also played an important ritual role in the enthronement of a new Oba, according to sixteenth-century Portuguese sources (Hodgkin, 1975, pp. 124–5). The new Oba sent an ambassador to the court of the 'Ogane', an overlord usually (though not invariably) identified with the Oni, or ruler, of Ife. From the Ogane the Oba received a brass staff, headdress and cross signifying the legitimacy of his rule.

An Ife head in the British Museum, dating from between the twelfth and fourteenth centuries (Plate 3.1.4), differs from the Benin heads in that it was formerly painted, and red pigment may be seen picking out the pattern on the hat. The holes in the beard area suggest that some other material, perhaps real hair, was attached to make the head look more lifelike. The head is open at the neck and at the top, and shows the extensive scarification that was characteristic of Ife heads. The features of this head are less heavily traced than the Benin heads, and the lifelike qualities even more pronounced, but this and numerous other examples show that the fashioning of heads of important rulers in bronze or brass was certainly a tradition common to both Ife and Benin. Ife bronzes or brasses of this early date were cast using very thin metal which, although a demonstration of the casters' skills, might also have been dictated partially by scarcity of materials.

The dating of the Benin brasses remains a vexed question. Although a very low proportion of zinc may indicate an early date (fifteenth and sixteenth centuries), the metallic composition cannot yet provide a reliable chronology (Junge, 2007). Where fragments of the clay core remain, the technique known as thermo-luminescence can be used to suggest which of the surviving brass works might date from the fifteenth or sixteenth centuries.

The Europeans and Benin

This section will explore the first cultural encounter between European explorers and the kingdom of Benin, which had artistic consequences for Benin in terms of the supply of raw materials for sculpture, new subjects and, crucially, new customers. Although brass sculpture in Benin is exclusively a royal art, ivory carvings were produced for export to Europe, and these hybrid works show clearly how Benin craftsmen adjusted their forms and subject matter to suit their new clients. Establishing the relative status of Benin's culture in the eyes of European explorers is problematic, but it will be argued here that at a time when Benin was a powerful kingdom in Western Africa, European explorers did not necessarily regard Benin as culturally, politically or racially inferior.

The late fifteenth and sixteenth centuries were a period of sea voyages of discovery, most famously Christopher Columbus's discovery of the West Indies and the coast of South America, and Vasco da Gama's discovery of a sea route round Africa to India via the Cape of Good Hope in 1498. Da Gama's voyage was the culmination of the gradual exploration of the west coast of Africa by the Portuguese, primarily in search of new trading opportunities. In 1469 Alfonso V of Portugal granted the monopoly of trade with the **Guinea** coast of Africa (as the western coast of Africa was then called) to Fernão Gomes, and Gomes continued to explore eastwards along the coast, reaching Benin probably by the end of his five-year trade monopoly in 1474. Until this date the kingdom of Benin had remained completely unknown to Europe. Even having discovered Benin, it was some time before the Portuguese ventured beyond the coast into the interior of the country. Initially they were based on the island of São Thomé, which they established as a trading colony. They established an inland trading post briefly at Ughoton, also known as Gwato, probably from the late 1480s, but the climate of the interior was unhealthy for Europeans and by the early sixteenth century the traders retreated back to the coast. João Afonso d'Aveiro, the first European to visit Benin City in 1485–6, was among those who died.

The Portuguese were in West Africa not as conquerors but as traders. Although valuable commodities were to be obtained from Benin, notably pepper and ivory, initially the main objective was the acquisition of slaves to be resold to pay for gold further west along the coast, nicknamed the 'Gold Coast'. Hitherto the gold trade had centred upon the legendary desert caravan centre of Timbuktu. Although later there was a demand for African slaves in the Americas and in Europe itself, initially the Portuguese participated in a slave trade indigenous to Africa.

Activity Read the extracts in Readings 1.1–1.3. These are from contemporary documents concerning Benin.

Reading 1.1 is an account by *Duarte Pacheco Pereira*, one of the Portuguese explorers of the West African coast, written *c*.1505–8 to advise fellow mariners. It may be taken as first-hand evidence of reasonable reliability, which was written not too long after the events it describes.

Reading 1.2 was written by a Portuguese historian, Ruy de Pina (writing 1497–1521), in the reign of John II of Portugal. His position would probably have enabled him to access accurate accounts of the visit of the Benin ambassador to Portugal *c*.1486.

Anthony Ingram's first-hand account of the 1588 English voyage to Benin (Reading 1.3) was recorded by Richard Hakluyt in *The Principal Navigations, Voyages, Traffics and Discoveries of the English Nation* (first published in 1589), an anthology justifying and charting England's contribution to the voyages of discovery.

In each instance, outline in one or two sentences what you think these documents tell us about European contact with the culture and art of Benin.

Discussion From Reading 1.1 we learn that the copper bracelets or brass manillas were used as currency in the slave trade. They could clearly be melted down to make the brass work for which Benin is famous, vastly increasing its supplies of metal. Pereira evidently has a low regard for Benin culture, but he acknowledges that Benin City is 'great'.

The Benin ambassador described by Ruy de Pina in Reading 1.2 was clearly treated with respect. Even bearing in mind the vested interest Portugal had in winning the favour of the Benin political hierarchy, there is little indication here that the ruler of Benin and his officials were regarded, or treated, as savages, though their religious beliefs are once again censured.

In Reading 1.3 Ingram pronounces Benin City to be a great city, where its nobles and factors are addressed in a manner not very different from persons of a comparable social rank in the west. The king's status was evidently supreme and it's of interest that he dealt with the English traders in person.

In none of these extracts do the Europeans comment on the art of Benin. Traders did not necessarily go to Benin City at all. Even for those who did, there is no first-hand evidence from this date that they entered the parts of the palace where the brass sculpture was kept.

There is little evidence that Benin brass work was exported to Europe other than the brass crucifix that Oba Esigie had made to be sent to the king of Portugal as a diplomatic gift. Work in ivory, conversely, seems to have been produced specifically for export. Englishman James Welsh, who visited Benin in 1588, commented on the 'spoons of elephants teeth very curiously wrought with diverse proportions of fowls and beasts made upon them' (Hodgkin, 1975, p. 144). Spoons were not used in Benin, so these were clearly produced specifically for the European market. One example in the British Museum shows a barefoot Portuguese boy in breeches and a cap with a dagger at his belt, balancing on the elegantly curved handle (see Figure 1.2). **Sapi** craftsmen in Sierra Leone also produced ivory spoons, according to Pacheco Pereira, and it was probably these that were imported into Lisbon as early as 1504–5 by the Casa de Guiné, or trading house of Guinea (Ryder, 1964).

The Casa de Guiné 1504–5 trading accounts also mention salt cellars, produced in both Sierra Leone and Benin, and again apparently for export. One double-chambered salt cellar attributed to Benin and now in the British Museum (Plate 3.1.5) has a Portuguese-style sailing ship on its lid, with a person crouching in the crow's nest at the top of the mast. Other carved figures wear tall hats, beards, decorated doublets and flowered stockings – apparently a fanciful version of Portuguese

Figure 1.2 Unknown artist, carved spoon, Benin, Nigeria, sixteenth century, ivory. British Museum, London, Ethno 9184. Photo: © The Trustees of the British Museum.

dress. They also carry European-style swords. The British Museum owns a duplicate of the central section of the salt cellar which differs only slightly in detailing and craftsmanship, so such salt cellars were evidently made in multiple versions. There are at least four other surviving versions of this design (Bassani, 2000, p. 299). It is possible that the two ivory salt cellars that the German painter Albrecht Dürer purchased in the Netherlands in 1521, which he believed to be from Calicut in India, were actually African, as confusion over the original place of manufacture was common (Bassani and Fagg, 1988, p. 53).

The third form of ivory export was carved hunting horns or oliphants, again adapted for European use by designing them to be blown from the end like a clarinet rather than from the side like a flute, which was African practice. One heavily carved example now in the British Museum (Plate 3.1.6) shows a Portuguese boy blowing a side-blown horn, an armillary sphere (an instrument of navigation and symbol of

Figure 1.3 Unknown artist, statuette of a Portuguese soldier holding a musket, Benin, Nigeria, seventeenth century, brass. British Museum, London, Ethno 1928.0112.1. Photo: © The Trustees of the British Museum.

Manuel I of Portugal (1469–1521)) and the coat of arms of Portugal, for which the carver had presumably been supplied with drawings or models.

Salt cellars, oliphants and spoons, whether from Sierra Leone or Benin, are recorded in aristocratic collections from before the mid-sixteenth century. In 1516, in the library of the collector Margaret of Austria, Regent of the Netherlands (1480–1530), were two ivory salt cellars described as having covers with strange animals on the top, which might conceivably have come from Africa (Finot, 1895, p. 236; Eichberger, 2005, p. 325). Vigorous trading relations between the Netherlands and Portugal would explain this import.

In addition to what has sometimes been called a tourist trade in Benin ivories, the impact of the Portuguese explorers was felt in the subject matter of Benin brasses. In the British Museum is a small statuette of a Portuguese soldier posed in the act of firing his musket (Figure 1.3). The half-crouching pose is exceptionally lifelike, and there is much intricate decoration surface detail on the armour. In the early sixteenth century Portuguese soldiers served on occasions as mercenaries for the Oba of Benin, although this statue has been dated provisionally to the seventeenth century. Portuguese figures recur in other Benin art forms, as we shall see.

Discovering Benin sculpture

So far we have established that the art of Benin existed before the arrival of Europeans and that its technology rivals any current in Europe at the time. The cultural encounter between the Portuguese and Benin fuelled the supply of metal in the form of brass manillas, the metal bracelets traditionally used as a medium of exchange, affected the subject matter of Benin brasses, and seems to have prompted the production of works in ivory specifically for export to Europe. In this section we will explore different strategies for uncovering the original meanings and motivations of Benin brasses.

In the absence of written explanations, the main sources of information are oral traditions preserved within Benin and evidence within the works of art themselves. Benin oral tradition suggests that different Obas might inaugurate specific ceremonies for which particular sculptures might be devised, though customs may have changed or been reinterpreted over time.

The remaining altar in the Oba's palace at Benin City includes several brass figures and brass heads of Obas, each with a huge ivory tusk fitted into their open tops. In 1897 there were several compounds with such altars within the Oba's palace, each dedicated to different deceased Obas. This suggests – and oral tradition bears this out – that brass heads were associated with the commemoration of former rulers. It is Oba Ewuare (*c.* 1440–*c.* 1473) whom oral tradition credits with first honouring royal ancestors (Ben-Amos, 1980, p. 20).

According to Benin brass caster Chief Ihama, the heads of defeated kings were cast as trophies and could be sent to subsequent rival rulers as a warning of possible retribution should they defy Benin power (Ben-Amos, 1980, p. 18). Hence some of the Benin brass heads appear to represent not Obas, but enemies.

With the exception of 'Queen Mother' heads, Benin brass heads were invariably open at the top, as indeed were Ife heads, but it is not known whether the practice of placing carved tusks in the heads began as early as the fifteenth or sixteenth century. The earliest such description was written over two centuries later, in 1702, by traveller David Nyendael, though a less precise reference survives from 1651–2 (Ben-Amos, 1980, pp. 32 and 39). Doubts have also been raised about whether the very thin metal of the earlier heads could have supported a carved tusk (Fagg, 1970).

Another genre of art particularly associated with Benin is the mask, made in either bronze or ivory. The eyes of an ivory mask of a 'Queen Mother' in the British Museum are outlined using copper wire and, as with many of the brass heads, two iron bars were formerly set into the forehead (Plate 3.1.7). The headdress is decorated with the tiny heads of Portuguese. The fact that the eyes, nose and mouth are solid, and that this mask is far smaller than an average human face, suggests that it was not intended to be used as a mask. By contrast some Ife bronze masks have eye slits and were clearly meant to be worn. In 1897, the British found this mask along with another very similar one in the Oba's bedchamber (Levenson, 1991, p. 182). This suggests a different significance from the brass heads that were discovered on altars. Carved loops above the ears suggest that a cord was intended to be threaded through them so that the mask could be worn around the neck.

Of the dozens of brass wall plaques from Benin now in the British Museum, one shows exactly how these plaques were originally used (Plate 3.1.8). It depicts four warriors in front of an open palace – evidently the palace of the Oba in Benin City. The palace roof is supported by pillars around which decorated brass plaques are bent and attached by nails. Many of the brass plaques in the British Museum show traces of this usage: nail holes are still visible, and sometimes the bent edges. The subject matter of some of the plaques bears witness to the cultural encounters between Benin and the Portuguese. One shows three warriors carrying bronze manillas, or bracelets, the commodity that the Portuguese traded with Benin (Plate 3.1.9). Another shows a Portuguese mercenary (Plate 3.1.10).

The palace of the Oba evidently included other sculptures in bronze, as shown in some of the bronze plaques. The roof of the Oba's palace in Plate 3.1.8 is decorated with a brass snake, possibly a python. In an engraving in a seventeenth-century book on West Africa by the Dutchman Olfert Dapper (Figure 1.4), the towers on the Oba's palace are surmounted by brass birds, said to bear symbolic associations.

Activity Study Dapper's engraving in Figure 1.4 and then the cast brass leopard in the British Museum (Plate 3.1.11). Look carefully at the dimensions of the leopard given in the plate caption.

1 Comment on the way that the leopard is represented. Think, for example, about any lifelike qualities and about decoration.

2 What do you think this leopard might have signified?

Figure 1.4 Unknown artist, a royal procession in front of the palace, Benin City, sixteenth century, engraving, from Olfert Dapper, *Description de l'Afrique. Avec des cartes & des figures en taille-douce. Traduite du flamand*, Amsterdam, Chez Wolfgang, Waesberge, Boom & van Someren, 1686, British Library, London, 457.e.4, plates 308–9. Photo: © By permission of the British Library.

Discussion

1 The leopard seems to me to be primarily decorative: look at its leaflike ear, for example, and the pattern covering the creature's body. Its upright stance and bared teeth make the creature look impressive.

2 If you look carefully at the Dapper engraving you will see that there are leopards in the foreground of the royal procession. This suggests that leopards were one of the many attributes of kingship in Benin. So the bronze leopard shown in Plate 3.1.11 was probably associated with the Oba in some respect. Note that cast leopards also appear at the entrance to the Oba's palace in Plate 3.1.8.

What cannot be seen in the photograph is that there is a channel in the top of the leopard's head through which water could flow and then stream out of the creature's nostrils. It has been suggested, therefore, that it served as an **aquamanile**, a vessel for pouring water in ritual ceremonies performed by or surrounding the Oba.

A royal art

We have seen that brass, coral and ivory were materials particularly associated with the Oba. Benin chiefs did commission works of art, but these tended to be of wood. At the time that the Portuguese arrived in Benin, metal casters (Igun Eronmwon) and ivory workers (Igbesanmwan) were grouped together in guilds within the royal compound of Benin City. (The brass quarter still exists in Benin City and is now a World Heritage Site.) The export trade in ivory spoons and salt cellars evidently took place with the Oba's consent unless these ivory workers were based in the port of Ughoton, beyond the control of the royal ivory guild.

In Benin, royal control over the arts was far more absolute than anything typical in Western Europe in the same period. In Western Europe in the fifteenth and sixteenth centuries the towns had guilds of craftworkers rather than the courts; those employed by royal or regional courts were usually exempt from guild control. The monopolistic control of raw materials, namely brass, and the heavy royal tax on ivory in Benin had no counterpart in European courts.

In Western Europe royal art was often used for propaganda. Maximilian I, Holy Roman Emperor 1493–1519, and therefore overlord of much of northern Europe excluding France and England, planned a lavish mausoleum intended to contain 40 over-life-size bronze figures of his ancestors (of which 28 were made), together with 100 figures of saints (of which 23 were completed) and 34 busts of Roman emperors which were never installed (Plate 3.1.12). A collaborative project that continued long after Maximilian's death, and eventually relocated from Vienna to Innsbruck, the mausoleum involved specialist bronze founders and sculptors in royal employment in Innsbruck, but also provided temporary employment of some of the best sculptors working in other German cities, with artists including Dürer producing designs.

In Benin the artwork was certainly on a scale and level of quality to compare with art produced under royal patronage in Europe at the time, but because much of it was kept in the palace of the Oba, neither the populace nor the Portuguese traders necessarily had access to it. The extent of the brass working tradition within Benin may have been revealed to Europeans only on the sack of Benin City in 1897.

Summary

Activity

1. How would you characterise the relationship between the Portuguese and the rulers of Benin in the fifteenth and sixteenth centuries?
2. How was the encounter with Western Europeans reflected in the works of art produced in Benin in the fifteenth and sixteenth centuries?

Discussion

1. The relationship between Portugal and Benin during this period was primarily one of trade. Portuguese trade appears to have been welcomed by the Obas of Benin. Although the Portuguese clearly condemned Benin religious practices, the Oba, his officials and the ambassador he sent to Portugal were treated with respect. Admittedly it was in Portuguese interests to maintain good relations with the Oba, but there is some evidence that when Europeans finally arrived at Benin City, they were genuinely impressed with what they saw. There is no evidence of hostilities between Western Europeans and Benin in this period. On the contrary, at one stage the Portuguese were serving as mercenaries for the Oba.
2. Reference to Western Europeans is to be found in bronze plaques, in the borders of the ivory mask of the Queen Mother, and in individual brass figures. The production of ivory work specifically for the European market implies that Benin craftsmanship was admired in Europe, or at the very least was sought for its curiosity value.

The frequent occurrence of Portuguese figures within Benin art, sometimes long after the Portuguese had been superseded by English and then Dutch traders, suggests that the encounter with the Portuguese was highly significant and later associated with a 'golden age' of Benin society (Blackmun, 1988).

Christian values always proved a stumbling block in the encounters between Western Europeans and non-Christian cultures. Christian missionaries were despatched to Benin in 1514 and the Oba Esigie's son Orhogbua was among the few who were baptised as Christians (Blake, 1942, Docs 29 and 36). The high death rate among the missionaries was among the causes of their ultimate failure, despite spasmodically renewed efforts. Neither conversion nor conquest was the primary motive behind western contacts with Benin: it was trade.

It would be anachronistic to propose that relations between Benin and the Europeans were grounded in modern ideas of equality, but they were certainly characterised by a notable absence of hostility. However much at variance the two cultures might have been, successful trading relations demanded a degree of mutual regard, and it is this mutual regard that sixteenth-century Benin art appears to reveal. As you will see, the situation altered radically by the end of the nineteenth century.

1.2 THE CONQUEST OF BENIN IN THE 1890s

Robin Mackie

In 1897 Benin was conquered by the British. This was not only a traumatic break in the history of Benin, which brought to a sudden end the independence of the centuries-old kingdom; it was also a key 'cultural encounter' in the discovery of Benin art by Europeans. This section will examine the occupation and why it happened. It will also focus on how we know about the occupation. Earlier in the course you have looked at the nature of evidence about the past and about how it has been used by historians. The occupation of Benin raises interesting questions about the relationship between the two: how the evidence available shapes how history is written.

The British occupation of Benin

Let us start with the occupation. In 1885, a British protectorate was declared over the coast of Nigeria; and in 1892, in the first official visit for thirty years, Captain Henry Gallwey, the new Vice-Consul for the Benin River section of the protectorate, visited Benin and signed a treaty with the Oba bringing Benin too under British protection. From the British perspective, however, this treaty proved to be a disappointment. In particular, trade continued to be a royal monopoly in Benin and subject to tight controls. By 1896, frustrated British traders and officials were openly calling for armed intervention, although in this the Foreign Office remained reluctant. On 2 January 1897, despite the absence of permission from London, the Acting Consul-General of the protectorate, James Phillips, set off for Benin, accompanied by a large if only lightly armed party. News of the approaching expedition caused alarm in Benin and messengers were sent to try to halt it. Phillips, however, insisted on continuing and, on 4 January, at less than a day's march from Benin City, his party was ambushed and most, including Phillips, were killed.

The British response was swift. A naval force was rapidly assembled to transport troops to the area, and an advance on Benin City began on 10 February. Eight days later, after fierce resistance, the town was captured, although the Oba and many of his chiefs escaped. In the subsequent days the town was destroyed by fire and during the next months the British extended their control. In August, the Oba surrendered and after a brief 'trial' was deposed, while two of his chiefs were executed. When the Oba failed to co-operate with the new British rulers, he was deported to Calabar on the coast. By 1899, after the capture, 'trial' and execution of further Benin chiefs, the country was firmly under British control (Ryder, 1969; Igbafe, 1970; Igbafe, 1979).

The two preceding paragraphs give a brief account of how Benin came to be absorbed into the British empire. Such narrative accounts are what we often look for from historians; they provide essential contextual information. But how do we know this is what really happened?

At the end of the paragraphs, I included references to the accounts I used to research the subject – the major *secondary works* on this topic. All three works are heavy with footnotes citing texts written at the time – the *primary sources* to which all subsequent accounts return. To a very great extent, therefore, the short answer is that we know what happened because of the records left by participants. We have a surprising amount of written material for the conquest of Benin. In addition to his official reports, Captain Gallwey gave a speech about Benin to the Royal Geographical Society which was later published. For the events of 1897, we have British government documents, a book by one of the two white men who survived the ambush (Boisragon, 1897), another by the intelligence officer of the invasion force (Bacon, 1897), and an eye-witness account by a doctor (Roth, 1972 [1903]). News travelled fast in a world recently linked by telegraphs: the *Times* carried a first report on the 'Massacre of a British Expedition in West Africa' on 11 January, seven days after the ambush; the first journalists arrived in Benin on 21 February, just three days after the capture of the city. These included

> Seppings Wright of the *Illustrated London News*, who was the foremost war correspondent of the day [...] He came with a great train of servants and baggage, scattering his largesse on the officers of the expedition – cigars and a ham to Lieutenant Haggard in whose tent he slept at the Crossroads Camp, and champagne and deck-chairs to those at Benin.
>
> (Home, 1982, p. 90)

Figure 1.5 and Plate 3.1.13 accompanied his report on the capture of the city. As will be explored in the next chapter, there was a ready market for accounts of adventure from Africa.

We have, therefore, no shortage of first-hand reports on the events surrounding the British conquest of Benin. As I hope you will have spotted, however, all the sources listed were written by British participants. Benin was an oral society and there are no accounts written at the time by the people of Benin. Nor is this simply a story of two sides. The British expeditions used large numbers of African carriers, and most of the soldiers involved in the conquest of Benin were also African. The written accounts all come from a small and quite atypical group of witnesses.

However, the written accounts were not the only way that the events were remembered. As in many oral societies, oral records were important in Benin society: 'the recounting of history has been a highly valued form of intellectual activity [...] The transmission of oral tradition in Benin is done through story-telling' (Layiwola, 2007, p. 84). A first written history of Benin based on such sources was published as early as 1934 (Egharevba, 1960 [1934]). Oral narratives, many of them relating to the royal house, and often supported by mnemonic devices – songs, proverbs, or visual artefacts which prompt memories and act as reference points – are an important source of information about Benin's past. The events of 1897 were also integrated into oral narratives, which are widely remembered in Benin to this day.

Such narratives, however, work in a different way from historical documents. Whereas a written source preserves the words used at the time, so that the problem for the historian is to understand the document in its contemporary context, in memories and oral

Figure 1.5 G. Montbard, 'In Quest of Water', drawing, 42 x 29 cm, reproduced in the *Illustrated London News* supplement, 27 March 1897. The caption reads: 'On the morning after the occupation of Benin three hundred water-carriers, with the seamen and marines of the "Theseus" and two companies of Houssas, went in search of water. After descending a gorge with banks two hundred feet high, they reached the Ikpobar Creek.'

traditions 'the past provides a subject in which the present continually interacts in order to produce a new consciousness' (Layiwola, 2007, p. 83). Oral tradition does not preserve the sources in an independent form. Instead, it provides a continually developing interpretation which helps explain past events.

It would be easy to see this distinction as the same as that between history and myth which you encountered when exploring Stalin's reputation earlier in the course. Myth, you will recall, was defined as a 'popular idea concerning historical phenomena', whereas history is 'an account of past events based upon the interpretation of all the available evidence' (see the introduction to Chapter 5 in Book 1). In fact, oral tradition has made a major contribution to African history. Later in this section we will look at one example of how it has contributed to our understanding of the conquest of Benin. The section, however, focuses on a different issue. What happens if 'all the available evidence' from the period was written by one party? Does the fact that all the documentary accounts of the conquest of Benin come from British records mean that any history based on them will be irretrievably biased? Can historians write 'history' when the evidence is tainted in this way?

1892: Gallwey in Benin

As I am sure you realise, the suggestion that those who write the records might be able to impose their version of events on the way history is written is an alarming one. In order to investigate this question further, let's look in more detail at some of the sources used to write the history of the occupation of Benin.

Activity Read Henry Gallwey's 'Report on visit to Ubini (Benin City) the capital of the Benin country' (Reading 1.4). In Book 2, Chapter 5 you were introduced to a set of standard questions one might apply to any historical source. Now apply them to this text.

1 Who wrote it?
2 Who was the intended audience?
3 When was it written?
4 What type of document is it (public, private, official, published, etc.)?
5 What is its historical context?
6 Do you have comments on specific points in the text?

Discussion

1 The document was written by Henry Gallwey, Deputy Commissioner and Vice-Consul.
2 The document is addressed to Gallwey's superior, the Consul-General Claude Macdonald. Macdonald forwarded it to London (as Gallwey presumably knew he might).
3 It was written on 30 March 1892, immediately after Gallwey's return to his Vice-Consulate.

4 The document is an internal government document.

5 The document can easily be fitted into the narrative account of the conquest of Benin. This is the official report of Henry Gallwey's visit and how he obtained the treaty (see Figure 1.6). In one sense it is a factual account – he tells us what happened, when, and how long it took. At the same time, he provides his readers with some impressions of Benin.

6 There are a number of points one might make. I will comment later on how Gallwey obtained the treaty. What struck me is how Gallwey talks about the religious beliefs of the people of Benin, for which he uses the word **fetish**. When Gallwey first mentions them, it is simply as an amusing (and perhaps convenient?) hiccup in the negotiations, but later 'fetish' is presented as the cause of 'Terror' and identified as a barrier to change.

Figure 1.6 Henry L. Gallwey with several Edo chiefs during his visit to Benin City, Nigeria, 1892. Photographed by J. H. Swainson. National Museum of African Art, Smithsonian Institution, Washington D.C., Eliot Elisofon Photographic Archives (Macdonald Calabar photographs, ca. 1895), EEPA 1996-0019-0135. Photo: Smithsonian Institution.

Edo and **Bini** are both used to describe the people of Benin. Edo refers to a language group in southern Nigeria, which includes the people of Benin as well as other peoples. Bini is the name of a subgroup of the Edo-language group and is often used to describe the people of the kingdom of Benin.

Having analysed the document, we can now ask how useful it is as an account of Gallwey's journey to Benin and examine it for information on Benin itself. Is it reliable? How can we know?

Obviously it would be very helpful if we could compare Gallwey's account with another, say from a Bini perspective. Although, as will be explored below, Bini oral traditions can give us insights into events surrounding the British conquest, they do not allow us to check the details of Gallwey's report. All too often in studying history, we cannot corroborate the source by comparing it with others and must look for evidence within the document itself. One way we might do this is to start from our answers above. Knowing what we do of the text, its author, audience and context, we might ask: was Gallwey likely to tell the truth? Is it probable that he could remember the events accurately? How much was he likely to have known about his subject matter?

Thinking about the value of the document in this way might lead to the following assessment:

- Gallwey was writing to his superiors and, if he had invented the whole episode, it would surely have cost him his job and his reputation. We might imagine him exaggerating his role or presenting it in a good light, perhaps even missing out some bits, but it would have been risky for him to stray too far from the truth.
- The account was written very shortly after the events. There is no reason why Gallwey should not remember them accurately, although a longer timespan might have given him the opportunity to place the events in a broader context.
- We might expect Gallwey to be most accurate when he writes about events he experienced personally.

On this basis we might conclude that Gallwey is likely to be fairly accurate when he recounts what he and his companions did. Where he is less likely to be reliable is when he writes about Benin – consider, for example, the paragraph starting 'At present the whole Benin country is, and has been for hundreds of years, steeped in Fetish'. How did he know this? It is clear from the account that Gallwey did not speak the local language and, indeed, relied chiefly on his own servant for communication. There was enormous room for misunderstanding in this cultural encounter.

This approach does allow us to make some progress in assessing the significance of the document. It suggests that we can accept Gallwey's report as a fairly accurate account, from a British perspective, of the events which led to the first treaty between Britain and Benin. The document is significant because it tells us when the treaty was signed and how this happened, although the fact that we only know this from one side is limiting. The document also provides some information about Benin, but here the limitations of the source loom larger. Note, too, that our assessment is not unqualified. It is linked to the questions asked: it is not that the document is or is not reliable, but that it is more likely to provide accurate answers to some questions rather than to others. Furthermore, there might be all sorts of factors which we do not know at present and which, if they emerged, would make us reassess our judgements.

Is this all that the document tells us? Historians have, in fact, read rather more in it, using it to reach some conclusions that Gallwey does not spell out. Look again at Gallwey's account of how he obtained the treaty. Although Gallwey did not know what was being discussed in the royal house, and is at pains to suggest that the Oba was happy with the treaty, there are hints that the Oba felt he was acting under duress. On the one hand, he was reluctant to meet Gallwey; on the other, he clearly felt he could not afford to let him depart without a meeting. When, on the third day, after many delays, he finally grants Gallwey an audience, he avoids touching the pen personally. We cannot know why this was so, but it does suggest some anxiety, as does his insistence that there should be no 'war palavers'. As A.F.C. Ryder concludes: 'the menace always implicit in Gallwey's attitude doubtless contributed to this nervous anxiety; failure to conclude a treaty would clearly entail unspecified unpleasantness' (1969, p. 270).

Gallwey left a second account of his trip to Benin, which we have reproduced as Reading 1.5, 'Journeys in the Benin country'. It is not essential that you read this, but it complements well his official report. This account was written slightly longer after the events, but still close to them. The audience was also different – the paper was first delivered to the Royal Geographical Society – and Gallwey tailored it accordingly. As a result, we must assess it differently. The extract (and this is indeed true of the whole document) focuses rather less on what Gallwey did (the information I suggested was most likely to be reliable) and rather more on Benin (where inaccuracies are more probable). Nevertheless, this is a learned audience and Gallwey is careful to emphasise what he *saw*. Does this mean it is more factual? Gallwey may still have misinterpreted what he was observing, and he offers opinions mixed in with the text. The document may tell us more about Benin than the first source, but we cannot be sure it is accurate.

1897: the 'punitive expedition'

Activity I would now like to jump forward five years and look at a document written in the aftermath of the British conquest. Read the extract from *Benin. The City of Blood* (Reading 1.6) and compare what its author, Commander Reginald Bacon, has to say about Benin with Gallwey's accounts.

Discussion I hope you started by analysing the document. If so, you will have noted that it was written by a participant shortly after the events, and that it was written for a very broad audience – the book-reading public. We might go on to question its accuracy, since it contains many judgements on Benin. Indeed, the contrast between the claim made in the Preface (quoted in the marginal note) and the extract selected is jarring: perhaps unfairly so, since most of Bacon's book is a long and factual account of the expedition, for which we can assume his knowledge was precise. But in this extract, in which he describes Benin City, the narrative is far from 'bald', and justifies the sensationalist title chosen for the book.

In places, the text contrasts sharply with the two extracts from Gallwey's documents. Consider, in particular, the issue of human sacrifice: this certainly figures in Gallwey's accounts and he does describe Benin as a 'city of skulls'. Human sacrifice, however, dominates Bacon's narrative. Nor is this just a question of style: whereas Gallwey saw 'no less than four crucified victims', Bacon implies that they were beyond counting. Gallwey was happy to sleep in the house provided and, indeed, describes it as 'very decent'; Bacon was 'practically sick' from the smell and his party slept in the open.

Figure 1.7 was printed in the chapter from which the extract was taken. Like Figure 1.5, it is a drawing and has clearly been dramatised. Yet photographs of very similar scenes also exist; an example is given in Figure 1.8. Human sacrifice undoubtedly occurred in Benin and one method used was described by British visitors as 'crucifixion'. Many societies in West Africa did practise human sacrifice and it figured prominently in European descriptions of such societies. For European visitors, human sacrifice was a deeply disturbing part of their encounter with West African cultures.

Yet, as we have seen, we need to interpret historical documents carefully, and this also applies to travellers' reports of human sacrifice, whether they are descriptions, drawings, or even photographs. As we know, both Gallwey and Bacon saw what they believed to be human sacrifices (corpses attached to crucifixion trees) or its results (the bodies strewn on the fields outside Benin City, blood on altars), but they did not necessarily fully understand what they were observing. They suggest different reasons for the corpses on the field before Benin, and, as the caption to Figure 1.8 shows, there were different ways of interpreting 'crucifixion'. The reasons for killing slaves or captives varied widely between West African societies (Law, 1985). European visitors often found it difficult to distinguish ritual killing for religious reasons or out of respect for ancestors, from capital punishment (which was, of course, widely used in their own countries) or, indeed, a desire not 'to contaminate the sacred earth with the bodies of criminals' (Isichei, 1978, p. 470; Wilks, 1988).

We can gain insights into the role of human sacrifice in Benin from oral traditions. These reveal that human sacrifice was linked to certain annual rituals surrounding the royal court. Drawing on such sources, historian Philip Igbafe argues that Bacon was certainly wrong about the *reasons* for human sacrifice. It was allowed only in special circumstances: 'the threat of a national calamity and the desire to appease the gods to avert the danger was one condition for making human sacrifices in the Old Benin kingdom. Other circumstances were comparatively few' (Igbafe, 1979, pp. 70–1). Thus, many sacrifices

Figure 1.7 W.H. Overend, 'The Crucifixion Tree', drawing, 15.5 x 9.5 cm, reproduced in Bacon (1897), p. 93.

were made in 1897 to stop the British advance (Egharevba, 1960 [1934], p. 52). One explanation for the contrast between Gallwey's and Bacon's reports is that the circumstances were different. When Gallwey visited Benin he represented a threat; Bacon arrived during the kingdom's terminal crisis.

Figure 1.8 Crucifixion tree, 1897. Photographed by Major N. Burrows. National Army Museum, London, Neg. No. 55546. Photo: Courtesy of the Council of the National Army Museum, London.

But to understand Bacon's account, we also need to investigate the British context. In his emphasis on human sacrifice, Bacon fits into a pattern of writing about Benin. Looking back, another visitor commented:

> Benin in the old days was more than squalid, it was gruesome. What the exact influence of the place was, or rather what the cause was of the influence felt, I cannot say, but the fact remains that no one who went there in the old days came away without being impressed. [...] the sense of the spirit of a long past of atrocities, which if not supernatural, were at any rate unnatural to a degree which is indescribable.
>
> (Quoted in Roth, 1972 [1903], p. vi)

To understand why Benin came to be seen in this way, we need to understand the wider context of the British conquest of what is now Nigeria.

For centuries, European relations with West Africa were dominated by the slave trade. Only with its gradual suppression in the middle of the nineteenth century did European traders begin to push inland, looking for what were described as 'legitimate products' and, in particular, palm oil. They were followed by missionaries and officers of the imperial powers, with Britain dominant in the Niger delta. The conquest of Benin was part of a process of British aggression throughout southern Nigeria which led to many small wars (Isichei, 1983). Some historians have highlighted economic reasons for British expansion and it is true that British traders were eager to see British power used to improve their access to the interior (Ikime, 1985). But merchants had little influence on government policy and London was often anxious to delay action on cost grounds. As important were often the actions of local officials: it is significant that Phillips set off for Benin without waiting for instructions. Men such as Gallwey and Phillips had contacts with merchants, but were hardly their agents – as soldiers and government officials they were often contemptuous of 'trade'.

More significant was the way in which Europeans thought about change in Africa. In their eyes, commerce and Christianity were closely linked; both were essential for the 'civilisation' of Africa. African societies, like others regarded as primitive, were seen as changeless or regressing (you can find this in the texts by both Gallwey and Bacon) and only western contact would lead to progress. Treaties, such as that with Benin, followed a standard format which included clauses opening acccss to both trade and Christianity. Resistance to merchants or missionaries was ascribed to the continued power of ancient superstitions. Thus, in forwarding Gallwey's report to London, Consul-General Macdonald claimed that 'trade, commerce and civilisation, however, are paralised [*sic*] by the form of fetish government which unfortunately prevails throughout the kingdom' and hoped that the treaty would overcome these barriers (quoted in Igbafe, 1979, p. 44).

In his report, Gallwey too was optimistic that 'the Treaty may be the foundation of a new order of things'. What changed expectations was the ambush of Phillips's expedition. Phillips set off determined to open Benin to trade; his ambush led to what was termed a 'punitive expedition'. When the Oba and his chiefs were put on trial, it was for 'the massacre of the unarmed white men of Phillips' peaceful expedition' (Roth, 1972 [1903], Appendix II, p. xiv). It was resistance to the British advance that provoked the invasion, not the practice of human sacrifice. Yet, in British eyes, the two were inextricably linked. Benin had failed to open itself to Britain and civilisation, and no clearer symbol of this existed than the continued prevalence of human sacrifice. When Bacon and his colleagues arrived in Benin City they expected to find certain things, and it was easy to interpret what they found in terms of their expectations.

The fire that destroyed the town in the next days changed it forever. Curiously, however, within the British records there is some evidence that sheds a rather different light on the last months of Benin independence.

Activity Read the 'Trial of Chief Ologbosheri' (Reading 1.7). What does this source tell us about the causes of Benin resistance?

Discussion Analysing the document throws up some unusual answers. The extracts are taken from the second Benin trial in 1899, when Ologbose (see Figure 1.9), who had recently been captured, was found guilty of organising the ambush. Although both statements are by natives of Benin, the texts must have been translated and written by someone else, and we cannot know how closely they correspond to what was said even though they were written at the time. Who was the audience? We might conclude that it was the British officers who, as the marginal note makes clear, ran the trial. Nevertheless, the extracts do give us a Bini voice, even if it is one that reaches us through British records and is likely to have been significantly affected by the context of its creation.

Contemporary British renditions of Benin names and titles are often different from the ways the names are written today. We have left the spellings in the Readings and in the figure caption as they are in the original. However, Ologbosheri is now written Ologbose; Omaregegboma and Idiaie are now written as Omorogboma and Idiaghe.

The texts create a confusing picture of messengers passing back and forth along the pathway between Ughoton and Benin City, and of contradictory instructions. Who gave the order to attack the British (if anyone did) is unclear. Yet, even if the leaders of Benin misjudged the intentions of Phillips and his colleagues, they correctly understood that the British expedition threatened their independence. The issue was how best to respond to this threat. Perhaps you noticed that there is no mention of gods or priests – nor is there elsewhere in the witness statements. Resistance was decided at a mass meeting of the Benin chiefs and not by a 'powerful theocracy of fetish priests'.

Looting the art of Benin

Activity At the beginning of this section, I asked how well we can write history when we rely so heavily on written documents written by one party. On the basis of the discussion of sources in this section, what answers can be given?

Discussion There are perhaps five points to make:

- It is essential to read and analyse sources carefully. To evaluate the significance of a document we need to think about the author, the audience and the context.
- A careful analysis of sources may reveal more information than was intended. Historians sometimes talk of 'reading against the grain' of the source. As well as considering what the author is telling us, we need to think what the source unintentionally tells us about the author's assumptions, what the source does not say, etc.
- The sources available may be more varied than might appear at first sight. Comparisons may reveal interesting differences between apparently similar texts. In this case, the British sources do in fact contain some evidence from Benin, even if we need to approach it with care.

Figure 1.9 Chief Ologbosheri after his capture, 1899. Unknown photographer. British Museum, London, Coll. Major Smartt, Archive AF-CA-79–15. Photo: © The Trustees of the British Museum.

- Sources need to be placed in a broader picture. Where possible, British documents need to be compared to Bini sources, or seen in the context of an expanding empire.
- Historians should not ignore evidence that comes from non-standard sources. In the case of Africa, oral sources and traditions have been used extensively to add to our knowledge of the past.

Is this enough to allay our concerns about a biased history? There is no doubt that a careful reading of the evidence will make an enormous difference. Nor should we assume that there is no common ground between different types of history: recent historians of Africa are keen to engage with popular accounts of the past. Nevertheless, I think we cannot entirely ignore this concern. The absence of contemporary texts from Benin remains a disadvantage. Historians of Africa have explored many ways to overcome such hurdles, but, for me, the witness statements made all too plain how frustratingly distant many aspects of Benin's past remain. Nor is this just an issue in Africa. Everywhere, those who leave records have a major impact on how history is written.

Activity Finally, what of the Benin bronzes? Look through the texts by Gallwey and Bacon again. What do they have to say about artworks?

Discussion Gallwey barely mentions it. In his paper for the Royal Geographical Society, he notes that Benin has a reputation for metal work, although he has not seen any himself. There is more in Bacon, however. He refers to tusks and bronze heads on the altars, brass work on the palaver and king's houses, and in the storehouse. He suggests it is left over from the past: the bronzes are discovered 'buried in the dirt of ages', the carved ivory is ancient, and there is no local industry, save a blacksmith's shop.

Activity Look now at Plate 3.1.14. What does this photograph tell us about the British capture of artworks?

Discussion Historical images, like written sources, need careful analysis. We need to think about context and composition: when and where the photos were taken, and what they are meant to show. This photograph has clearly been carefully arranged with the artefacts in the foreground and the men posing in the centre. In the background we can see what seems to be an important Benin building: perhaps the palaver house described by Bacon with its serpent. The captured artefacts are displayed as booty. One does not know who the intended audience is, but the whole effect suggests triumph.

As will be explored in the next chapter, the discovery of the Benin bronzes took Europeans by surprise. The extract from Bacon shows that they were discovered all over the city, but no attempt was made to record where. Seen as 'the only things of value' in the city, they were collected together (see Figure 1.10) and distributed: officers received trophies according to their rank, and items deemed of value were taken back and sold in Britain to pay for the expedition (Home, 1982, pp. 100–1).

What became of the art of Benin is explored in the next chapter. Yet we can note here that the circumstances of their seizure meant that they were immediately ripped from their locations, with the result that much information about their context was lost forever (Plankensteiner, 2007, p. 28). For Bacon and his colleagues, they were simply war booty to be removed from a city which they saw as the epitome of

Figure 1.10 Interior of the royal palace after the fire, Benin City, Nigeria, 1897. Unknown photograper. Pitt Rivers Museum, Oxford, PRM 1998.208.15.11. Photo: © Pitt Rivers Museum, University of Oxford. The photograph is inscribed on the back: 'Interior of the royal palace, destroyed in a fire, bronzes on the ground. Capt. C.H.P. Carter 42nd, E.P. Hill.'

barbarity. How the Benin bronzes were captured, and how Benin was imagined, are crucial to understanding their reception in Europe.

REFERENCES

Bacon, R.H. (1897) *Benin. The City of Blood*, London, Edward Arnold.

Bassani, E. (2000) *African Art and Artifacts in European Collections 1400–1800*, ed. M. McLeod, London, British Museum.

Bassani, E. and Fagg, W.B. (1988) *Africa and the Renaissance: Art in Ivory*, New York, Center for African Art, Prestel Verlag (exhibition catalogue).

Ben-Amos, P. (1980) *The Art of Benin*, London, Thames and Hudson.

Blackmun, B.W. (1988) 'From trader to priest in two hundred years: the transformation of a foreign figure on Benin ivories', *Art Journal*, vol. 47, no. 2, pp. 128–38.

Blake, J.W. (trans. and ed.) (1942) *Europeans in West Africa 1450–1560*, London, The Hakluyt Society.

Boisragon, A. (1897) *The Benin Massacre*, London, Methuen.

Egharevba, J.U. (1960 [1934]) *A Short History of Benin* (3rd edn), Ibadan, Ibadan University Press.

Eichberger, D. (2005) *Women of Distinction: Margaret of York, Margaret of Austria*, Mechelen, Brepols (exhibition catalogue).

Fagg, W. (1970) *Divine Kingship*, London, British Museum (exhibition catalogue).

Finot, J. (1895) Inventaire sommaire des archives départmentales antérieurs à 1790, Nord, archives civiles, sér. B, Chambre des comptes de Lille, nos 3390–65, vol. 8.

Herbert, E.W. (1973) 'Aspects of the use of copper in pre-colonial West Africa', *Journal of African History*, vol. 14, no. 2, pp. 179–94.

Hodgkin, T. (1975) *Nigerian Perspectives* (2nd edn), Oxford, Oxford University Press.

Home, R. (1982) *City of Blood Revisited*, London, Rex Collins.

Igbafe, P.A. (1970) 'The fall of Benin: a reassessment', *Journal of African History*, vol. 11, no. 3, pp. 385–400.

Igbafe, P.A. (1979) *Benin under British Administration. The Impact of Colonial Rule on an African Kingdom, 1897–1938*, London, Longman.

Ikime, O. (1985) 'Nigerian reaction to the imposition of British colonial rule, 1885–1918' in S. Forster, W.J. Mommsen and R. Robinson (eds) *Bismarck, Europe and Africa. The Berlin Africa Conference 1884–1885 and the Onset of Partition*, London: German Historical Institute and Oxford University Press.

Inneh, D. (2007) 'The guilds working for the palace' in Plankensteiner, 2007.

Isichei, E. (1978) 'The quest for social reform in the context of traditional religion: a neglected theme of West African history', *African Affairs*, vol. 77, pp. 463–78.

Isichei, E. (1983) *A History of Nigeria*, London, Longman.

Junge, P. (2007), 'Age determination of commemorative heads: the example of the Berlin collection' in Plankensteiner, 2007.

Krautheimer, R. (1970) *Lorenzo Ghiberti*, 2 vols (text and plates), Princeton, Princeton University Press.

Law, R. (1985) 'Human sacrifice in pre-colonial West Africa', *African Affairs*, vol. 84, no. 334, pp. 53–87.

Layiwola, A. (2007) 'The Benin Massacre: memories and experiences' in Plankensteiner, 2007.

Levenson, J.A. (1991) *Circa 1492: Art in the Age of Exploration*, Washington, National Gallery of Art (exhibition catalogue).

Mauny, R. (1962) 'A possible source of copper for the oldest brass heads of Ife', *Journal of the Historical Society of Nigeria*, vol. 3, pp. 393–5.

Plankensteiner, B. (ed.) (2007) *Benin. Kings and Rituals. Court Arts from Nigeria*, Kunsthistorisches Museum, Vienna (exhibition catalogue).

Roth, H.L. (1972 [1903]) *Great Benin: Its Customs, Art and Horrors*, Northbrook, IL, Metro Books.

Ryder, A.F.C. (1964) 'A note on the Afro-Portuguese ivories', *Journal of African History*, vol. 5, no. 3, pp. 363–5.

Ryder, A.F.C. (1969) *Benin and the Europeans, 1485–1897*, London, Longman.

Wilks, I. (1988) 'Asante: human sacrifice or capital punishment? A rejoinder', *The International Journal of African Historical Studies*, vol. 21, no. 3, pp. 443–52.

RESOURCES

Reading 1.1

From Duarte Pacheco Pereira, *Esmeraldo de Situ Orbis*, *c.* 1505–8

By this channel towards the sea is a village called Teebuu and on the other side are some more villages. A league up this river on the left two tributaries enter the main stream: if you ascend the second of these for twelve leagues you find a town called Huguatoo [Ughoton], of some 2,000 souls: this is the harbour of the great city of Beny [Benin], which lies nine leagues in the interior with a good road between them. Small ships of fifty tons can go as far as Huguatoo. This city is about a league long from gate to gate; it has no wall but is surrounded by a large moat, very wide and deep, which suffices for its defence. I was there four times. Its houses are made of mud-walls covered with palm leaves. The Kingdom of Beny is about eighty leagues long and forty wide; it is usually at war with its neighbours and takes many captives, whom we buy at twelve or fifteen brass bracelets each, or for copper bracelets which they prize more; from there the slaves are brought to the castle of S. Jorze da Mina where they are sold for gold. The way of life of these people is full of abuses and fetishes and idolatries, which for brevity's sake I omit.

Source: Hodgkin (1975), pp. 120–1 (footnotes omitted).

Reading 1.2

From Ruy de Pina, *Chronica del Rey Dom João II*, ch. 24

The king of Beny sent as ambassador to the king a Negro, one of his captains, from a harbouring place by the sea, which is called Ugato [Ughoton], because he desired to learn more about these lands, the arrival of people from them in his country being regarded as an unusual novelty. This ambassador was a man of good speech and natural wisdom. Great feasts were held in his honour, and he was shown many of the good things of these kingdoms. He returned to his land in a ship of the king's, who at his departure made him a gift of rich clothes for himself and his wife: and through him he also sent a rich present to the king of such things as he understood he would greatly prize. Moreover, he sent holy and most catholic advisers with praiseworthy admonitions for the faith to administer a stern rebuke about the heresies and great idolatries and fetishes, which the Negroes practise in that land.

Source: Hodgkin (1975), p. 125.

Reading 1.3 From 'A Voyage to Benin' by Anthony Ingram

Whereas we departed in the month of December from the coast of England with your good ship, the *Richard of Arundel*, and the pinnace, we held on our direct course towards our appointed port, and the 14th day of February following we arrived in the haven of Benin, where we found not water enough to carry the ship over the bar, so that we left her without in the road, and with the pinnace and ship boat, into which we had put the chiefest of our merchandise, we went up the river to a place called Goto, where we arrived the 20th of February, the foresaid Goto being the nearest place that we could come to by water to go for Benin. From thence we presently sent negroes to the King to certify him of our arrival and of the cause of our coming thither: who returned to us again the 22nd day with a nobleman in their company to bring us up to the city, and with 200 negroes to carry our commodities. Hereupon the 23rd day we delivered our merchandise to the King's **factor**, and the 25th day we came to the great city of Benin, where we were well entertained. The six and twentieth day we went to the Court to have spoken with the King, which (by reason of a solemn feast then kept amongst them) we could not do: but yet we spake with his veadore, or chief man, that hath the dealing with the Christians: and we conferred with him concerning our trading, who answered us that we should have all things to our desire, both in pepper and elephants' teeth.

The first of March we were admitted to the King's presence, and he made us the like courteous answer for our traffic.

Source: John Hampden (ed.) (1970) *The Tudor Venturers: selected from The Principal Navigations, Voyages, Traffics and Discoveries of the English Nation made by Sea or over Land [by] Richard Hakluyt*, London, The Folio Society, pp. 254–5.

Reading 1.4 H.L. Gallwey, 'Report on visit to Ubini (Benin City) the capital of the Benin country', Enclosure in Consul-General C.M. Macdonald to Marquess of Salisbury

Henry Gallwey (1859–1949) was Vice-Consul for the Benin River section of the Oil Rivers (later Niger Coast) Protectorate of which Claude Macdonald (1852–1915) was Consul-General. The Marquess of Salisbury (1830–1903) was Minister of Foreign Affairs in 1892, a post he combined with that of Prime Minister.

I left my Vice-Consulate on the morning of the 21st March 1892, my object being to visit Ubini the capital of the Benin country, and to see the King with a view to concluding a Treaty between him and Her Majesty the Queen of England.

[...]

The next morning, the 24th, on arrival at the King's residence, I was informed that the King could not see me till later – and to make a long story short, I did not see him until the afternoon of the 26th. His messages which kept coming to me all day, were a series of lies and excuses.

I fancy he is afraid of doing anything without the full concurrence of his big men. On the 25th I had an interview with all the leading men of the place and fully explained to them the object of my visit, and also what a treaty was, and what it meant. They were fully satisfied, or said they were, at my suggestions generally: and promised to conduct me to the King that morning. However, as I stated before, they did not do so. The following day I determined to bring matters to a crisis – and so sent word to the King that I was leaving that day, and had no intention of returning any more – i.e. as a friend – and to complete the ruse, I sent off a number of carriers with baggage that was not required – telling them to wait at Egoru for me.

The King immediately sent and begged me not to be 'vexed' – and that if I would see his big men once more, they would bring me straight to him. I said I would on no account see them again, as they had already told me enough lies. Eventually after receiving several begging messages, I consented to see the 3 leading men.

They asked me to wait till the sun went down that day, as it was too hot for me to go out during the day, and asked me not to be 'vexed'. I said far from being 'vexed', I was amused – and although it might be too hot to see the King, it was not too hot for me to return to Gwato [another name for Ughoton]. I then dismissed them. Finally, two of the leading men came and said the King was ready to receive me. I told them I would think about it, and in the meantime told them to wait – I kept them waiting some time, and eventually about 2 p.m. I went to the King's residence, accompanied by Mr. Hutton, Mr. Swainson, and Dr. Hanley.

[...]

The rest of the 'palaver' [talk] was most satisfactory – the King and chief men being more than anxious to sign the 'Book', as they called it. Owing to the King being in the middle of celebrating some big fetish custom, he explained to me that he could not touch the pen – but that all his big men would do so, and that it would be the same as if touched by him, provided his name was written. I found the interpreter that I took up with me was, owing to his fear of the King, useless – but fortunately, my man Agaie, proved a most efficient interpreter. He fully explained each Article of the Treaty, as propounded by me, in the Acure tongue (a country bordering on Benin) – this was passed on to the King's chief adviser, who passed it on to the King.

Eventually the king signed the Treaty in full, and I gave him one copy – it having being signed in triplicate.

[...]

I then had a talk with the King on several matters – and I found him most sensible, and willing to listen to reason. He laid great stress upon the fact that there should be no 'war palavers' – I informed him that as long as he kept to the terms of the treaty, that the Queen of England would always be his friend.

[...]

At present the whole Benin country is, and has been for hundreds of years, steeped in Fetish. The Town of Ubini might well be called 'The City of Skulls' – I saw no less than four crucified victims during my few days there in addition to numerous corpses – some mutilated fearfully – which were strewn about in the most public places. The rule appears to be one of Terror, and one can only hope that the Treaty may be the foundation of a new order of things throughout the vast territory ruled over by the King of Benin. [...]

H.L. Gallwey
Dep. Com. and Vice-Consul

H.B.M.'s Vice-Consulate
Benin
30th March 1892

Source: Gallwey, H.L., 'Report on visit to Ubini (Benin City) the capital of the Benin country', Enclosure in Consul-General C. M. Macdonald to Marquess of Salisbury, Public Record Office, Foreign Office 84/2194. Reprinted in A.F.C. Ryder (1969) *Benin and the Europeans, 1485–1897*, London, Longmans, pp. 344–8 (editorial notes added).

Reading 1.5

H.L. Gallwey's paper 'Journeys in the Benin country, West Africa', read at a meeting of the Royal Geographical Society on 5 December 1892

Benin city lies about 25 miles [40 km] from Gwato, the whole route being through a dense forest, with the exception of the last mile or two. We slept at Gwato that night, and started early next morning on our march halting at a place called Egoru for the night, having done 16 miles of the journey. Just before reaching the city we had to pass through rather an unpleasant half mile of fairly open country. We presumed it was the place where all criminals' bodies were deposited. The path was strewn on both sides with dead bodies in every stage of decomposition; skulls grinned at you from every direction – a gruesome experience in its way. On reaching the city we found the king had told off a couple of very decent houses for our use. One we took possession of, and put our carriers in the other. These houses were built of red clay, having a high wall all round forming a sort of courtyard. There were two fair rooms and many uncanny alcoves; skulls, human and otherwise, hung around promiscuously. The walls were adorned with the impressions of a very large hand in lime and blood. The roof was a thatched one, full of creeping things.

I will not weary you with an account of our five days' stay in this extraordinary place. The king had promised to see me on my arrival, but it was three days before he gave me an audience. However, the result was very satisfactory, so one cannot complain. Benin city is the seat of a very powerful theocracy of fetish priests. The king is all-powerful, though he would appear to be somewhat in the hands of his big men, and very much tied down by fetish customs. He only goes amongst his people once a year, the occasion being one of general rejoicing and feasting. Human sacrifices are of frequent occurrence, and the rule is one of terror. The usual form of sacrifice is crucifixion. We saw several crucified victims during our stay in Benin city, on the plain outside the king's residence. It is, however, to be hoped that now this country is under Her Majesty's protection these terrible practices will be put an end to, though it must take time. Punitive measures are all very well in their way, but in a country like Benin the effect would probably be to drive the natives into the bush, and make them greater savages than ever; one cannot reasonably hope to abolish in a short time customs that have been in practice for centuries. The Benin people are free, but are treated as slaves by the king, the title of king's slave being considered an honour.

[...]

It might prove interesting to compare the Benin city of to-day with what it was two or three hundred years ago. The Portuguese called it Great Benin. Among the Benin people it is known as Ado, meaning the place where the king lives, whilst the Jakris call it Ubini. According to Dapper the city was surrounded by a high wall, and contained many towers and spires. Nyendale, a Dutchman, would appear to be the best authority on the subject in the seventeenth and eighteenth centuries, he having visited the city on two occasions. He describes the streets as being 'prodigious long and broad,' and says that the town is 'four miles large.'

The state of the place to-day is very different, the so-called city being but a straggling collection of houses, built in clusters here and there, in little or no order. The number of ruins testify to the fact that it was once very much larger; but in our wanderings through the place we saw nothing that suggested 'prodigious long and broad streets.' The only market-place we saw was on the plain outside the king's residence. The whole aspect seemed to bespeak anything but a prosperous state of affairs. [...]

The Benin people at one time had the reputation of being great weavers of cloth and workers in metals. They undoubtedly practise these industries now, though we saw nothing of the kind going on during our few days in the place. We saw, however, many specimens of brass ware of very clever workmanship.

Source: H.L. Gallwey (1893) 'Journeys in the Benin country, West Africa', *Geographical Journal*, vol. 1, no. 2, February, pp. 128–30.

Reading 1.6

From R.H. Bacon, *Benin. The City of Blood*

As the title page of the book explains, Commander R.H. Bacon (1867–1947), Royal Navy, was the intelligence officer on the expedition to capture Benin in February 1897. In the preface to his book he explains his reasons for writing it: 'to have a full account of what happened, and [...] to leave on record certain details of organisation and equipment which may be useful in future to officers serving on similar expeditions. All tendency to enlarge has been carefully avoided, and the reader must kindly accept the baldness of the narrative as surety for its lack of exaggeration' (p. 7). The following extracts are taken from Chapter 7, describing the city of Benin.

To describe one of these **Juju** places will be to describe all of them, as they only differed in position and size.

[...]

The altar was made by three steps running the whole length under the shelter of the shed; slightly raised for some distance in the centre, on which raised portion were handsomely-carved ivory tusks placed on the top of very antique bronze heads. Near these tusks were carved clubs, undoubtedly for use upon the victims of the sacrifice. The altar was deluged in blood, the smell of which was too overpowering for many of us. This same awful smell seemed to pervade the whole compound, as if the grass had been watered with blood.

[...]

The one lasting remembrance of Benin in my mind is its smells. Crucifixions, human sacrifices, and every horror the eye could get accustomed to, to a large extent, but the smells no white man's internal economy could stand. Four times in one day I was practically sick from them, and many more times on the point of being so. Every person who was able, I should say, indulged in a human sacrifice, and those who could not, sacrificed some animal and left the remains in front of his house. After a day or so the whole town seemed one huge pest-house.

[...]

Blood was everywhere; smeared over bronzes, ivory, and even the walls, and spoke the history of that awful city in a clearer way than writing ever could. And this had been going on for centuries! Not the lust of one king, not the climax of a bloody reign, but the religion (save the word!) of the race. The Juju held sway for a hundred miles all round, and that in the older and more flourishing times of the city must have been practised with, if possible, greater intensity than at the present day.

[...] the atrocities of Benin, originating in blood lust and desire to terrorise the neighbouring states, the brutal love of mutilation and torture, and the wholesale manner in which the caprices of the King and Juju were satisfied, could only have been the result of stagnant brutality.

Behind these three main Juju compounds, lay the Palava House and the King's House, side by side. The former a large oblong building, with a roof running over the side and end walls, leaving the centre open. The roof was of galvanised iron, and down the south portion of it ran a huge bronze serpent with a most forbidding looking head. Red mud seats ran round the walls, for the use of the chiefs taking part in the palava. The doors were covered with stamped brass, as were also portions of the woodwork of the roof. This place was turned into the hospital, and any article of value found in the town was stored here.

The King's House was almost identical, but smaller, and had rooms leading off it. The archway over the King's sleeping-place was decorated roughly with stamped brass and squares of looking-glass.

The remainder of the compound consisted of storeroom, medicine house, and houses for the King's followers, as well as some other Juju compounds. After which it straggled away into ruined and uninhabited houses, used probably as burial-places for the men of note.

The storehouses contained chiefly cheap rubbish, such as glass walking sticks, old uniforms, absurd umbrellas, and the usual cheap finery that traders use to tickle the fancy of the natives. But buried in the dirt of ages, in one house, were several hundred unique bronze plaques, suggestive of almost Egyptian design, but of really superb casting. Castings of wonderful delicacy of detail, and some magnificently carved tusks were collected, but in the majority of cases the ivory was dead from age, very few of modern date were to be seen, and those mostly uncarved. Silver there was none, and gold there was none, and the coral was of little value. In fact, the only things of value were the tusks and bronze work. In one well forty-one tusks were discovered. Of other ivory work, some bracelets suggestive of Chinese work and two magnificent leopards were the chief articles of note; bronze groups of idols, and two large and beautifully-worked stools were also found, and must have been of very old manufacture.

Leaving the compound and facing north there was immediately in front a clear space, forming, so to speak, the delta of the road leading to the water at Ikpoba. On the right was a crucifixion tree with a double crucifixion on it, the two poor wretches stretched out facing the west, with their arms bound together in the middle. The construction of this tree was peculiar, being absolutely built for the purpose of crucifixion. At the base were skulls and bones, literally strewn about; the débris of former sacrifices. [...]

Down the avenue to the right was a tree with nineteen skulls, the result of more or less recent murders, and down every main road were two or more human sacrifices.

[...]

Beyond one blacksmith's shop there was little sign of any native industry or evidence of much trade with the interior, in fact, it is known that the King was ruining the country by placing a Juju on nearly every article of merchandise. But now we may hope for a revival in trade, and the wealth and produce of the Hinterland is sure to flow through the city to the river as soon as peace and security are established.

Source: Bacon, (1897) pp. 87–93, 97 (editorial notes added).

Reading 1.7

Trial of Chief Ologbosheri, 27 June 1899

Although this was described as a 'trial' held at the 'native court', Benin City, the trial was not conducted according to any formal body of law. Present were Sir Ralph Moor (1860–1909), Consul-General for the Niger Coast Protectorate, and four other British officers, as well as eleven Benin chiefs. The trial was conducted by the British, but the verdict was officially decided by the 'Chiefs of Native Council'. The trial record contains statements from four witnesses and from the accused, Chief Ologbosheri (Ologbose) (c.1850–99), the war-chief of Benin and son-in-law of the Oba. Ologbose was found guilty, and was hanged the next day. Joseph Chamberlain (1836–1914) was Colonial Secretary.

2nd witness, *Omaregboma*, being duly sworn, states:–

I was a slave the king. I remember the time when the white men were killed. It is about two years, or five native years, since. I was placed at Gwatto by the king to meet the white men when they landed there. When the white men landed I sent a message to the king by Idiaie. I asked the white man for his stick, which I told him I would send to the king. The white man gave me his stick, and I sent it by Idiaie. I told Idiaie to tell the king that many white men had landed with plenty of boys; but they had no guns or arms to fight with. The white man told Idiaie that he wanted him to get to Benin City that night, and to come back with the king's answer the next morning, but before Idiaie returned the white men had started and gone towards Benin City and the massacre took place. I tried to persuade the white man to wait till the messenger returned with the staff from the king, but he would not wait. [...]

[Omoregboma went on to explain that the Phillips expedition set off without him, but he overtook it and encountered the ambush party.]

I asked the chiefs why were they all come to lay wait in the bush with guns and matchets, and told them that the white men were coming, and that a messenger had been sent to the king to tell him so, who had not yet returned. [...] I told Ologbosheri that I had sent a messenger to the king with the white man's staff, but had not received an answer yet. I told Ologbosheri that he was the head war chief of the king, and pressed him to stop the people firing. Ologbosheri said he had orders from home before he came out, and how would he go back if he did not carry out the orders. [...]

Prisoner's statement

Prisoner *Ologbosheri* states: I was at home one day when the king sent word to me that he wanted to send me somewhere, in the presence of all these chiefs, except Ojumo. The king told me that he had heard that the white men were coming to fight with him, and that I must get ready to go and fight the white men. I told the king that this was not my work [...] While still at Egbini, Omaregboma came and told me that the white men were coming, but had neither guns nor matchets to fight with, and I told him that I had sent a messenger to the king about the white men, and when he came back I would know what to do. I asked Omaregboma why he allowed the white men to come out of Gwatto before his messenger returned from the king. Since I was born in Benin City I had never been to the water side – I never went as far as Jebu – but when all the people called the mass meeting at Benin City and selected me to go and fight the white men, I went. I had no palaver with the white men before. The day I was selected to go from Benin

City to meet the white men all the chiefs here present were in the meeting, and now they want to put the whole thing on my shoulders.

Source: HMSO Cd. 9529 'Correspondence Relating to the Benin Territories Expedition, 1899', Parliamentary Papers, 1899, LXIII, 395. No. 3: 'Commissioner and Consul-General Sir R. Moor to Mr. Chamberlain (received August 1, 1899)'. Enclosure 1, 'Trial of Chief Ologbosheri'. Held at the Native Court, Benin City, on Tuesday, June 27, 1899, at 8 a.m.'

2 THE ART OF BENIN: CHANGING RELATIONS BETWEEN EUROPE AND AFRICA II

Donna Loftus and Paul Wood

MATERIALS YOU WILL NEED

- DVD ROM: The Art of Benin
- Illustration Book

AIMS

This chapter will continue to:

- introduce you to the art of Benin, a kingdom in West Africa which was home to a unique tradition of sculpture
- explore the ways that Europeans encountered this art in the late nineteenth and twentieth centuries
- discuss how the context in which art is encountered shapes how it is understood
- give you some understanding of the ways that the meaning of artistic objects can undergo translation as they move from one context to another
- consider why the ownership and location of Benin's art remains a controversial issue today
- demonstrate how the two disciplines of Art History and History can both contribute to our understanding of artworks.

INTRODUCTION

This chapter takes up the history of the Benin artworks from their arrival in Europe after the punitive expedition of 1897. It continues to explore how cultural encounters between Europe and Africa have influenced the meanings ascribed to the bronzes and, in particular, how the changing relationship between Europe and Africa impacts on the status of the objects as art. These issues will be taken further in the DVD ROM which you will be referred to at the end of the chapter.

2.1 THE ART OF BENIN IN BRITAIN

Donna Loftus

The events surrounding the invasion of Benin in 1897 were followed closely in Britain and Europe. Stories of imperial adventures in Africa were very popular in the late nineteenth century. Accounts of travel, exploration and war in foreign lands emphasised the moment of encounter between white European 'civilised' culture and the 'dark, dangerous' people and places of Africa. There was, however, another encounter that was less easy to fit into the established ways of talking about Africa. As the reports of the time noted with some curiosity and uncertainty, when the British expedition entered Benin City in February 1897, they found magnificent works of craftsmanship and art as well as scenes of great horror.

This section picks up the story, introduced in Chapter 1, of Benin, through the artefacts that were discovered by the British on their arrival there. These artworks and objects were confiscated by the British forces and brought to Britain where they were sold, in part, to pay for the expedition. Museums, private collectors, art historians and scholars in America and Europe were quick to realise the significance of the Benin artworks and competed to acquire the best pieces. One such collector, Felix von Luschan (1854–1924), made a careful account of where the looted Benin works ended up. According to von Luschan, 2,400 objects arrived in Europe after the punitive expedition. The largest collection of 580 was acquired, with von Luschan's help, by the Royal Museum for Ethnography in Berlin, where he worked as a curator and ethnographer (Völger, 2007, p. 217). Other works were sold to museums and private collectors around the world. Some were bought by Liverpool's Mayer Museum, the Pitt Rivers Museum in Oxford, and London's Horniman Free Museum. This section will focus in particular on the British Museum's treatment of the Benin sculptures.

In its acquisition of artworks and in the production of scholarship, the British Museum had to compete vigorously with museums and scholars abroad. The rush to acquire the Benin artworks and to produce research about them generated a lot of debate. In this section you will be asked to study this debate in the order in which it emerged.

In particular, you will need to consider how immediate reactions to the Benin artworks drew on contemporary images and ideas of Africa. You will then explore how evidence that emerged from the detailed studies of the artworks was accommodated to the existing notions about Africa. Did the study of the Benin artworks challenge common ideas about Africa in the late nineteenth century? You will also consider the role that certain institutions and agencies, such as the British press, the British Museum and the *Encyclopædia Britannica*, played in giving authority to, and disseminating, certain perspectives on Benin.

Benin and British newspapers

In the Resources section at the end of this chapter you will find extracts from two British newspapers about Benin and the artefacts that were found there. The first report, reprinted in Reading 2.1, and the accompanying image shown in Figure 2.1, are from the *Illustrated London News* special supplement on Benin, published on 27 March 1897. The *ILN*, established in 1842, was the first illustrated weekly newspaper. It combined gossip on fashion and royalty with features on world affairs, and included drawings to highlight key events. It produced many stories about the British empire, but was particularly interested in reporting on the many small wars of empire that took place in the late nineteenth century. As with many newspapers of the time, the *ILN* sent journalists and artists to convey dispatches and sketches from the front line. The extract in Reading 2.1 was produced from eyewitness accounts. As you will see, this resulted in a style of reporting that created a sense of drama. The extract in Reading 2.2 is taken from *The Times* which – as you may know – was, by the late nineteenth century, a well-established daily newspaper. Although it is more serious in tone, it also displays an interest in the British empire and the place of Britain in relation to the wider world.

Activity Read the extract from the *ILN* (Reading 2.1) and look at the image in Figure 2.1.

How is Benin described? Are the Benin artworks mentioned?

Discussion This extract presents an eyewitness account of the scene that British forces encountered when they arrived in Benin City in February 1897. It is sensationalist in tone and was probably intended to grab the newspaper reader's attention.

The language used to describe Benin and the accompanying illustration emphasises the brutality and savagery of the scene that met the British party when they arrived. Benin is described as a 'city of blood' with pits full of 'dead and dying'. The art of Benin appears here as 'grotesque' appendages to torture and human sacrifice. You may also have noticed that the arrival of British troops is presented as a form of liberation; bringing order and humanity to a place locked in barbaric and brutal practices associated with less civilised periods and places.

Figure 2.1 H.C. Sepping Wright, 'The Golgotha, Benin', drawing, 42 x 29 cm, reproduced in the *Illustrated London News* supplement, 27 March 1897.

Activity Now read the extract from *The Times* (Reading 2.2).

Again, consider the kinds of words which are used to refer to Benin. How is the art of Benin discussed?

Discussion This extract is a review of the exhibition of 300 bronze plaques from Benin City held by the British Museum in September 1897. It appears to be written by someone with specialist knowledge of antiquities, possibly acquired from the British Museum. The report refers to the 'brutal savages of Benin', but also to the 'technical perfection' of the bronzes. Although described as 'strange' and 'fantastic', these are seen as 'surprising evidences' of Benin skill and craftsmanship.

You may have noticed that the report hints at the problem the British Museum had in accommodating Benin's supposed brutality with evidence of skilled craftsmanship displayed in the bronzes. The use of images and markings is explored in trying to find links between Benin and ancient civilisations of North Africa such as the Gnostics, a second-century people of much interest in the nineteenth-century study of antiquity for their religious beliefs. Eventually, however, the report concedes with surprise that the bronzes are the work of the people of Benin, an 'unexpected phase of negro craftsmanship'.

How does the historian accommodate these descriptions of Benin – one that emphasises the brutality of the people, the other their skill and craftsmanship? Why was such Negro craftsmanship so 'unexpected' by scholars? What does this tell the historian about British attitudes to Africa? To answer these questions we need to look further into the context of debates about Benin.

Victorian attitudes to race

The Benin artworks arrived in Britain at a time of great interest in the British empire, the history of humankind, and the significance of race in the development of societies. Throughout the nineteenth century, the expansion of British interests overseas was accompanied by comment, enquiry and descriptions of the people and places encountered in foreign lands. In 1890 there was a general and widespread interest in Africa, a trend that reflected a new phase in British imperialism (Bolt, 1971, p. 109). In the 1880s and 1890s Africa was aggressively colonised by European powers, and the ensuing struggle for influence brought the European nations into conflict with Africans and each other. As British imperialism made ever greater inroads in Africa, travellers, missionaries, capitalists and civil servants sent objects, letters, drawings and accounts of the landscape and people to Britain, where they were reproduced in books, museums, exhibitions and newspaper reports. These accounts were diverse, but stories that told of encounters with native people and emphasised stark differences in appearance, beliefs and practices such as witchcraft and cannibalism were particularly popular. This popular interest in Africa corresponded with a growth in debates about the history of the human race, some of which were associated with the expansion of scientific knowledge.

In 1843 the Ethnological Society of London was founded, 'for the purpose of inquiring into the distinguishing characteristics, physical and moral, of the varieties of Mankind which inhabit, or have inhabited the Earth; and to ascertain the causes of such characteristics' (editorial in the *Journal of the Ethnological Society of London*, vol. 1, 1848, p. 3). The Ethnological Society was essentially a humanitarian organisation which believed in the common descent of mankind.

In 1850 Robert Knox, a trained anatomist and popular lecturer, published *The Races of Men* (a second edition was published in 1862). In his book Knox argued that various races had different lines of descent and that, as such, humankind was made up of a range of species with unequal qualities and abilities. This, he argued, was based on observation and experience: 'Look all over the globe, it is always the same; the dark races stand still, the fair progresses' (Knox, 1850, p. 222). As such, Knox concluded that 'there must be a physical and, consequently, a psychological inferiority in the dark races generally' (Knox, 1850, p. 224).

Followers of Knox formed the Anthropological Society of London in 1863, which undertook the study of humankind based on the assumption of racial differences born of physical difference. This understanding of race was influenced by **craniometry** (the study and measurement of skulls) and **phrenology** (study of the shape of the cranium), two pseudo-sciences that perceived the size and shape of the skull to be indicators of character and abilities. Alongside such studies, new trends in scientific thought investigated the ability of living things to adapt and change. In 1859 the naturalist Charles Darwin published *On the Origin of Species by Means of Natural Selection, or the Preservation of Favoured Races in the Struggle for Life* in which he argued that life on earth progressed, or evolved, through long periods of change in which the advantageous characteristics of organisms gradually overtook the bad. In 1864 the social theorist Herbert Spencer published his *Principles of Biology*, which suggested that the concept of evolution might be applied to human society. He coined the phrase 'survival of the fittest' to describe the successful adaptation of humans to their environment.

In the context of imperial expansion overseas and competition within Europe for industrial and imperial supremacy, ideas of race, both popular and scientific, were increasingly used to justify hierarchies and legitimise imperial power. British industrial, imperial and administrative capacity was seen by some as evidence of a superior ability to adapt and respond to changing environments. The perceived backwardness of other societies, such as Benin, was taken as evidence of their inability to improve without help. As such, some British contemporaries believed that they had a 'civilising mission' to undertake, and that the supposed superiority of the British imbued individuals and the government with the responsibility to eradicate the backwardness and superstition they believed existed in other countries. As the *Illustrated London News* stated, in applauding the invasion of Benin, 'no successful attempt has up to now been made to rescue the native population from grovelling superstition and ignorance' (Plankensteiner, 2007, p. 201).

In this context, as the photograph in Figure 2.2 shows, the artworks were removed from Benin with little attention given to the nature of the objects or the way that they had been displayed and used there. In an atmosphere of intense rivalry between museums and collectors across Europe, they were separated out and sold. But, given the interest across Europe in the history of humankind, they were soon subjected to more sophisticated analysis, and were used to inform debates about race and culture. German and British ethnographers and art historians were anxious to acquire the finest pieces: for such collectors, the Benin 'war booty' consisted of objects and artworks that could afford valuable insight into the 'artistic life of the Negro'.

Figure 2.2 Transport of artworks out of Benin, 1897 photographed by H.S. Measham. British Museum, London, AF-A79-17. Photo: © The Trustees of the British Museum.

The British Museum and the Benin 'antiquities'

As mentioned above, well-known museums such as the British Museum, the Victoria and Albert Museum, and the Natural History Museum emerged as world leaders in the collection, preservation and display of objects in the nineteenth century, in close competition with their German and French counterparts. The very ability of western culture to create such institutions was itself seen as an indicator of superiority over other cultures (Pointon, 1994, p. 3). The British Museum, first opened in 1759, soon became a forum for the exhibition of antiquities from around the world. The museum was organised into different departments which together told the story of the emergence of civilisation from prehistory.

In the nineteenth century, the growth of the British Museum corresponded with the rise in the study of **anthropology** and **ethnography** and their struggle for scientific recognition, and the relationship between the museum and the study of ethnography was strong. In 1886 the British Museum opened an ethnographic gallery to the public to house and display the many objects it had acquired from overseas. The publicity given to debates about evolution in the 1860s had raised the profile of both the Ethnological Society and the Anthropological Society. The two societies amalgamated in 1871 and founded the Anthropological Institute which had a close relationship with the ethnographers of the museum, Charles Hercules Read and Ormonde Maddock Dalton, both of whom worked hard to upgrade the status of ethnography at the museum. The character of the collection gradually changed to reflect the 'scientific' concerns of ethnographers and included objects and art from Africa. The 1899 Guide to the exhibition galleries of the British Museum claimed that ethnography was the study of

> manners and customs of particular peoples and of their development from savagery towards civilisation [...] The purpose for which a collection such as the one here exhibited is brought together, is to enable us to understand by what methods man, in his earlier efforts of development towards civilisation, supplies the wants of existence, protects his life, expresses his religious idea, and gradually advances towards the cultivation of the industrial and ornamental arts.
>
> (Coombes, 1994b, p. 110)

The display of spears, shields, pots and utensils was used to represent ideas about how so-called primitive races lived; artworks were seen somewhat differently as evidence of progress and civilisation. Although the British Museum was keen to acquire some of the artworks from Benin for the contribution they made to the history of humankind, fitting them in to the established theories of progress was not easy.

From 1897 onwards there was considerable debate about the origin of the Benin bronzes among collectors, ethnographers and art historians in Britain and Germany. The skill, craftsmanship and **aesthetic** qualities shown in the artworks did not fit with sensational stories of human sacrifice and brutality that had reached Britain from Benin, or with existing stereotypes of Africa and Africans that were more generally held. Questions were raised about how a society such as Benin, which was perceived as savage and brutal, had managed to create such sophisticated works of art. There was speculation that the artworks were 'relics' of a lost African civilisation, which had since degenerated into savagery and brutality. However, some, such as Justus Brinckmann, an art historian and founder of the Hamburg Museum of Arts and Craft, speculated that they were evidence of contact between Benin and the more 'civilised' peoples of ancient Egypt (Plankensteiner, 2007, p. 206). The anthropologist and collector Augustus-Pitt Rivers, who had acquired a number of bronzes for his Oxford museum, argued that they could only have been made as a result of European influence, probably as a consequence of contact with the Portuguese in the sixteenth century. Henry Ling Roth, Director of the Bankfield Museum in Halifax, acknowledged that there was considerable difference between the 'crude castings of the average native African' and the 'beautiful results' from Benin, but he conceded in 1898, after a detailed study of the castings, that the technique for their production predated the arrival of the Portuguese. His conclusion caused a stir by arguing that the bronzes were of African origin alone (Coombes, 1994a, pp. 45–6).

In their detailed study, *Antiquities from the City of Benin and from Other Parts of West Africa in the British Museum*, published in 1899, Read and Dalton went further in arguing for a purely African origin of the bronzes. Their earlier studies had argued that the skilled craftsmen of Benin produced work equal to that of the Italian Renaissance of the fifteenth and sixteenth centuries, but they dated the artworks from the mid-sixteenth century around the time of the arrival of the Portuguese. Their later study used the oral accounts of local Benin leaders which had been collected by Captain Roupell of the British expeditionary force. It provided clear evidence of the ancient history of Benin society, together with a close analysis of the artworks to suggest that the Benin castings may have emerged independently of European or Egyptian influence (Coombes, 1994a, p. 57). The acknowledgement that the people of Benin had produced sophisticated artworks in the sixteenth century, and the inability of ethnographers to find evidence of more recent pieces of the same quality, raised further questions about Benin's progress. For many commentators the ultimate suggestion was that, as contact with Europeans declined, Benin had degenerated into a savage and brutal society. The artworks were regarded as 'relics' and 'antiquities', objects that demonstrated an African civilisation now long gone.

Institutional politics and rivalry may well have prompted Ling Roth and Read and Dalton to publicise their conclusions about an African origin for the bronzes in the 1890s. Dalton and Read were keen to promote the ethnography within the British Museum; the museum was keen to promote itself as a benevolent educator and, in the process, to cast the British as the civilised keeper of the world's history. Such representations featured heavily in campaigns orchestrated by the museum for financial support from the British government. In this context, the Benin artefacts offered Read and Dalton the opportunity to put the Ethnographic Gallery 'on the map'. The plaques on display in the museum were on loan from the Foreign Office, but it was hoped that they would become the property of the museum if funds could be raised. In the meantime, as the image in Figure 2.3 shows, Germany, one of Britain's main imperial competitors in the 1890s, was busy building its own national ethnographic collections with generous government grants and donations from private benefactors (Coombes, 1994a, pp. 59–60).

Activity Read the extract from Henry Ling Roth, 'On the British loss of antique works from Benin' (Reading 2.3). In it Ling Roth laments the British government's failure to fund the permanent acquisition of the bronzes for the British Museum at Bloomsbury. Why does Ling Roth think it important that the British Museum should have a permanent display of the art of Benin?

Discussion Ling Roth thinks that such artefacts are important to the study of anthropology – or the study of 'native races' – knowledge which he sees as important for successful international trade and imperial government. Such knowledge would enable the officials to govern and trade more effectively. He is also concerned that, with its acquisition of African art, Germany will surpass British scientific knowledge and increase its imperial and economic superiority. Roth's reasoning shows how entwined cultural, national and imperial politics were in the 1890s.

The representation of the history of Benin and the artworks as African by Read and Dalton may have something to do with their campaigns to establish the significance of the ethnographic collection to world history and thereby to ensure funding and space for the artefacts in the museum. Ultimately their perspectives did little to challenge stereotypes of African inferiority. Instead, the explanations for the art of Benin that gained pre-eminence were those that fitted the story of the Benin 'antiquities' into established narratives of African backwardness by presenting them as relics of an African civilisation that had since degenerated.

Activity Now read the entry on 'Negro' from the eleventh edition of *Encyclopædia Britannica*, published 1910–11 (Reading 2.4), and consider how debates about the Benin artworks were presented to the public. You will need to apply your knowledge of the debates about the Benin artefacts to a close reading of the encyclopedia extract.

Figure 2.3 Display cabinet with objects of the Berlin Benin collection, prior to 1926, Museum für Völkerkunde, Berlin. Unknown photographer. Ethnologisches Museum – Staatliche Museen zu Berlin, 40.009.687. Photo: bpk/Ethnologisches Museum, Staatliche Museen zu Berlin.

1. Who is the article written by and how is his authority shown in the entry in the encyclopedia?
2. Can you identify the influence of 'scientific ideas' of race? How are these ideas used in the entry?
3. What does the author say about bronzes produced by the 'natives of Guinea'? How does he use the 'bronzes' to inform broader arguments about race?
4. How valuable a source is this for the study of British and African history?

Discussion

1. The *Encyclopædia Britannica* was, and still is, presented to readers as a comprehensive account of recent knowledge on key subjects, prepared by experts in the field. This article was written by T.A. Joyce. His authority is shown by his status as Assistant in the Department of Ethnography, British Museum and Secretary of the Anthropological Society. He would have been familiar with all the debates about an African origin for the bronzes. He also writes in a manner that gives little indication of the diverse range of argument and opinion on theories of race. He refers to evidence frequently to support his argument without any suggestion that it is controversial or contested.
2. There is evidence in the text of the influence of theories of evolution. The entry attempts to chart the progress of 'the negro', mentally and physically, on an 'evolutionary plane' in relation to the 'white man'. There is also evidence of the anatomical science in which characteristics of the body are taken as evidence of mental and cultural capabilities. The extract also talks of the 'progress of the white race'. In addition, you may have detected reference to the influence of the environment on the progress and development of the races, a formulation that may have its roots in the ideas of natural selection. At each stage, ideas about race informed by 'science' are used to justify or explain the inferiority of black people and the superiority of whites.
3. The extract concedes that bronze castings found in Guinea show that the 'natives' were capable of skilled craftsmanship. Joyce states that skilled craftsmanship, such as that demonstrated by the bronzes, could only be produced by Africans with European inspiration. The apparent decline in production of bronze work after the sixteenth century is used as evidence that such craftsmanship was not normal for Africans, but was temporarily inspired by contact with Europeans. He uses the 'exceptional' case of the bronze craftsmanship to prove the general inferiority of all black people.
4. The value of this source depends on how you would use it in the study of history. If taken at face value, it is not a good source for the study of African history as it is clearly informed by racist stereotypes. However, it does provide a valuable insight into the way knowledge about Africa and Africans was produced and communicated in Britain at that time. In particular, the entry shows how much-debated and controversial racist ideas were presented to the public as authoritative and

uncontested knowledge. It is always difficult for the historian to know how material was interpreted by contemporary readers, but the appearance of this entry on 'Negro' may well have persuaded people that equality between races was impossible.

Institutions and agencies such as British newspapers, museums and encyclopedias are important mechanisms for the dissemination of information about science and history. Through their publications, displays and writings, these agencies define 'accepted knowledge'. In museum displays and the resulting scholarship, collections of objects are used to integrate new ideas and established theories. The way artefacts are displayed, and the catalogues and captions used to describe objects to the public, are important mechanisms for communicating expert knowledge about history, science and art to the general public. The subjection of the Benin artworks to analysis, and the new knowledge this created, did little to challenge racist ideas. The perspective on Benin that gained predominance in the late nineteenth century was one that presented the sophisticated and skilled people of the sixteenth century as an exception. Africa was largely confirmed as 'backward' and incapable of progress without the intervention of white and western, Christian culture.

African sources?

As Chapter 1 demonstrated, history tends to be written by the victors. Added to this, the nineteenth-century view of Africans as having little history worthy of serious scholarship, as well as the privileging of written sources in western history writing, has meant that Benin's perspective on the invasion of 1897 was not recorded. Dalton and Read did make use of the witness statements of Benin rulers that were recorded by Captain Roupell, but, on the whole, African accounts of colonisation, race and culture, which were passed down through stories, objects and art, have been largely ignored.

There were, however, different perspectives on Africa that emerged in the late nineteenth and early twentieth centuries, informed by men and women who were motivated to challenge the supposed superiority of white, western culture. West African newspapers, such as the *Lagos Weekly Record* and the *Sierra Leone Weekly News*, provided an outlet for voices critical of colonial rule and western racism. Writers and thinkers such as Edward Wilmot Blyden (1832–1912) worked with British individuals and institutions in campaigns to promote a better understanding of Africa in Britain. Blyden was born in the West Indies and grew up in America, but he spent his adult life as a writer, intellectual and statesman in Liberia, Lagos and Sierra Leone. He is now well known as the founder of West African nationalism and a campaigner for Black history writing. Blyden was supported by Mary Kingsley (1862–1900), a traveller and writer on West Africa. Together they promoted the view that Africans were a people with a distinct culture and history who could not be made European.

Figure 2.4 Edward Wilmot Blyden, nineteenth century. Unknown photographer. Photo: © Corbis.

The African Society was founded in London in 1901, in part by funds from Blyden and the Lagos merchant R.B. Blaize, to educate British society about Africa. But as a review of the society written in 1935 noted: 'The Society did not thrive well. Lectures upon African subjects and the customs of the natives did not attract Londoners' (Shelford, 1935, p. 224).

Activity Read the extract from a speech made by Blyden to the African Society in 1903 (Reading 2.5). Can you identify any ways in which Blyden's version of African history and society challenges the one you encountered in the *Encyclopædia Britannica*?

Discussion

Blyden challenges the association made in European scientific thought between physical characteristics and mental capacity. Blyden sees this simplistic association to be the result of the 'superficial knowledge' and the 'unthinking' assumption of European superiority. This, he argues, has blinded Europeans to the fact that Africa has institutions and a history worthy of study. Blyden counters the representation of Africa as godless and reminds listeners of the ancient association between Africa and God.

What then, in Blyden's opinion, had happened in Africa to destroy this history? Blyden became well known for his argument that it was encounters with Europeans that had led to degeneration in Africa. Blyden pointed out that Europeans had ruined Africa by destroying its institutions and attempting to remake them in a European style. Blyden's arguments about Europe and Africa were complex and they changed much during the course of his life. He self-consciously fashioned history to support the cause of African nationalism. But his argument that contact with Europeans led to African degeneration adds a different perspective on Africa and Britain that needs to be considered.

Summary

The sources you have encountered on Benin and its artworks may be biased but, in tracing the way that they are partial, the historian can identify how ideas about Africa were produced in relation to Britain. The racialised systems of knowledge that emerged in the 1890s around Benin were contested and challenged, particularly from emergent writers in Africa such as Blyden. Nevertheless, certain representations gained credibility and became reproduced as the accepted norm. History means understanding the range of arguments put forward and using context to see which ones gain predominance and why. In the case of the Benin artworks, the arguments that gained acceptance were those which could be accommodated with existing stereotypes and which fitted with national and imperial political agendas. In the following part of this chapter you will consider how the changing relationship between Europe and Africa has impacted on the status of the bronzes as art and resulted in questions over whose cultural property they might be.

2.2 THE BENIN BRONZES AND MODERN ART

Paul Wood

In this final part of the chapters on Benin, I move away from a discussion of history as such, to refocus on the question of art. What makes the annexation of Benin and the looting of its treasures a *cause célèbre* even today is the value of what was taken away. Considered simply on a financial level, works of art change hands for extraordinary amounts of money. But art is widely seen as transcending mere economic value. This can be characterised as 'aesthetic' value; sometimes it may be talked of as a 'spiritual' value. In certain exceptional cases, works of art may even come to symbolise the values of an entire people or civilisation. Such is the case with the Benin bronzes. It is this dimension that gives contemporary debate about the bronzes its urgency. At the end of this chapter (and in the accompanying DVD ROM), issues concerning the ownership and display of the sculptures will be discussed further. But first I want to look at the relationship of the Benin bronzes, and of African art more generally, to modern art in the West.

Exotic encounters

It is widely acknowledged that African art had a profound impact on modern art. Avant-garde artists as eminent as Pablo Picasso, Henri Matisse and the sculptor Constantin Brancusi owed an explicit debt to a variety of African artworks they encountered in the early years of the twentieth century (see Figure 2.5 and, for a higher-quality image, Plate 3.2.1). Influenced both by their example and through renewed encounters with African originals in museums, later artists working in the 1920s and 30s continued to mine African art for a range of formal experiments and expressive effects. It would be natural to assume that the Benin bronzes, which are among the most sophisticated works of art to have been made in Africa, and which were widely known in Europe, would have been in the forefront of this African influence on modern art. Yet they were not. The reasons they were not, however, can tell us a great deal about some of the core values of modern art and about the relation of European culture to Africa more generally. In terms of the relationship between African art and the modern western avant-garde, the Benin bronzes are an exception that proves the rule.

There are numerous stories of how avant-garde artists first encountered non-western art. The French painter Paul Gauguin left Europe in the 1890s and spent the rest of his life working in Polynesia, incorporating exotic motifs and forms into his pictures (Plate 3.2.2). In Germany, in the first decade of the twentieth century, a group of young artists in Dresden, known as the *Brücke*, discovered carvings and other artefacts from the South Pacific and from Africa in the local ethnographic museum, and incorporated their stylistic features into their own paintings and sculptures (Plate 3.2.3). In Paris, around 1905, André Derain acquired an African mask from a fellow artist who had come across it in a local café, and showed it to Matisse and Picasso, among others (Plate 3.2.4). Also in Paris, in 1907 Picasso himself was overwhelmed by a visit to the Trocadero museum, where he encountered many masks and what he called 'dusty manikins' (quoted in Richardson, 1996, p. 11) (see Plate 3.2.5). More interesting than the circumstantial details of these encounters, however, is the question of *why* these artists were so affected by what they saw.

Figure 2.5 Pablo Picasso, *Les Demoiselles d'Avignon*, 1907, oil on canvas, 238 x 244 cm. Museum of Modern Art, New York. Photo: Lauros/Giraudon/The Bridgeman Art Library.

'Modern' and 'primitive'

Modernity

When it first emerged in Paris in the mid-nineteenth century, modern art was primarily a response to urban circumstances. New technologies and new forms of life – steam engines, railways, big cities, with their emerging obsession with commodities and fashion and exacerbated class conflict – all of these added up to an experience of life that could not adequately be dealt with in the language of the classical tradition. As early as 1846, the poet Charles Baudelaire had written of the 'heroism of modern life', and in the visual arts it is possible to see the work of Edouard Manet and then the Impressionists as a response. Manet walked the Parisian boulevards with a top hat and a cane observing the edginess of urban existence. Edgar Degas incisively represented the tensions inherent in scenes of modern work and leisure in bars, cafés, the theatre and the laundry. Before he turned to painting neutral subjects such as water lilies and haystacks, Claude Monet had worked out a new visual language – 'impressionism' – with which to capture the fleeting sensations of modernity: the experience of a crowded street, or of a smoky railway station (Plate 3.2.6). But after some years, for a new generation of artists coming to the fore in the late 1880s and 90s, the vitality seems to have drained out of representations of modern life.

Just as the long academic-classical tradition had lost its vitality when faced by the new forms of life associated with urban modernity, now it seemed modernity itself could not sustain the sense of a fulfilled and expansive life, but had become cramped, constrained and conventionalised. In the words of the German sociologist Max Weber (1864–1920), modernity was on the way to becoming an 'iron cage', rather than a place for modern heroes (Weber, 1904–5). In this crisis of the modern, what we find is that certain artists of the avant-garde sought to find a way out of the problem by looking back. It is here that we can begin to piece together an answer to our question about the Benin bronzes and modern art: that is, why they are exceptions to the rule about a profound African influence on modern art.

The idea of a 'primitive' art

It was in this situation that a positive value of the 'primitive' arose. Hitherto, 'primitive' had been a partial synonym for 'barbaric'. Not many years before, the Victorian critic John Ruskin had said that there had been no 'pure and precious ancient art' in Africa, Asia or America (Ruskin, 1857, p. 122). The concept of 'art', that is to say, was largely reserved for the European, Christian tradition. 'Fine art' was identified in the European post-Renaissance tradition with, above all, painting and sculpture; and painting in turn meant the representation of believable illusions of figures in coherent space, while sculpture was similarly identified with the representation of idealised bodies in bronze or marble. The qualification 'largely', in the sentence above, is merited because of the grey area presented by the architecture, book illustration, pottery and textile design of manifestly sophisticated cultures such as those of the Islamic, the Chinese and the Indian. Nonetheless, these were not seen as properly producing 'Art' in the western sense. There was, of course, no question at all about Africa, or the South Seas.

Activity Look at Plates 1.3.12 and 3.2.5. Imagine you are a middle-class Victorian with conventional tastes. Do you think you would be inclined to regard the objects in both of these images as 'works of art'? If not, try to say why not.

Discussion Both of these offer full-length representations of figures. But beyond that they are very different indeed. The oil painting – which is itself a medium closely associated with 'fine art'– has as its subject one of the traditional genres of art, the nude. On the other hand, your Victorian alter-ego's answer may have involved a belief that African figures were 'primitive'. Art with a capital A tended to be seen as the product of civilisation; indeed, a criterion *for* civilisation. It was widely felt that non-western, non-Christian cultures were less advanced (i.e. more 'primitive') than those of post-Renaissance western societies. Only with the emergence of the avant-garde, which challenged conventional western bourgeois cultural values, were the products of non-western cultures re-evaluated, such that 'primitive' became a positive value identified with authenticity, rather than a negative value associated with barbarism.

In the world of the European powers towards the end of the nineteenth century, imperialism – as you have seen – was a major force. And where the soldiers and businessmen went, scientists and teachers followed. Artefacts of all kinds flowed back from the colonies to newly constituted anthropological museums in Germany, France, England and elsewhere – the artworks of Benin included. These objects were, of course, accompanied by words: books, newspaper and magazine articles, even labels in the museums themselves. They were all dedicated to explaining the 'primitive' forms of life that generated this bewildering array: utensils and weapons, clothes and fetishes, ornaments, altars and furniture, which were all so different from the products of western modernity and classicism alike.

That was precisely what the artists fell upon. Increasingly outsiders within their own materialistic capitalist societies, they found intellectual and emotional succour in the work of peoples even more fiercely marginalised than they were themselves. Avant-garde artists recognised – or thought they recognised – imaginative 'affinities' between their own strivings for artistic truth in the face of bourgeois hypocrisy, and the forms produced by other unfortunates on the receiving end of European power.

Form

That word 'form' is crucial here, and it is worth pausing for a moment to explore its implications. You will be familiar from Book 1, Chapter 3, on Cézanne with how the search for a new visual language appropriate to modernity involved a rejection of the conventions of academic modelling: gradations of light and shadow, smooth finishing, modulated light falling on different materials, rounded forms in space – all the technical devices for producing a coherent spatial illusion. It is a short step from here to seeing avant-garde art as a 'distortion' of the characteristic forms of academic art, in two or three dimensions: a distortion that became all the more jarring when the subject was a familiar one from the European canon of 'fine art', such as a grouping of nude figures (see Cézanne's *Bathers*, Plate 1.3.5). The important point to grasp is that these distortions do not result from an inability to produce typically academic forms but from a rejection of them, or, more particularly, from the values they were felt to embody. By extension, the distorted forms of avant-garde art were seen as embodying other values: deep feelings, truthful responses, profound emotions, rather than the superficial veneer of 'civilised' convention.

To use another key term, these distorted forms were seen not as depicting such emotions, but as *expressing* them. A shift of emphasis has taken place. For the avant-garde artist the accuracy with which a painting depicts its subject matter is not at issue. What does matter is the power with which the colours and shapes in combination with each other express the feeling the artist wants to capture. The orchestrated composition matters more than what the marks may or may not be a picture of. That is to say, for the open-minded viewer, one not hidebound by academic convention, these colours and shapes could convey feeling directly: not by accurately – illusionistically – imitating an expression of fear or love on a human face, but in themselves, in a way comparable to the feeling produced by a succession of notes in music.

That cluster of ideas, about form and feeling and the direct expression of emotion, was central to late nineteenth- and early twentieth-century modernist art. In more recent times, such ideas have been challenged, but their historical impact is unquestionable. The artists who espoused them seemed to find confirmation and reinforcement in the forms of objects and images produced by peoples who, through their very 'primitiveness' itself, were outside the orbit of civilised convention: a civilisation found wanting by its avant-garde critics (Plate 3.2.7). In brief, 'primitive' form, and by extension, the avant-garde's emulation of it in their own 'primitiv*ism*', was felt to inhabit a realm of truth; academic convention one of bourgeois falsehood.

The avant-garde and imperialism

The flaw in this reasoning, it goes almost without saying, is that the avant-garde were in effect working within the stereotype of the empire builders, for all that they turned it upside down. They attributed more or less the same set of qualities to Africa as did Europeans generally: simplicity, timelessness, and an absence of 'civilising' decorum.

The difference was that whereas these qualities were anathema to orthodox taste, they were highly valued by the avant-garde. Picasso, Matisse and others were not remotely interested in the actual historical situation of the work they admired, nor how it may have functioned in the indigenous societies of Africa and elsewhere. What they were interested in was the stimulus it could provide for their own 'expressive' art.

Figure 2.6 Unknown artist, mask, Etoumbi region, Republic of Congo, Hongwe or Ngare, polychromed semi-hardwood, height 36 cm. Musée Barbier-Mueller, Geneva, inv. 1021-33. Photo: © abm–archives barbier-mueller–studio Ferrazzini-Bouchet, Genève.

Activity Look at the illustrations of *Les Demoiselles d'Avignon*, painted by Picasso in 1907 (reproduced as Figure 2.5 and Plate 3.2.1), and of a mask from the Etoumbi region, Congo (reproduced as Figure 2.6 and Plate 3.2.8). Are there any similarities, and differences, that immediately strike you?

Discussion Clearly the two works are very different: one is a large multi-figure oil painting, the other a single, relatively small, carved wooden mask. But three of the faces of the nude figures in the painting appear to be 'mask-like': the profile face on the left, and the two at the right. In particular, the one at the top right seems to bear quite a strong resemblance to the Etoumbi mask, especially in the long curved nose, but also in the stripes on the cheek and the 'black holes' of the eyes and mouth.

African objects and modernism

For writers in the 1930s, who were beginning to map the modern movement and its 'Masters' as fully fledged equivalents to the 'Old Masters' of the Renaissance, claims for a profound relationship between avant-garde art and the unvarnished truth of the 'primitive' became standard. The whole equation was concisely formulated by Robert Goldwater in his innovative survey of 1938, which contained the following 'Definition of Primitivism': 'the assumption that the further one goes back – historically, psychologically or aesthetically – the simpler things become; and that because they are simpler they are more profound, more important and more valuable' (Goldwater, 1986 [1938], p. 251).

In 1936 an important exhibition was held in New York under the title 'Cubism and Abstract Art', which did much to establish the idea of a 'mainstream' for the modern movement. The most important modern style, on this account, was Cubism. Cubism had emerged around 1910 in the work of Picasso and Georges Braque, and with its fractured forms, inconsistent pictorial space and relative abstraction it set the agenda for much of what followed in avant-garde art (Plate 3.2.9). In the catalogue accompanying the exhibition, its curator, Alfred H. Barr, forged some of the connections we have been rehearsing here. Picasso was accorded prominent status in the development of modernism principally because of his role in the development of Cubism. Barr designated Picasso's work of *c.*1907, the crucial transitional period immediately before the inception of Cubism, as his 'Negro period' (Barr, 1974 [1936]). In a page of illustrations, he succinctly made the connection between *Les Demoiselles d'Avignon* ('the Negro period at its most barbaric'; p. 30), smaller figure studies for it, and African sources (Plate 3.2.10). In a slightly later book, Barr described the characteristics of this head explicitly: 'a flat-ridged nose, a sharp chin, a small oval mouth and deleted ears' as being 'characteristic of certain African Negro masks of the French Congo', and he illustrated the 'Itumba' (Etoumbi) mask, to prove the point (Barr, 1975 [1946], p. 55).

However, in the 1980s the American writer William Rubin showed that none of the four masks that have been put forward by art historians as models for Picasso's *Demoiselles* could actually have been seen by him in 1907. In the case of the Etoumbi mask specifically, 'none of the three masks of this type known to exist came out of Africa before 1929' (Rubin, 1984, p. 262). Hence, although there is no question that Picasso did see some African sculpture around the time he was working on *Les Demoiselles*, and although some artists – such as members of the *Brücke* group in Germany – did base their paintings and sculptures directly on particular 'tribal' models, this instance reinforces the need for care in mapping the relations between 'primitive' and 'modern' art. It can be argued that, rather than simply 'copying' African models, Picasso and others were picking up on what they felt to be 'affinities' between the emotional responses to modernity that were driving their own formal experiments, and the characteristics they observed in 'primitive' carvings. It remains very much a moot point in art historical accounts as to the extent to which African art 'changed the course' of modern art or enriched a series of developments that had already begun. African carvings are an undeniable element in the constellation of factors out of which Picasso made his painting, but they are not the simple cause of it.

The Benin bronzes and 'primitivism'

Let us now turn back to the Benin bronzes, and see where they stand in this relationship between modernist art and the idea of a 'simpler, more profound' past.

Activity Look at the Benin head (reproduced as Figure 2.7 and Plate 3.1.1) and the Grebo mask from the Ivory Coast (Plate 3.2.11).

Note down what you perceive to be similarities and differences – in the subject, as well as in the material – and try especially to comment on the forms and techniques employed to shape them.

Discussion The first thing I would say is that, despite the difference in appearance, the subject matter of both is essentially the same: a human head. Perhaps it is precisely that shared subject that dramatises the differences. The material, of course, is different. The Benin head is made of cast metal, brass, in one integral form, while the mask is made of wood, with the addition of fibre for the hair. If you look closely you will be able to see that two techniques are employed on the mask. One is additive: the fibrous 'hair', and the wooden rings and bars making up the eyes and mouth are stuck on. The other is a process of carving directly into the wood, as geometric patterns are incised on the brow and the 'horns'. There is also the fact that the Benin head is free-standing: it was probably placed on an altar, whereas the mask, of course, was meant to be worn. Despite that difference, however, it is also worth noting that both would ultimately have gained their meaning in the first instance from being used in ceremonies of one sort or another, involving circumscribed spaces of some kind, and human actions, as well as words and, possibly, music.

Figure 2.7 Unknown artist, Queen Idia, commemorative head of the Queen Mother, Benin, Nigeria, early sixteenth century, brass, height 39 cm. British Museum, London, Ethno 1897.10-11.1. Photo: © The Trustees of the British Museum.

Casting and carving

In the western tradition, sculpture, broadly speaking, had been of two types: carvings, in wood or stone, and casts in materials such as bronze. Bronze casting was known in ancient China and Egypt, though the earliest bronze sculptures in the western tradition are from ancient Greece. Bronze casting was then further developed in the Italian

Renaissance and in the post-Renaissance academic tradition. Carving, as in the case of saints on the façade of a medieval cathedral, came to be regarded as an archaic method, even – to use that loaded term again – 'primitive'. The late nineteenth-century sculptor Auguste Rodin, for example, was not a carver. He modelled in clay, from which multiple bronze casts were subsequently taken (Plate 3.2.12). Even a well-known piece such as *The Kiss*, though made of marble, was not actually carved by Rodin, but was mechanically squared-up by assistants from a clay model (at most, Rodin would sometimes finish a piece off with a chisel).

Not surprisingly, given what you have already encountered about ideas of 'truth', 'originality' and 'authenticity' in the avant-garde, such practices were regarded as problematic – and after Rodin's death there was a major scandal about the provenance of multiple copies of his works. In the early twentieth century, avant-garde artists began to investigate once more the expressive possibilities of direct carving into their chosen material (Plates 3.2.13–16 and Figure 2.8). All of these artists were impelled by the power of a sense of direct contact with the material, and, needless to say, by the relation of that idea to the notion of a 'primitive' and hence 'authentic' expression.

Recategorising the Benin bronzes

On the few occasions when avant-garde artists did refer to the Benin bronzes, they seem to have simply assimilated them to the discourse of 'primitive art', despite the evident sophistication of their manufacture. Thus the German Expressionist Ernst Ludwig Kirchner made a drawing of a Benin plaque in the Dresden ethnographic museum in 1911 very much as if it was a 'primitive' carving (Plates 3.2.17–18). Still more dramatically, one of his colleagues in the *Brücke* group, Max Pechstein, made a coloured woodcut based on another Benin plaque (Plates 3.2.19–20). Here again you can see how he has rendered the quite rounded forms of the bronze cast into more jagged shapes, and added vibrant, pure colours in order to answer to a felt need for a primitive, and hence more 'expressive', power. Yet another Expressionist, Ernst Macke, writing in 1912, simply included the bronzes in a list of primitive works: 'The cast bronzes of the Negroes from Benin in West Africa, the idols from the Easter Islands in the remotest Pacific, the cape of a chieftain from Alaska and the wooden masks from New Caledonia speak the same powerful language' (Macke, 2006 [1912], p. 89).

In this context, then, the Benin bronzes are in a peculiar situation. They came from a non-western context, from what was then perceived to be a 'primitive' society, yet they themselves were anything but primitive. In terms of their material, and the sophisticated manufacturing process involved, they shared more with academic sculpture than with the values of the modernists. In fact, for this very

Figure 2.8 Constantin Brancusi, *King of Kings*, *c.*1938, oak, 300 x 48 x 46 cm. Solomon R. Guggenheim Museum, New York, 56.1449. Photo: David Heald © The Solomon R. Guggenheim Foundation, New York. © ADAGP, Paris and DACS, London 2008. For a higher-quality reproduction of this image, see Plate 3.2.16.

reason, the early twentieth-century avant-garde critic Carl Einstein argued that, from a point of view informed by the technical radicalism of the modern movement in general, and of Cubism in particular, 'despite their technical sophistication', the Benin artworks 'seem to us of no decisive significance' (Einstein, 1921, quoted in Heymer, 2007, p. 250).

When the Benin bronzes entered museum collections at the end of the nineteenth century, the anthropologists and museum curators who tried to explain them had to square a bizarre circle. On the one hand they had been taken from people who were demonised as barbarous and bloodthirsty – the epitome of the 'primitive' – and as such, justification for the civilising mission of empire. Yet on the other hand the bronzes themselves were extolled as comparable in technical mastery to the sculpture of the Italian Renaissance, that cornerstone of western civilisation itself (see, for example, Read and Dalton, 1899b, p. 372; Reading 2.6). The disparity between the avant-garde's 'translation' of the artworks into the discourse of 'the primitive' – when they were mentioned at all – and the more conservative/academic comparison with the products of the Renaissance, is symptomatic of the problems they caused for western artistic categories of all kinds.

Changing categories: from 'primitive art' to 'world culture'

However enabling they may have been to the early twentieth-century avant-garde, ideas of 'authenticity', 'direct expression' and, above all, that of the 'primitive', have proved deeply problematic. For all that they helped the avant-garde break free from academic convention, they traded in the currency of the wider culture when it came to the west's relations with the rest of the world. It would be an oversimplification to equate the beliefs of avant-gardists, such as Picasso, Matisse, Kirchner and others retrospectively identified with the discourse of 'primitivism', with imperialist politics. Indeed, a generation after them, the artists and poets of the Surrealist avant-garde developed an explicit political critique of colonialism. Moreover, those artists who did espouse the values of contemporary imperialism tended not to be avant-garde artists, but to work in an academic style (Plate 3.2.21). Nonetheless, when Picasso spoke of the *Demoiselles* as an 'exorcism painting' (André Malraux, quoted in Richardson, 1996, p. 24), he was drawing on a set of beliefs about Africa current in early twentieth-century Europe that bear little scrutiny now. Quite what he did mean is not exactly clear. But it seems likely that he was making a connection between the magical powers ascribed to African carvings on the one hand, and on the other to his own deep feelings about women, sex and violence *and* the ability to overcome them through art. In short, it seems he was trying to tap what he regarded as the power of the primitive fetish to overcome dark forces. The implication of all this, it seems to me, is not to assume an easy retrospective moral superiority over Picasso and other avant-garde artists working in the age of imperialism. It is, rather, to come to an understanding of the ambivalent power of 'Africa' as an idea, rather than as a real place with a history and a politics. Through their embrace of the 'primitive', avant-garde artists sought liberation from bourgeois constraints by breaking with the conventions of academic art. But primitivism had the effect of condemning those cultures it praised for their 'authenticity' to a state of timelessness and lack of development. When we consider primitivism in this way, we can see that it does indeed sit within the wider ideology of imperialism. A symptom of modernity itself, primitivism disenfranchised its non-western subjects from modernity, exiling them from human history and re-situating them in a perpetual 'nature'.

It is in this complex web of forces, then, that we can trace the most important thread in the relation of the Benin bronzes to artistic modernism. Not that the former in some sense 'influenced' the latter, because they didn't, for the reasons we have discussed. My point is this. The modern movement effectively expanded the definition of art, so that works of art came to be seen as intentionally complex bearers of meaning in their own right, rather than trivially accurate imitations of something in the world. So, regarded as 'works of art' in that sense – that is, as fully fledged works of art in themselves rather than as 'influences' on some other art – the Benin bronzes gave the lie to the de-historicisation of the rest of the world by prevailing western mythology. They are not the 'natural' or 'spontaneous' responses of a people outside history, defined solely by their relationship to nature, but the products of an at least partially urbanised civilisation, characterised by complex social divisions, including an elaborate guild system for the production of art, and a technology comparable to anything before the advent of modern industrialisation.

Once we have learned not to misread them as 'primitive', but to read them as 'art' – that is, as complex cultural representations – then the Benin bronzes resist the typical western misunderstanding of Africa and stand as evidence of a shared human history. They thus open the prospect of being able to think a genuinely world culture: a 'world culture' not in the sense of an increasingly unified situation produced by economic globalisation, but a world made up of equal and different cultures, evolving in different places and times – a sense quite distinct from an assumption of the pre-eminence of western art, against which all others are in various ways marginalised or diminished.

key

Displaying the Benin bronzes today

The last third of the twentieth century saw the eclipse of primitivism in fields such as cultural studies, anthropology, comparative literature and art history. As we have moved away from a sense of the culture of the rest of the world existing as a kind of fuel for western art while being denied the status of art itself, so there have been consequences for how such work is presented in western museums. I want to conclude this discussion by looking at two examples, both in London: the British Museum and the Horniman Museum.

Anthropology and aesthetics

In earlier times, ethnographic museums tended to run together the display of what we now like to regard as art – such as paintings and carvings – with the display of functional items such as utensils, weapons and even boats. To some extent the Pitt Rivers Museum in Oxford has retained this archaic mode of display deliberately: rows of glass cases stuffed with objects of every description, accompanied by explanatory labels which themselves betray the assumptions of the past about human social evolution (see Figure 2.9 and Plate 3.2.22). The British Museum used to display its Benin plaques as a sort of collective wall decoration, halfway up the main stairs, one more element in the eclectic mosaic of artefacts drawn from all over the world, the only cohering element of which was their container: the museum itself. This has now undergone substantial revision with the creation of the African Galleries.

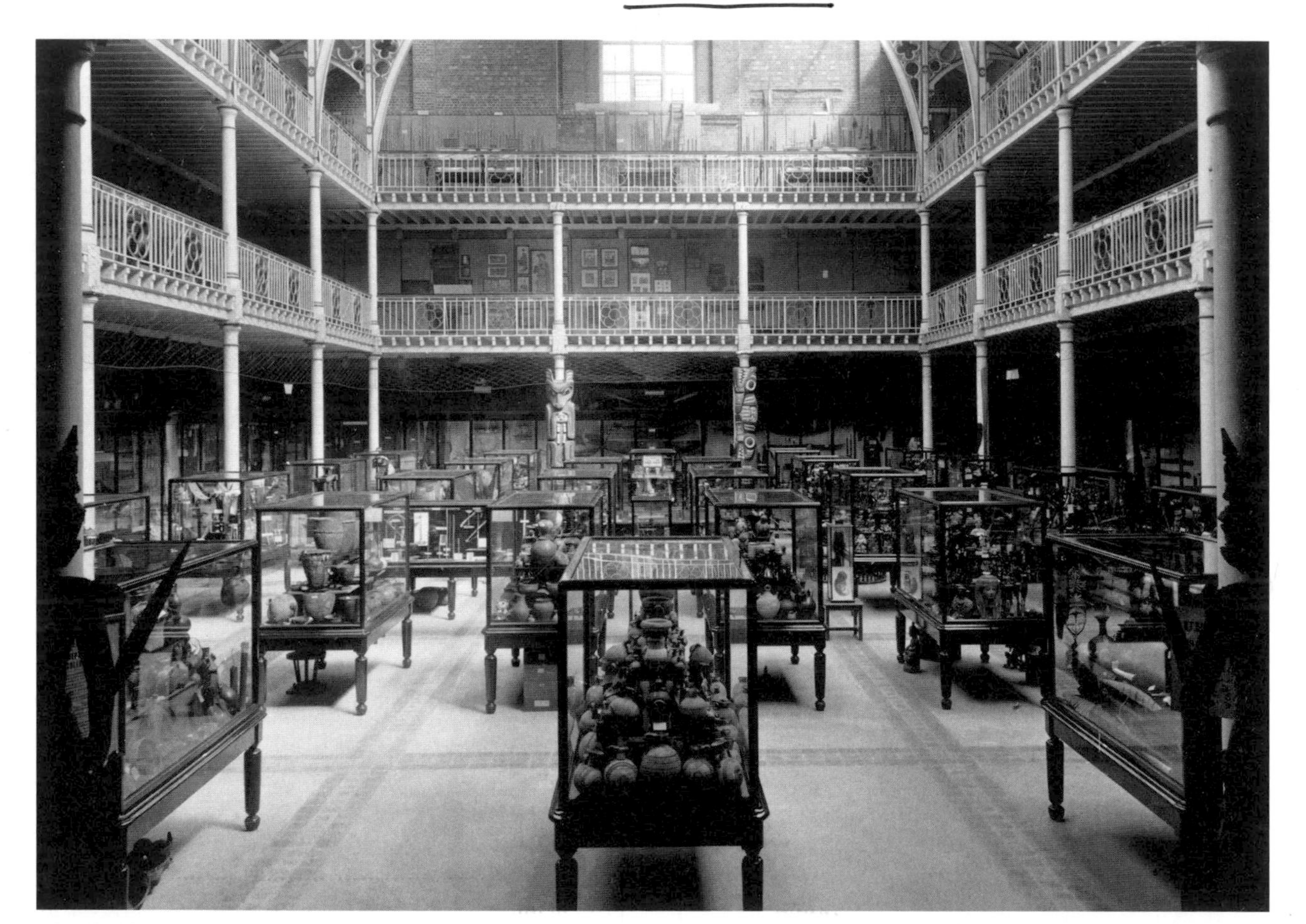

Figure 2.9 General view of the collection, Pitt Rivers Museum, Oxford, *c.*1904. Unknown photographer. Pitt Rivers Museum, Oxford 1998.267.95.3. Photo: © Pitt Rivers Museum.

One of the key shifts that the modern movement brought about in the display of art was to exhibit paintings in neutral spaces with the works widely separated to aid uninterrupted aesthetic contemplation. This was in contrast both to the way in which paintings had traditionally been displayed (where works were often piled on top of each other from floor to ceiling), and also to the way artefacts were exhibited in ethnographic museums: usually in cases with explanatory labels. The British Museum African Galleries move somewhat uneasily around these precedents, as the display tries to shift the meaning of objects such as the Benin bronzes from the sphere of the ethnographic artefact to the domain of 'art'.

While this chapter was being written, a large banner hung in the British Museum's Great Court, deep red below, golden yellow above, with leaves silhouetted at the top, suggestive, perhaps, of an African sunrise, and announcing the 'Sainsbury African Galleries' with all the prestige one would associate with a major art collection. The polished granite staircase leading down to the galleries themselves bears a dedication to the English modernist sculptor Henry Moore. Interestingly, given what we have already discussed about the European modern movement and Africa, an accompanying statement by Moore celebrates the African 'carvers', who could 'interpret' – that is, alter or 'distort' – 'the human figure to this degree but still keep and intensify the expression'. Despite the qualifications which might now be raised about this kind of assessment, embodying as it does many earlier modernist assumptions about African and western art alike, the intended message is clear: to elevate the whole collection to the status of art, and avoid the criticism that the museum does not treat African culture with the dignity it deserves.

However, the explanatory text on one African Gallery wall remains somewhat ambiguous. On the one hand, what it refers to as 'artefacts drawn from the entire continent and from many historical periods' are displayed in categories such as 'Pottery', 'Textiles', 'Personal Adornment' and, indeed, 'Brass Casting': all compatible with traditional ethnographic display. On the other hand, however, these are shown alongside what the text has no hesitation in describing as 'important works by some of Africa's foremost contemporary artists': such as the man's cloak by the Ghanaian artist El Anatsui (Plate 3.2.23). The result is a kind of blurring. The Benin display itself sits somewhat uncomfortably between historical weaponry and textiles and contemporary art – part ethnographic display, part art exhibition. Fifty-six of the plaques are displayed on vertical metal posts. On the one hand, this is meant to evoke the way they were originally mounted on the Oba's palace. But the arresting grid format, in its stripped-down, spotlit austerity, is also clearly an 'art' display, inviting aesthetic contemplation as an end in itself (see Figure 2.10 and Plate 3.2.24). Yet the rest of the Benin objects, both ivory carvings and the brass heads and figures – including the famous 'Queen Mother' head – are subject to a much more traditional display in glass cases complete with maps and technical information about their manufacture. It clearly remains a difficult circle to square.

Figure 2.10 Display of Benin bronzes in The Sainsbury African Galleries, the British Museum, 2005. Unknown photographer. British Museum, London, 24041. Photo: © The Trustees of the British Museum.

Activity How would you describe the difference between the two displays in Figures 2.9 and 2.10 (Plates 3.2.22 and 3.2.24)?

Discussion To describe Figure 2.9 (Plate 3.2.22) I would use words like 'crowded' or 'cluttered'. There is no differentiation between things we would now regard as 'art' and useful things like tools, weapons and even forms of transport.

In Figure 2.10 (Plate 3.2.24), the display of the Benin bronzes reminds me of contemporary installation art – an empty space, a geometric grid and the frisson of contrast between figurative and abstract elements.

Anthropology and aesthetics revisited: art and contemporary Africa

The Horniman Museum has taken things even further in its African Worlds gallery, seeking explicitly to shift the display of its seven Benin plaques out of the traditional anthropological encounter but also, significantly, beyond the modernist art exhibition. Each plaque is displayed in its separate space, dramatically spotlit to highlight the depth and complexity of the casting, in much the same way that a gallery of modern art would light an exhibition (Plates 3.2.25–6). But the point here is that with its art status now secured, the object is not presented as if the moment of aesthetic contemplation were an end in itself. Rather, the moment of concentrated attention on the work of art is seen as a prelude to a more prolonged encounter, involving a variety of texts and photographs, with the entire culture of Benin, past and present. New information based on contemporary research by a Nigerian historian, Joseph Eboreime, seeks to read the meaning of the plaques through ceremonies in present-day Benin, supplemented by the oral traditions in which they have their resonance. Eboreime's essay in the accompanying book pairs images of the plaques with photographs of the same ceremonies and costumes. Crucially, also in the Horniman Museum's displays, the plaques are captioned in the language of the Edo people, with English as a translation below (Eboreime, 2000; Reading 2.7).

Activity You should now read through Readings 2.6 and 2.7, paying particular attention to the two short paragraphs at the end of each extract describing the images on two of the plaques (Plates 3.2.27 and 3.2.28). Compare and contrast the description by Read and Dalton, published in 1898, with that by Eboreime, published just over a century later in 2000.

Discussion Both the tone and the content of the descriptions seem markedly different, to represent, as it were, two different stages of anthropological thought, two distinct ways of thinking about another culture. Read and Dalton speak in the supposedly objective voice of the Victorian scientist. One thing that is quite clear is that, beyond the level of description, they literally do not know what they are looking at (a 'god' or a 'king', a 'fish resembling a catfish'), and that even in their description, they are drawn to compare the image to non-African examples: 'recalling a Persian form', 'the fashion represented in Sassanian carvings'. Moreover, not only can they not understand what is represented, they do not expect to be able to find out: there is no 'hope that a clue to their origin or use might be found in Benin itself', since its people are now 'entirely barbarous'. In complete contrast, Eboreime, drawing on his familiarity with Benin ritual, and his ability to communicate with the people there, not only describes various features of the image, indicating their significance and providing their correct African names, he is able actually to name the depicted figure and say what he is doing.

Eboreime's treatment serves to underline the shift which has recently taken place in thinking about non-western art, how museums should display it, and what meanings these displays should seek to bring to the fore. For Victorian anthropologists the Benin bronzes were puzzling artefacts that were difficult to fit into a racist picture of 'primitive' ways of life. Increasingly throughout the twentieth century they took on the status of works of art to be admired in themselves rather than as a kind of historical evidence. In Eboreime's text, the terms of reference change again. For him, rather than being an end in itself, looking at the art of Benin properly becomes a gateway to African history. To sharpen the point, it may even be the case that the road passing through that gateway leads away from the western concept of 'art' itself. Rather than the contemplation of art being an end in itself, as it has become in modern western culture, free from the jurisdiction of political, religious and overtly moral criteria, the move implicitly reasserts a sense of art not as independent but as embedded in the manifold priorities of lived society: a means to an end, rather than an end in itself. If this point is pressed to its limit, a fundamental revision of the relations between art and society as we have come to experience them in western modernity would beckon.

Cultural property

These two contemporary displays of Benin bronzes at the British Museum and the Horniman Museum clearly attempt to negotiate a hazardous terrain. In one sense, they testify to a changed relationship between Europe and Africa: confirming the sense of a historical dimension to African culture that had been denied by the ideology of primitivism, and inviting a geographical and historical expansion of the concept of 'art'. But the result is far from a consensus in which everyone is happy. The debate as to whether the bronzes can be regarded as 'art' or not may have been resolved. Very much alive, however, is the question of who they belong to, whose cultural property they are, and, as a corollary of that, the question of how to decide between competing definitions of art per se. Precisely to the extent that they encourage equality between African and European cultural histories, the bronzes have become active elements in contemporary debate about a genuinely reciprocal post-colonial culture. Ironically, for all their assumption of the status of 'art', rather than becoming pristine figureheads in a sanctified space, they have entered controversy on another level. The Benin bronzes, along with the 'Elgin marbles' from ancient Greece, are embroiled in the argument about the legitimacy of their holdings into which all major western museums are now plunged. The many-sided debate about 'cultural patrimony' (about who rightfully 'owns' the arts of the past or of the non-western world), about the pros and cons of returning objects to their place of origin, about the status of the 'global' museum claiming to hold objects in trust for the whole of humanity: this is where the bronzes have their resonance now. To that extent, their significance, their *meanings*, are as contested, and as open, as ever.

Activity
You should allow two hours to work through the material on the DVD ROM.

Now turn to the DVD ROM 'The Art of Benin'. You will find that this has been divided into four main sections. The first section gives you the opportunity to examine five Benin artworks in detail. The next two sections allow you to hear different voices in the debate on where the art of Benin should be held and how it should be displayed. First you can watch a short film showing some of the Benin artworks in the context of a major exhibition at the Musée du quai Branly in Paris in 2007 and then you can listen to interviews expressing different views on the issue of repatriation. The final section returns to the concluding discussion of this chapter by asking you to think about how the display of Benin art affects its meaning through an activity on images from various exhibitions. The DVD ROM also includes a timeline and a map which you can consult at any time.

REFERENCES

Barr, A.H. (1974 [1936]) *Cubism and Abstract Art*, New York, Museum of Modern Art.

Barr, A.H. (1975 [1946]) *Picasso: Fifty Years of his Art*, London, Secker and Warburg.

Baudelaire, C. (1846) 'On the heroism of modern life' in Harrison, C., Wood, P. and Gaiger, J. (eds) (1998) *Art in Theory 1815–1900*, Oxford, Blackwell, pp. 300–04.

Bolt, C. (1971) *Victorian Attitudes to Race*, London, Routledge and Kegan Paul.

Coombes, A.E. (1994a) *Reinventing Africa: Museums, Material Culture and Popular Imagination in Late Victorian and Edwardian England*, New Haven, Yale University Press.

Coombes, A.E. (1994b) 'Blinded by "science": ethnography at the British Museum' in Pointon, M. (ed.), pp. 102–19.

Eboreime, O.J. (2000) 'Recontextualizing the Horniman's collection of Benin Bronzes', in Arnault, K. (ed.) *Re-Visions: New Perspectives on the African Collections of the Horniman Museum*, London, The Horniman Museum and Gardens, pp. 61–72.

Goldwater, R. (1986 [1938]) *Primitivism in Modern Art*, Cambridge, MA and London, The Belknap Press of Harvard University Press.

Heymer, K. (2007) 'The art of Benin in German-speaking countries: notes on its reception history in the context of avant-garde art', in Plankensteiner, B. (ed.), pp. 246–53.

Knox, R. (1850) *The Races of Men*, London, Henry Renshaw.

Ling Roth, H. (1898) 'Primitive art from Benin', *The Studio*, vol. 15, no. 69, pp. 174–85.

Macke, A. (2006 [1912]) 'Masks' in Kandinsky, W. and Marc, F. (eds) *The Blaue Reiter Almanac*, London, Tate Publishing.

Plankensteiner, B. (ed.) (2007) *Benin. Kings and Rituals: Court Arts from Nigeria*, Kunsthistorisches Museum, Vienna (exhibition catalogue).

Plankensteiner, B. (2007) 'The "Benin Affair" and its consequences' in Plankensteiner, B. (ed.), pp. 199–211.

Pointon, M. (ed.) (1994) *Art Apart: Art Institutions and Ideology across England and North America*, Manchester, Manchester University Press.

Read, C.H. and Dalton, O.M. (1898) 'Works of art from Benin City, *Journal of the Anthropological Institute*, vol. 27, pp. 362–82.

Read, C.H. and Dalton, O.M. (1899) *Antiquities from the City of Benin and Other Parts of West Africa in the British Museum*, London, The British Museum.

Richardson, J. (1996) *A Life of Picasso, vol. 2: 1907–1917*, London, Jonathan Cape.

Rubin, W. (ed.) (1984) *'Primitivism' in Twentieth-century Art: Affinity of the Tribal and the Modern*, 2 vols, vol. 1, New York, Museum of Modern Art.

Ruskin, J. (1857) 'The political economy of art: a lecture given at Manchester', London, Smith, Elder & Co.

Shelford, F. (1935) Review, *Journal of the Royal Society of Africa*, vol. 34, July, pp. 224–6.

Völger, G. (2007) 'Curator, trader, Benin scholar Felix von Luschan – an Austrian in Royal-Prussian museum service' in Plankensteiner, B. (ed.), pp. 213–25.

Weber, M. (1904–5) 'Asceticism and the spirit of capitalism' in Harrison, C. and Wood, P. (eds) (2003) *Art in Theory 1900–2000*, Oxford, Blackwell, pp. 136–7.

RESOURCES

Reading 2.1 The horrors of Benin City

Benin is indeed a city of blood, each compound having its pit full of dead and dying; human sacrifices were strewn about on every hand, hardly a thing was without a red stain, and one road was lined on each side with more than sixty victims. The city consists of a number of huge compounds of oblong shape, surrounded by walls made of red mud, about nine inches thick, and of extraordinary strength. At the top of these compounds there was usually a covered space, the ground underneath being raised about two feet. Here the people of Benin hold their hideous rites to their gods or fetishes, which are ranged along the wall, and which comprise elephants' tusks and carved figures of ivory, brass, and bronze, having the most grotesque appearance. In the centre of the sheltered part was an orifice, from the sides of which blood was streaming. I must not omit to mention the huge crucifixion-trees which were in the wide road leading past the compounds, and on which the remains of victims could still be seen.

[...]

The blood of our countrymen has been avenged, and a system of barbarism rendered hideous by the most savage, horrible, and bloodthirsty customs that even Africa can show has been effectually broken up. Now that the cause of civilisation has been advanced in this benighted district, the only wonder is that such a state of things should have been allowed to exist so long.

Source: *Illustrated London News*, 27 March 1897. Special Illustrated Supplement on Benin, p. 10.

Reading 2.2 Benin antiquities at the British Museum

An exhibition of a remarkable kind has been arranged within the last few days at the British Museum in the Assyrian basement, a part of the building better known to those who attend lectures there than to the general public. The bronzes from Benin now shown have but little in common with the rest of the contents of the room, and their exhibition in such uncongenial surroundings is due only to the want of any other gallery in which a temporary display of this kind can be made. Two long screens in the middle of the room are covered with bronzes or brass plaques, about 300 in number, with figures in high relief, cast and slightly finished by tooling, which, both by the novelty of the subjects and the technical perfection of the work, are surprising evidences of the skill of the Benin native in the casting of metal. From time to time strange, fantastic carvings in ivory or in wood, and more rarely objects in bronze, have come from parts of the coast of West Africa, and all large collections have a few such pieces which could not be assigned to any of the known tribes. These we now know to have been made at Benin, as the numerous objects that have been brought home by officers from the recent expedition have precisely the same strange appearance and are designed in the same fantastic style. [...]

Among the figures of natives are some which are deserving of special mention, notably one type on which the figure, which otherwise resembles the rest, has in place of legs two snakes, the heads of which curve upwards on either side, recalling in a striking manner the monstrous figures found upon Gnostic gems [Roman period amulets carved from hard, often semi-precious stones, with images of deities or demons and short Greek inscriptions]. That this has special meaning there can be no doubt. It occurs upon several of the bronzes, and every one of the many tusks that formed a considerable part of the Benin spoils had the same figure repeated upon it in different ways. Whether there was at any time a link between the brutal savages of Benin and the Gnostics is a question not easy to solve. It is hard to believe; but the coincidence is not the less remarkable. There was a faint hope, among those who thought of the possibilities, that among the loot from Benin might be found some traces of the more ancient civilizations of Northern Africa, drifted down among the unheeding negroes through the trade routes which have served from time immemorial as the avenues by which the great natural riches of Central Africa reached the Mediterranean. No such treasures have appeared, but in their place we have an entirely unexpected phase of negro craftsmanship, although West Africa, Ashanti especially, is noted for its metal workers.

Source: *The Times*, 25 September 1897, p. 12.

Reading 2.3 On the British loss of antique works of art from Benin

When on the return of the members of the Punitive Expedition it became known that fine specimens of bronze castings and ivory and wood carvings had been found in the old city of Great Benin, Mr. Charles H. Read, the Keeper of Antiquities at the British Museum, with characteristic energy at once endeavoured to secure for the national collection good representative specimens of these bronzes, and he succeeded in gathering together the finest collection of plaques that is to be found in any Museum. But owing to the want of proper pecuniary support, he was not able to obtain possession of any of the more expensive, and in many cases equally interesting, articles. Not only was the national institution thus deprived of its lawful acquisitions, but at the same time another government department sold for a few hundred pounds a large number of castings which had cost thousands to obtain, as well as much blood of our fellow countrymen. Hence it is that so many Bini articles are not represented at all at Bloomsbury. [...]

From what I can ascertain, the bulk of these bronzes has been secured by the Germans [...]

For many years the Germans have foreseen that the study of native races and their development, a study known to us under the awkward name of Anthropology, is essential to every civilised community which trades with, or is called upon to govern native communities [...]

Politically, it is of the first importance that our governing officials should have a thorough knowledge of the native races subject to them – and this is the knowledge that anthropology can give them – for such knowledge can teach what methods of government and what forms of taxation are most suited to the particular tribes, or to the stage of civilization in which we find them. In connection with this, there can be no doubt that with adequate knowledge much spilled bloodshed could have been saved in the past, both on our frontiers and in our colonies.

Source: Henry Ling Roth (1972 [1903]) *Great Benin: Its Customs, Art and Horrors*, Northbrook, IL, Metro Books, pp. xviii–xix.

Reading 2.4

Negro

In certain of the characteristics mentioned [above] the negro would appear to stand on a lower evolutionary plane than the white man, and to be more closely related to the highest anthropoids. The characteristics are length of arm, prognathism, a heavy massive cranium with large zygomatic arches, flat nose depressed at the base, &c. But in one important respect, the character of the hair, the white man stands in closer relation to the higher apes than does the negro.

Mentally the negro is inferior to the white. The remark of F. Manetts, made after a long study of the negro in America, may be taken generally as true of the whole race: 'the negro children were sharp, intelligent and full of vivacity, but on approaching the adult period a gradual change set in. The intellect seemed to become clouded, animation giving place to a sort of lethargy, briskness yielding to indolence. We must necessarily suppose that the development of the negro and white proceeds on different lines. While with the latter the volume of the brain grows with the expansion of the brainpan, in the former the growth of the brain is on the contrary arrested by the premature closing of the cranial sutures and the lateral pressure of the frontal bone.' This explanation is reasonable and even probable as a contributing cause; but evidence is lacking on the subject and the arrest or even deterioration in mental development is no doubt very largely due to the fact that after puberty sexual matters take the first place in the negro's life and thoughts. At the same time his environment has not been such as would tend to produce in him the restless energy which has led to the progress of the white race; and the easy conditions of tropical life and the fertility of the soil have reduced the struggle for existence to a minimum. But though the mental inferiority of the negro to the white or yellow races is a fact, it has often been exaggerated; the negro is largely the creature of his environment, and it is not fair to judge of his mental capacity by tests in mental arithmetic; skill in reckoning is necessary to the white man, and it has cultivated this faculty; but it is not necessary to the negro.

On the other hand negros far surpass white men in acuteness of vision, hearing, sense of direction and topography. A native who has once visited a particular locality will rarely fail to recognise it again. For the rest, the mental constitution of the negro is very similar to that of a child, normally good-natured and cheerful, but subject to sudden fits of emotion and passion during which he is capable of performing acts of singular atrocity, impressionable, vain, but often exhibiting in the capacity of servant dog-like fidelity which has stood the supreme test. Given suitable training, the negro is capable of becoming a craftsman of considerable skill, particularly in metal work, carpentry and carving. The bronze castings by the *cire perdue* process, and the cups and horns of ivory elaborately carved, which were produced by the natives of Guinea after their intercourse with the Portuguese of the 16th century, bear ample witness to this. But the rapid decline and practical evanescence of both industries, when that intercourse was interrupted, shows that the native craftsman was raised for the moment above his normal level by direct foreign inspiration, and was unable to sustain the high quality of his work when the inspiration failed.

Source: Entry on 'Negro' in the *Encyclopædia Britannica*, 11th edn (1910–11). Written by T.A. Joyce, Assistant in the Department of Ethnography, British Museum, and Secretary of the Anthropology Society.

Reading 2.5

West Africa before Europe

Scientific Europeans, who have any time to give to the subject at all, look upon a being whose physical characteristics are so different from their own as possessing also mental peculiarities which require special study. The unthinking European partly from superficial knowledge and partly from a profound belief not only in an absolute racial difference, but in his own absolute racial superiority, rushes to the conclusion that this difference of external appearance implies not only a physical difference, but an inferior mental or psychological constitution, and that the man possessing it must by assiduous culture by the European be brought up to the level of his teacher.

[...]

Miss Kingsley was a providential instrument raised up in the course of human evolution to save Europe from imbruing her hands in her brother's blood. She dreaded, as Europe with further light will dread, the guilt of murdering native institutions, and thus if not actually destroying the people, impairing their power of effective co-operation with their alien exploiters. Every race, it is now being recognised, has a soul, and the soul of the race finds expression in its institutions, and to kill those institutions is to kill the soul – a terrible homicide. 'Fear not them which kill the body but are not able to kill the soul.'

Europe had so long been taught to regard the people who drink the waters of the Niger, the Gambia, and the Congo, who dwell on the borders of the great Lakes and roam the plains of Nigeria as hopelessly degraded, that it came as a surprise – to not a few an agreeable surprise – to learn that these people had institutions worthy of study, of respect and of preservation.

[...]

When we consider the zeal and energy with which generous Europeans have for the last hundred years been trying to introduce religion into Africa, it is interesting to look back to ancient times and study the place which the Continent then occupied in the religious history of the world. It was for many ages the seat and centre of religious impulse – so regarded, it would appear, by the Almighty Himself, as we are taught in the Bible, and by the gods of Greece and Rome, as taught by their Poets. The founders of the Hebrew religion, Abraham, Isaac, Jacob, Moses – received religious instruction in Egypt. The greatest of all the Prophets was in helpless infancy sheltered in Egypt. Great Kings and warriors went to Africa to learn the will of God at the Oracle of Jupiter Ammon. Alexander the Great did homage to it and made costly offerings at its shrine.

[...]

The opinion, then, throughout the civilised world of that time – among the most enlightened nations of Greece, Asia, and Egypt – was that God revealed himself only in Africa, that 'He buried His great truths in Afric's sands.' If Africa is the 'last home of the devil' as it has been recently said, it was the first home of God.

Now things have so changed that it is the opinion of some that God is everywhere except in Africa.

Source: Edward W. Blyden (1903) 'West Africa before Europe', *Journal of the Royal African Society*, vol. 2, no. 8, pp. 359–74 (extracts from pp. 363, 365, 368–9).

Reading 2.6 Works of art from Benin City

The panels which are our principal subject, form part of a series of about three hundred which are now in the British Museum [...] When it was announced that Benin had been taken and that many curious objects had been discovered there, official representation was made to the Government on behalf of the British Museum, so as to secure at any rate some of the specimens, and samples of these tablets were in consequence sent from the coast [...]

Their appearance seemed to point to their originally having been buried, for they were, and many of them still are, covered with a fine red earth, in some to such an extent that the details could not be made out. It is not easy to understand why they are covered with this earth, but it seems certain that they were not buried, for Major Gallwey in a letter written just before he went out again, says, 'The plaques were found heaped up anyhow on the floor of an empty house in the king's compound. None of them were hanging up nor were any buried. They appeared to be simply thrown in a heap and uncared for. [...]' This is the only account of their finding that we have, and it effectually destroys any hope that a clue to their origin or use might be found in Benin itself, and we are thus thrown back upon the tablets themselves to solve their own mystery.

It need scarcely be said that at the first sight of these remarkable works of art we were at once astounded at such an unexpected find, and puzzled to account for so highly developed an art among a race so entirely barbarous as were the Bini, and it must be confessed that the latter problem has not yet been solved.

[...]

The method by which the tablets were produced can only be that known as the '*cire perdue*' process. By no other is it conceivable that so much extravagant relief and elaborately undercut detail could be represented with success. [...]

This '*cire perdue*' process is that by which many of the finest Italian bronzes of the best period were produced, and we thus find the Benin savages using with familiarity and success a complicated method which satisfied the fastidious eye of the best artists of the Italian renaissance.

[...]

A description of one of the plaques (Plate 3.2.27).

A god, or king considered as god. He wears a helmet-like headdress, with vertical top, recalling a Persian form. This is apparently covered with beadwork made of cylindrical coral beads. To the front are attached three larger beads or possibly some sort of charm. He wears a jacket covered with similar beadwork, from the lower border of which are suspended small human masks, possibly of cast metal. On his wrists are large (carved ivory) armlets. He wears the usual 'beluku' or long loin-cloth, with guilloche border and covered with chased ornament [...] He has broad anklets, probably of coral beadwork, which were a sign of higher rank than necklaces. A fish resembling a catfish, of a kind constantly repeated in both casts and carvings, issues from each of his sides, while in each hand he swings a leopard by the tail, after the fashion represented in Sassanian [ancient Persian] carvings.

Source: Read and Dalton (1898), pp. 370–2, 377 (footnote omitted).

Reading 2.7 Recontextualising the Horniman's collection of Benin bronzes

The redisplay of the Benin bronzes in the *African Worlds* gallery, was turned into an occasion to advance iconographical and historical research on pieces in the Horniman Africa collection. In this paper I mean to present some of the material which was generated from fieldwork aimed at eliciting contemporary interpretations of bronze plaques and pieces. For this I drew on my familiarity with Edo historical and ritual discourse [...]

The aim of the interpretative enterprise was a historical iconographical reconstruction which was intended to illuminate the central question of how the bronze plaques reflected the history of the Benin Kingdom and court life from about the middle of 16th century to the beginning of 17th century [...]

Reinterpretation of the Benin bronze plaques

Interpretation of the bronze plaques and pieces in the *African Worlds* gallery has similarly drawn impetus from my Edo background, indigenous knowledge and cognition facilitated by comparison with ongoing rituals and practices in Benin.

Photographs of the Horniman collection of bronze plaques were taken to the field. With the help of my field assistants who were groomed in the palace, the motifs and themes from the plaques were compared with living traditions and rituals witnessed during the annual *Igue* festivals. The reason for the presence or absence and significance of motifs were explained in detail through private interviews held in the houses of chiefs, priests and women. The burial rites of the Queen Mother in 1999 provided a unique opportunity to witness ancient practices, songs and rituals, made public; while the centenary celebration of 1997 provided a corpus of corroborative materials to help in the analysis of the plaques.

Images, texts, histories

What follows are iconographical interpretations of seven bronze plaques that are in the Horniman collection. They can be said to reflect the history of the Benin kingdom, court life, as well as [to] speak of the contact with immediate neighbours and foreigners, from about the middle of 16th century up to the beginning of 17th century.

[...]

A description of one of the plaques (Plate 3.2.28).

Although he [Ezomo Agban] is standing alone, the Ezomo's posture and ceremonial war regalia suggest that he is dancing the victory dance, Isi' Okuo, at the victory parade after defeating an enemy.

[...]

The deputy commander is wearing a high pyramidal helmet with flaps covering the ears (*erhu iy'ewu*) and the leopard teeth necklace encased in a brass base (*akon atalakpa*). A brass pectoral war-bell (*egogo amen u'yan re*) is hanging from the necklace to guarantee a warrior's safe return.

The Ezomo is also wearing leaded brass body armour (*ewu'oze*) engraved with the image of a leopard's face, a royal symbol that invoked awe and reverence. Underneath the body armour he is wearing a leather dress with straps and brass bells. The brocade wrapper is designed in the *guilloche* pattern (*Oba n'urhi*) and edged with coral beads. The background of the plaque is decorated with six 'the sun never misses a day' and water leaf motifs.

According to Benin legend, while Ezomo Agban was relating his war exploits to the new Oba, Ehengbuda N'Obo, he was interrupted by a thunder clap. In vexation, Ezomo Agban declared war on the inhabitants of the sky.

Source: O.J. Eboreime (2000) pp. 61, 64–5, 70.

Media notes

Glossary for the DVD ROM

This list contains key terms and names that can be found on the DVD ROM and which are not defined in the book glossary.

aestheticising the act of regarding something in terms of its formal properties. In the film on the musée du quai Branly, it is used to refer to the treatment of Benin artefacts as works of art to be appreciated as such in their own right. See **aesthetic** in the glossary at the end of the book.

Chirac, Jacques (b. 1932) President of France from 1995 to 2007. Chirac actively supported the building of the Musée du quai Branly as a showcase of non-western art.

discourse the discussion of a topic in text or spoken language. The term assumes that this language contains meanings which have the power to provoke certain interpretations.

ethnocentrism the tendency to evaluate other cultures through preconceived ideas originating in one's own.

Le Fur, Yves assistant director at the Musée du quai Branly.

Musée de l'Homme Museum of Mankind in Paris created in 1937 to supersede the Musée Ethnographique du Trocadéro (Ethnographic Museum at the Trocadero) which was founded in 1878 to house and display collections of artefacts and curiosities from around the world.

Musée des Arts Africains et Océaniens a museum in Paris built for the colonial exhibition of 1931 to house African and Oceanic artefacts.

Musée du quai Branly a museum and gallery, commissioned by the French President Jacques Chirac, dedicated to the display of non-western art.

Nouvel, Jean (b. 1945) French architect who designed the Musée du quai Branly in Paris.

othering the act of treating someone or something as different. In this case it refers to the treatment of non-western art as essentially different from – and, by implication, inferior to – western art.

patrimony inheritance usually handed down from a male ancestor. It is used by Anne-Christine Taylor in the film about the musée du quai Branly to refer to cultural inheritance (usually referred to in English as 'heritage').

repatriation the sending back of people to their country of origin. In the debate on the Benin bronzes the term is applied to artefacts and their possible return to the place where they were produced.

restitution the restoration of lost or stolen objects to their rightful owner. In the context of debates over ownership of the Benin artefacts, 'restitution' is regarded by some as a solution to the debate over ownership.

Taylor, Anne-Christine Director of Research and Information at the Musée du quai Branly.

3 CULTURAL ENCOUNTERS AND CULTURAL EXEMPTIONS

Jon Pike

MATERIALS YOU WILL NEED

- Audio CD: Discussing Cultural Exemptions

AIMS

This chapter will enable you to:

- follow a debate that arises within the philosophical tradition of liberalism
- understand the terms 'difference-blind liberalism' and 'autonomy'
- gain some experience in assessing and manipulating arguments: in particular, argument by analogy, moving from particular cases to general principles.

INTRODUCTION

In this chapter, we are going to look at some issues that arise when cultures encounter each other, and when they encounter political and philosophical traditions. The idea that there can be philosophical traditions was mentioned in Book 2, Chapter 1 on Plato's *Laches*, where it was stressed that philosophical traditions are open to questioning and criticism. In this chapter, we shall investigate the philosophical tradition known as **liberalism**. In particular, we shall consider how liberalism deals with the claims of people who belong to minority cultures – for example, Roman Catholics or Sikhs living in the UK, or Musqueam Indians living in Canada. This is not to suggest that liberalism itself is somehow outside or above culture: that is certainly not the case. Rather, in Western Europe and North America, liberalism as a philosophical tradition is a part of the dominant culture.

The tradition of liberalism has changed and developed in response to an increasingly diverse world. Rather than looking at the whole set of ideas covered by the term liberalism, we will focus on a particular version, which is known as **difference-blind liberalism**. This version of liberalism has been much discussed in recent years (Barry, 2001; Taylor, 1995). Difference-blind liberalism is a set of ideas about the way in which governments and other public institutions should treat different groups of people. We are going to look at that set of ideas in a rather abstract way. But ideas do not exist in a vacuum. They have historical roots, and they develop against a changing social background.

One important influence on the development of difference-blind liberalism has been the emergence, in Western Europe and North America, of societies that include many different cultural groups. This is, in part, a consequence of colonial rule – a topic that you have already encountered in the chapters on Benin. In recent history, the European empires have been in retreat – a process that began in the eighteenth and nineteenth centuries with the independence of the Americas; and which continued, after the Second World War, with the independence of many other former colonies, particularly in Africa, South East Asia, and the Indian subcontinent. The period after colonialism has seen major shifts of peoples; and as a result, Western European countries have become home to a variety of minority cultures. The trend towards multicultural societies is seen most clearly in Britain, France, Belgium and the Netherlands, reflecting their histories as colonial powers (see Figure 3.1). In North America, the picture is a little different: the story of the emergence of the USA, for example, has been one of different cultures forming one state, albeit with huge tensions and struggles along the way. There continue to be tensions and disputes between the dominant culture and a variety of minority cultures, including religious and Native American minorities.

Figure 3.1 Eid celebrations held in Trafalgar Square, London, 28 October 2006. Photographed by Daniel Berehulak. Photo: 2006 Getty Images. This was the first time the Muslim festival of Eid ul-fitr, which marks the end of Ramadan, was celebrated in Trafalgar Square.

But not all cases of cultural difference result from colonisation and the movement of peoples. As John Wolffe showed in his discussion of English Christianity (Book 2, Chapter 3), cultural differences can also arise when religious and other cultural traditions change, diverging from the practices and beliefs of long-established groups. For example, Roman Catholicism is now practised by only a minority of people in England, where it was once the dominant religion.

As the discussion of Benin in Chapters 1 and 2 made clear, cultural encounters have many different aspects. The story told in those chapters is, in part, a story of conflicting values; of an encounter shaped by assumptions of cultural and racial superiority; and of violent confrontation. But it is also a story of discovery and exchange, and of the way in which the traditions of one culture can be enriched through an encounter with the traditions of another. In this chapter, we will focus on the idea that cultural diversity within a society can produce a certain kind of ethical or political *problem*. The problem arises because the values of minority cultures sometimes clash with the values of the dominant culture, and it is not obvious how these clashes should be resolved. Should members of minority cultures be expected to conform to the values of the majority? Or should members of minority cultures sometimes be exempted from laws or policies that conflict with their beliefs or traditions? In other words, should they sometimes be granted what have become known as **cultural exemptions**? This issue forms just one small part of a much wider public debate about cultural diversity and multiculturalism that has developed in recent years. As you come to the end of this chapter, you will be able to listen to some discussion of this wider debate on the Audio CD 'Discussing Cultural Exemptions'.

In the following sections, we are going to look at a range of real-life cases, including Sikhs and Catholics in the UK; Rastafarians and the Amish in the USA; and the Musqueam people in Canada. In studying these cases, you may find yourself reacting quite strongly. Some of the examples may make you feel uncomfortable, or encourage you to think again about assumptions you make. The aim of this discussion is not to force you to change those assumptions, but to allow you to recognise them *as* assumptions, which are open to question and challenge. This should help you to think further about these examples, and about other similar cases. In the *Laches*, Lysimachus and Melesias were trying to resolve a practical problem: how to educate their sons. But this practical problem prompted Plato's characters to reflect on their assumptions about the nature of courage (Book 2, Chapter 1). In this chapter, practical concerns should prompt philosophical reflection in the same way.

Before we look at these cases, I shall introduce some of the key principles of liberalism; and I shall explain how difference-blind liberals think about issues concerning public policies and cultural diversity.

3.1 LIBERALISM, FREEDOM AND EQUALITY

What are the rules that should govern society? In Western Europe and North America, this question has most commonly been answered by appealing to the principles of liberalism.

Liberalism, in this sense, is only very loosely related to the views of political parties that describe themselves as 'liberal'. Liberalism is a historical tradition, and belongs to a particular time and place. It arose in the seventeenth century as a reaction to earlier traditions, in particular traditions that assumed that there is a natural hierarchy among human beings. Liberalism also stood in opposition to certain kinds of discrimination. These included the religious discrimination that arose out of the shifts in religious traditions which you studied in connection with English Christianity (Book 2, Chapter 3). One of the founding documents of liberalism was John Locke's *Letter Concerning Toleration* (1689). Locke (1632–1704) argued that there should be much more toleration of religious diversity, and an end to religious persecution. Even so, he did not push his conclusions as far as he might: atheists, he thought, could not be trusted, because they did not believe in an afterlife in which they would be held accountable for their misdeeds.

John Locke was an English philosopher, known both for his rejection of rationalist theories of knowledge, of the kind espoused by Plato, and for his contribution to liberal political theory. He argued that the legitimacy of a government depends on the consent of the governed, and that people have a right to overthrow a government that threatens their liberty or property. In *The Letter Concerning Toleration*, he argues that the state should not interfere in religious matters, though he makes exceptions for atheists and for members of religions with beliefs or practices that threaten the security of the state or its members.

Figure 3.2 Unknown artist after Sir Godfrey Kneller, portrait of John Locke, *c.*1704, oil on canvas. The Bridgeman Art Library. Photo: © Philip Mould Ltd, London/The Bridgeman Art Library.

The tradition of liberalism has continued to develop and to diversify, but there remain some key ideas that are typical of liberal views. In particular, liberalism is thought of as focusing on the rights of the individual. These rights are supposed to guarantee the freedom of individuals to live and to express themselves as they choose. In addition, they are supposed to guarantee that individuals will be treated equally, for example, by ensuring that everyone receives due process under the law. I mentioned earlier that liberalism was, in part, a reaction to the idea that there is a natural hierarchy among human beings, and that some people deserve better treatment than others. In contrast, liberals hold that every human being is of equal moral value, and that justice is a matter of treating people equally. But what exactly does 'equal treatment' mean?

Figure 3.3 Unknown artist, statue of Justice. Photo: © Jürgen Priewe/Alamy. Justice is depicted as a blindfolded woman with a set of scales – in one way, carefully measuring differences, in another way, completely disregarding them. But what should Justice measure, and what should she ignore?

There are some very obvious ways in which I am equal to you. There is just one of me and, taking you (the reader) as an individual, there is just one of you. We are both human beings; warm-blooded; capable of making rational choices about our lives. But there are also likely to be many important differences between us: I am unlikely to be exactly the same age and height as you; and we may well have different hair colour, religious beliefs, political views, musical tastes, living arrangements and so on. There seem to be many contexts in which it is perfectly appropriate to take differences of these kinds into account: for example, when I chat to friends, it is appropriate for me to take account of their age, musical tastes, political views and so on. But in other contexts, it seems, it is not appropriate to take account of these differences. Suppose that a young man is on trial for murder. In deciding on a verdict, what the jury needs to consider is whether or not he committed the murder. They do not need to consider whether he is over or under six foot, or whether he prefers classical music to pop, or what he looks like. In a court of law, all defendants are supposed to be treated equally, and treating them equally means ignoring things like height, musical tastes and appearance.

Activity Until quite recently, especially at the older universities, students sitting an examination would begin by writing their name on the top of their answer sheet. Almost all universities have now changed to anonymous marking, in which a student is identified by a number rather than by a name. How might this help to ensure that all the candidates are treated equally?

Discussion This shift in practice has helped to ensure equal treatment in marking by making sure that markers don't take account of irrelevant information in assigning marks to students' scripts. It's often possible to tell someone's gender or ethnicity from their name. By removing this information, anonymous marking ensures that there's no possibility of someone's gender or ethnicity affecting their mark. It also means that a marker can't tell who a student is, so they can't give high marks to a student whom they like or low marks to a student whom they dislike.

So, treating people equally involves ignoring certain kinds of difference between them. Exactly which kinds of difference should be ignored seems to depend on the context: academic achievement is not relevant to the jury's decision, but it is relevant to someone who is marking examination scripts.

I mentioned earlier that liberalism is primarily concerned with the rules and institutions that govern society. Liberals hold that, in making laws and setting policy, governments and other public bodies should treat people equally. As we have seen, this involves ignoring certain kinds of differences between them. But which differences should governments ignore? There is some room for liberals to disagree on this point. In this chapter, I am going to focus primarily on a version of liberalism that has become known as difference-blind liberalism. (The label is a little unhelpful: as I have just been saying, the issue among liberals is not *whether* some differences should be ignored, but *which* differences should be ignored. However, since the label is now commonly used among philosophers, I shall stick with it here.) Difference-blind liberals argue that, when it comes to making laws and setting policies, governments should ignore differences of gender, ethnicity, culture and religion. Instead, they emphasise universal and common features of our humanity, and insist that it is these universal features that are relevant when it comes to making laws and setting policies. Differences in religion, culture, gender and ethnicity are seen as a private matter, which ought not to be the concern of public institutions. This is how difference-blind liberals interpret the claim that every human being is of equal moral worth.

The story of the development of liberalism is not straightforward. Those who have called themselves liberals have not always stood by its ideals of freedom and equality. Nevertheless, liberalism has

The system of apartheid was in place in South Africa from 1948 to 1991. Under this system, voting rights were restricted to the white minority; members of different racial groups were made to live in different areas, attend different schools and use different amenities; members of the majority black population and other racially defined groups suffered a wide range of legal, educational, economic and social disadvantages.

provided a basis for opposition to legally instituted racism in South Africa and in the southern states of the USA. One form of opposition to racist laws, like those that made up the South African Apartheid state or those that fuelled the Civil Rights Movement in the USA, appeals to difference-blind liberalism to insist that the laws of a country should not take account of racial differences (see Figures 3.4 and 3.5). To be racist is to discriminate in favour of or against people for no other reason than that they belong to one particular racial group. Difference-blind liberals hold that a person's racial origins do not alter his or her value as a person, and that they are irrelevant to questions of citizenship and employment; so racist laws are unjust.

In this chapter, we are concerned with cultural differences, rather than differences of gender, race or ethnicity. Cultural differences might include differences in moral values; different tastes in art, literature or music; differences in social customs and traditions; and differences in belief – particularly religious belief. For many people, cultural identity will line up with ethnic identity, but this is not always the case: for example, people from the same ethnic background do not always share

Figure 3.4 A beach near Cape Town, South Africa, reserved for white people only during the South African apartheid, 1979. Unknown photographer. Photo: Keystone Features/Getty Images.

Figure 3.5 Civil rights protest in Memphis, Tennessee, 29 March 1968. Unknown photographer. Photo: © Bettmann/Corbis. Civil Rights protestors on Beale Street in Memphis, USA, walk past a row of National Guard riflemen with signs saying, simply, 'I am a man'.

The Civil Rights Movement in the USA was at its most active in the 1950s and 1960s. The movement used protest marches, sit-ins and boycotts to oppose the numerous forms of racial segregation and discrimination affecting African Americans at the time. Its members campaigned for the desegregation of schools, public transport, libraries, cinemas and other facilities, and for equal access to voting rights, jobs and education.

the same religion or social customs. With this in mind, it is possible to define the aspect of difference-blind liberalism that I am interested in as follows:

> *The difference-blind principle*: Laws and public policies should treat everybody in the same way, regardless of their cultural identity or religious beliefs.

We might wonder whether this principle is correct. Deciding that, though, would be a huge task. Instead, I am going to ask a more specific question. Is adopting this principle the best way to apply the values of liberalism? Should liberals be difference-blind?

3.2 WHAT IS DISCRIMINATION?

One reason that might be given for endorsing difference-blind liberalism is that treating groups of people differently is wrong. Treating groups differently is discrimination, and discrimination is unfair or unjust. But what is discrimination?

Very generally, discrimination takes place whenever one group of people is treated differently from another group of people. However, this happens all the time, and often we do not think that it is unfair.

Activity

- Think of an example in which one group of people is treated differently from another group of people, and note whether you think the difference in treatment is fair or unfair.
- If the example that you have thought of is a case of unfair discrimination, say why you think it is unfair. Can you change the example in a way that would make the discrimination fair?
- If it is an example of fair discrimination, can you change the example to make the discrimination unfair?

Discussion

Some examples I came up with are:

- Architects discriminate between men and women when they plan separate changing facilities at swimming pools. This doesn't seem (to me) to be unfair. But it would be unfair if the actual provision differed significantly – if, for example, men were given twice as much room to change in than women.
- Examiners discriminate between students when they give some high marks and some low marks. If the different marks are distributed according to the academic worth of the student's work, this doesn't seem to me to be unfair. Perhaps it would be unfair to give everyone the *same* mark. But if the marks were given out on the basis of which students the examiner found most witty or charming, then that would be unfair.
- In the UK, people aged over 60 get a free bus pass. Opinions may differ over whether this is fair or not. A reason for thinking that this might not be fair is that some people over 60 are much wealthier, and so find it much easier to pay for bus tickets, than some people under 60. But perhaps it is possible to agree that it would be unfair if, say, only Roman Catholics over 60 received a free bus pass.

From your answers and from mine as well, we have some raw materials to do some philosophy. The aim is to get a general sense of the difference between cases of discrimination that are unjust, and cases of discrimination that are not unjust. To do this we are going to need to look at a range of particular cases, and try to extract some general principles from them. As you will see, we are not going to end up with a polished account of justice. Philosophers since Plato have struggled to say what justice is, and I am not going to try to resolve this question right now. What I am aiming to do is to identify some of the considerations that are relevant in thinking about discrimination and justice. If we can do this, we will at least have made a start on the problem.

3.3 WHEN IS DISCRIMINATION UNJUST?

First, it looks as if we ought to distinguish between treatment that is *better* or *worse*, and treatment that is merely *different*. It is when treatment is worse for one group and better for another that discrimination starts to look unjust. (But we should also bear in mind that sometimes treatment is worse *because* it is different.)

It is not always unfair to treat one group of people less favourably than another: it is not unfair, for example, for examiners to award lower marks to people who have performed less well in an examination; but it is unfair for markers to award high marks only to students whom they find witty or charming. The difference seems to be that academic achievement is *relevant* to examination marks, whereas wit and charm are not. Which properties are relevant and which are irrelevant depends on the case in question: it does not seem unfair to consider wit or charm when choosing someone to deliver an after-dinner speech.

This might be taken to suggest that discrimination is unjust when it is based on something that is irrelevant to the particular case. So we might try adopting this principle:

> *Principle 1*: It is unjust to discriminate between people on the basis of considerations that are irrelevant to the situation.

Principle 1 is supported by the case of the examiners. But in order to test whether it applies more generally, we need to find out whether we can imagine a case in which it does not apply so well.

Activity

Suppose that you are an impresario and that you are looking for a tightrope walker for a circus. You put an advertisement in the paper, asking that people write to you, outlining their tightrope-walking skills, by a certain date. Once you have the replies and the closing date has passed, you then select between those who wrote in, perhaps by giving them an audition.

Now suppose that a woman writes to you, complaining that you did not consider her for the job. She saw the advertisement, she says, but chose not to answer it because she was too busy. She points out that the ability to answer a letter by a certain date has no bearing on the ability to perform a high-wire act. Next time, she suggests, you should not hold an audition, but instead scout for talent, to make sure that you have considered everyone who might be able to do the job. Otherwise you will be guilty of unfairly discriminating against people who are particularly busy.

Does she have a good case? If not, why not?

Discussion

Here's my own response to this case. I don't think that the woman has a good case. I agree that the ability to write a letter by a certain date is irrelevant to the ability to perform a high-wire act, but I also think that there are some other considerations that are important. One is that the woman *chose* not to write in. She could have written in, but she chose not to do so, and she can be held responsible for the choice that she made.

If this is right, Principle 1 does not apply to every case: there are some cases in which it is not unjust to discriminate on the basis of something that is not directly relevant to the case. Nevertheless, the tightrope-walker example might be taken to suggest a different principle. The case appears to suggest that it is not always unfair to discriminate on the basis of characteristics that are a matter of *choice*. This is because discrimination is one way of holding someone responsible, and we hold people responsible for what they choose to do. In contrast, it might be thought, it is unfair to discriminate on the basis of characteristics that are simply a matter of chance. For example, it may be that part of what is unjust about sexual discrimination is that gender is a matter of chance, not choice.

This suggests a second principle that we might adopt:

> *Principle 2*: It is unjust to discriminate between people on the basis of considerations that are not a matter of choice.

Once again, though, we need to consider whether Principle 2 applies to all cases. Is it unfair to discriminate against someone in the selection of a basketball team because they are, through no fault of their own, short? Height is not a matter of choice. On the other hand, shorter people are, generally speaking, worse at basketball than taller people: so height is at least a relevant consideration. If choosing the tallest available players is not unjust, then Principle 2 will not apply in all cases.

It seems, then, that neither Principle 1 nor Principle 2 applies to all cases, and so we have not succeeded in finding a simple way to define unjust discrimination. Nevertheless, it does look as if we have identified two considerations – relevance and choice – that have an important role to play in deciding whether a particular case of discrimination is just or unjust. Certainly, it does seem to be unjust to discriminate between people on the basis of considerations that are *neither* a matter of choice, *nor* relevant to the situation. In what follows, we will be investigating whether it can be just to make laws or set public policies that discriminate between members of different cultural groups. In thinking about this issue, we will need to bear these two considerations in mind.

Before moving on, there is one last question that I would like to raise: if cultural discrimination is an injustice, how serious an injustice is it?

A restaurant may, arbitrarily and unreasonably, fail to provide brown sauce for its diners, and instead offer only tomato ketchup. This might be an arbitrary injustice, but there is not a systematic pattern of discrimination in society against those who prefer brown sauce to tomato ketchup. It is not true that brown sauce aficionados have bad housing, miss out on jobs, get a rough deal from the criminal justice system and so on. So the injustice in the lack of full provision of sauces in that restaurant is a trivial injustice. If, on the other hand, an employer only employs Protestant job applicants, that is quite another matter, especially on the island of Ireland and in west-central Scotland. That is a form of arbitrary injustice, but it is not at all trivial, because it chimes in with other ways in which non-Protestants have been discriminated against. This suggests that the seriousness of the injustice will depend to a large degree on the extent to which it fits into a broader pattern of deep-seated, long-lasting and substantial inequalities. On this measure of seriousness, then, treating people from different cultures differently is likely to be much more serious than treating people with different tastes in sauce differently. That is one reason why debates over cultural discrimination matter.

3.4 RULES AND EXEMPTIONS

In liberal democracies, it is generally assumed that laws and public policies should be formulated in such a way that they apply equally to everyone. For example, UK law forbids anyone to drive a car if they do not have a driving licence; there are no exemptions. However, in a culturally diverse society, laws acceptable to the majority will sometimes conflict with the values of a cultural minority. In Western Europe and the USA, these conflicts of value have sometimes been managed using the **rule and exemption approach**.

Suppose that there is a law that prohibits a certain activity. Under the rule and exemption approach, an exemption can be granted for a specific group of people if they can show that the activity has a particular religious or cultural significance for them. Here are some examples in which members of a cultural minority sought exemption from law or a public policy. In each case, you have (a) the general law or policy; (b) a sketch of the case for the exemption; and (c) a report of the outcome.

1 Exemption from the prohibition of cannabis use (USA).
  (a) Consumption of cannabis is prohibited in the USA.
  (b) The Ethiopian Zionist Coptic Church appealed for an exemption on religious grounds: 'The core of Rastafarian religiosity resides in the revelatory dimensions induced by the sacramental use of Ganja in which a new level of consciousness is attained. Adherents to the movement are enabled more easily to perceive Haile Selassie as the redeemer and to appreciate their own identities' (Poulter, 1998, p. 356; quoted in Barry, 2001, p. 39).
  (c) The appeal was finally turned down by the US Supreme Court in 1990.

2 Exemption from the compulsory wearing of crash helmets (UK).

   (a) Between 1972 and 1976 in the UK, all motorcycle riders were required by law to wear a crash helmet.

   (b) Sikhs sought an exemption, on the grounds that Sikh religious observance requires Sikh men to wear turbans (Barry, 2001, pp. 296–7).

   (c) In 1976, the Motor-Cycle Crash Helmets (Religious Exemption) Act was passed, establishing the exemption in law.

3 Exemption from anti-discrimination legislation concerning same-sex adoption (UK).

   (a) Under the Equality Act (2007) in the UK, adoption agencies must not discriminate against same-sex couples in adoption cases.

   (b) The Catholic Church requested an exemption from the provisions of the Act on religious grounds: 'to oblige our agencies in law to consider adoption applications from homosexual couples as potential adoptive parents would require them to act against the principles of Catholic teaching' (Letter from Cardinal Cormac Murphy-O'Connor, sent to the British Prime Minister on 22 January 2007).

   (c) The request for an exemption was turned down, in favour of a temporary delay in the application of the Equality Act to Catholic agencies.

4 Exemption from fishing quotas (Canada).

   (a) In 1983, the Canadian Department of Fisheries banned the use of fishing nets over a certain length in some coastal waters.

   (b) In 1984, Ronald Sparrow, a member of British Columbia's Musqueam band, was charged with fishing with a net longer than was permitted by his food fishing licence. Mr Sparrow did not dispute the facts, but argued that he was exercising an existing aboriginal fishing right, constitutionally protected under section 35(1) of the Constitution Act (1982).

   (c) In a series of Supreme Court judgments, Canada upheld exemptions to general fishing restrictions on the basis of aboriginal fishing rights. Their decision turned on the finding that: 'for the Musqueam, the salmon fishery has always constituted an integral part of their distinctive culture' (R. v. Sparrow (1990) 1, SCR, 1075).

5 Exemption from requirement to display 'slow-moving vehicle' sign (USA).

   (a) In Minnesota, slow-moving vehicles are required to display a red and orange reflective triangle (see Figure 3.6).

   (b) The Swartzentrubers (a subgroup of the Amish) objected on the grounds that the signs are 'wordly' and 'using them would mean trusting in the symbols of man rather than in the protection of God' (Zook, 1993, pp. 145–60; quoted in Barry, 2001, p. 184).

   (c) Gideon Hershberger was sentenced to jail for seven days after refusing to pay fines incurred when he failed to display a 'slow-moving vehicle' sign. But, in 1989, the ruling was overturned by the Minnesota Supreme Court.

6 Exemption from particular elements in the school curriculum (USA).

(a) In the USA children attending a publicly funded school must follow the school curriculum.

(b) In 1987, a group of fundamentalist Christian parents claimed a right to exempt their children from the basic reading curriculum of the school system in Hawkins County, Tennessee. They objected to exposing their children to any idea that conflicted with their religious beliefs, which they took to be based on the literal word of the Bible (Barry, 2001, pp. 245–7).

(c) The court refused to grant the parents the right to select which elements of the school curriculum their children should follow.

Figure 3.6 Amish man travelling in a horse-drawn courting buggy, displaying a slow moving vehicle sign, Lancaster County, Pennsylvania. Photographed by Chuck Pefley. Photo: © Chuck Pefley/Alamy. Most Amish communities do not object to displaying 'slow-moving vehicle' signs.

It is worth pausing to note the seriousness of these cases. For some people, the requested exemption goes to the heart of their identity – to what makes them the sort of person that they are. The exemption may seem essential in order to protect deeply held values or to preserve a long-established way of life. On the other hand, the granting of the exemption may have momentous consequences for some of the people affected by it. For example, in the Hawkins County case (example 6), at issue were not only the values of a religious group, but also the standard and breadth of the education offered to their children. In these cultural encounters with difference-blind rules, there is a lot at stake.

Figure 3.7 Special Constable Jabbal, the first British policeman to wear a turban on duty, London, 1970. Unknown photographer. Photo: © Hulton-Deutsch Collection/Corbis. Sikh police officers in the UK are permitted to wear a turban in place of a cap.

All these cases have the same basic structure. In each case, a minority group requests an exemption from a difference-blind rule on the grounds that the exemption is required in order to protect their cultural identity, or their religious practices, or to preserve a long-established way of life. But there are also some differences between the cases. You might have noticed that in some case the requested exemption was granted but in others it was not. In some cases, the requested exemption was likely to have had a direct impact on third parties, while in others – such as cases (1) and (2) – this was not the case. Finally, you may also have noticed that, although in most cases there was an appeal to religious beliefs or practices, case (4) turned solely on the cultural identity of the Musqueam people.

How did you react to these cases? You might have thought: 'At last, people are starting to accept that they ought to be sensitive to cultural differences, rather than forcing their way of life on others.' On the other hand, you might have thought: 'This looks like Political Correctness gone mad! When in Rome, you should do as the Romans do.' In what follows, I want to try to stand back from these initial reactions, and consider some of the principles that might be used to evaluate the rule and exemption approach. In particular, I will explore a tension between the rule and exemption approach and the principles of difference-blind liberalism.

Activity Look back at the definition of difference-blind liberalism presented at the end of Section 3.3. Why should a difference-blind liberal object to the rule and exemption approach?

Discussion Difference-blind liberalism implies that justice is a matter of treating everyone equally, regardless of their cultural identity. But the rule and exemption approach involves treating members of cultural minorities differently. Hence, a difference-blind liberal will object that the rule and exemption approach is unjust.

So, difference-blind liberals are committed to the view that the rule and exemption approach is unjust. It might be argued that the injustice is not as serious as it is in cases in which cultural minorities are treated less favourably by the law, especially where this forms part of a pattern of unfavourable treatment. Nevertheless, the rule and exemption approach clashes with the principles of difference-blind liberalism. By itself, this does not imply that the rule and exemption approach should be abandoned. We might choose to defend the rule and exemption approach on pragmatic grounds, while allowing that it does involve a certain degree of injustice. Alternatively, we might decide to reject difference-blind liberalism – perhaps in favour of a version of liberalism that takes account of cultural differences.

In what follows, I am going to consider three arguments that aim to show that the rule and exemption approach is consistent with the broader principles of liberalism, and that liberalism should not be difference-blind. As we shall see, the first of these arguments is not successful, but the second and third do raise some significant questions for the claim that laws and public policies should ignore cultural differences.

3.5 THE AUTONOMY ARGUMENT

The first argument we are going to consider goes like this. It might be said that I ought to wear a crash helmet when I ride a motorcycle because I ought to protect myself from injury. But perhaps it should be up to me whether I do this or not: after all, it is my head. So perhaps I should not be prevented by law from riding a motorcycle without a helmet. Making the point more general, if I should be allowed to wear whatever I want when I ride a motorcycle, Sikhs should be allowed to do so too. It is a matter of personal freedom.

Let us call this the 'autonomy argument' against compulsory motorcycle helmets. **Autonomy** means 'self-rule': an autonomous person is able to make his or her own choices about how to live. To treat someone as autonomous involves respecting them as a rational being, with the right to make up his or her own mind as to how to live. The notion of autonomy plays an important role in liberal theories: as we saw in Section 3.3, liberals value the freedom of each individual to live as he or she chooses. So, if the autonomy argument proves to be a good argument in favour of cultural exemptions, this might give us a reason to reassess the claim that liberals should reject the rule and exemption approach. Unfortunately, though, the autonomy argument does not succeed in establishing this.

Activity Why does the autonomy argument fail to show that Sikhs should be granted an exemption from the law that requires motorcycle riders to wear crash helmets? (It might help to start by thinking about what it does show.)

Discussion You will probably see quite quickly that the autonomy argument isn't an argument that favours granting an exemption to Sikhs. Rather, it's an argument against the law that forces motorcyclists to wear helmets. It certainly implies that Sikhs ought to be allowed to ride motorcycles while wearing turbans, but that's because it implies that everyone, regardless of culture or religion, should have that right. In fact, it is a difference-blind criticism of legislation designed to protect people from harm that they may cause to themselves.

Take any of the six cases above: you could appeal to the importance of autonomy to argue that:

1 Cannabis should be legalised.
2 People should be free to ride motorcycles without crash helmets.
3 It should be legal to discriminate against same-sex couples.
4 The state ought not to restrict fishing.
5 'Slow-moving vehicle' signs ought not to be a legal requirement.
6 Parents ought to have a legal right to determine what their children learn at school.

Each of these claims might be defended on the grounds that some things are up to the individual, and that the government should not interfere with people's autonomy. But in each case, the objection is to the rule itself, not to the suggestion that it should be applied to everyone, regardless of cultural identity.

Autonomy arguments, then, are arguments that should be taken seriously by liberals. They give liberals a reason (though not necessarily a conclusive one) to be cautious about any legislation that restricts personal freedom. But they do not give liberals a reason to reject difference-blind liberalism in favour of the rule and exemption approach, because they do not imply that members of cultural minorities should be treated differently.

In Section 3.8 we shall consider a different way of appealing to autonomy to defend cultural exemptions.

3.6 THE UNEQUAL IMPACT ARGUMENT

The second argument against difference-blind liberalism might be labelled the 'unequal impact argument'. It goes as follows.

Difference-blind liberals reject the rule and exemption approach because they hold that laws and public policies should apply equally to everybody, regardless of their cultural identity. But there is another important sense in which difference-blind laws and policies do not necessarily treat everybody equally. This is because they do not always affect everybody in the same way. Arguably, for the majority of people living in the USA, the prohibition on cannabis impacts, at most, on how they choose to relax or socialise; but, as we saw in Section 3.4, for members of the Ethiopian Zionist Coptic Church, the prohibition prevents them from doing something that has a particular significance and value for them. So, there is a sense in which the prohibition of cannabis does not treat everyone equally: although the law *applies* equally to everyone, it has a heavier *impact* on members of the Ethiopian Zionist Coptic Church. Thus the law might be said to discriminate unjustly against members of that church.

In your work on Plato's *Laches* (Book 2, Chapter 1), you learned how to clarify how an argument works by breaking it up into premises and a conclusion. Let's do that here:

The unequal impact argument

Premise 1: If a law or policy does not have the same impact on everybody, it is not just.

Premise 2: The blanket prohibition of cannabis does not have the same impact on everybody.

Conclusion: The blanket prohibition of cannabis is not just.

This is a valid deductive argument. But should the difference-blind liberal accept that all its premises are true?

Looking at the two premises, it seems to me that the difference-blind liberal is likely to reject the first premise. The difference-blind liberal is likely to reply that this is not what is meant by the claim that laws and public policies should treat everyone alike: what is meant is that laws should apply in the same way to everyone, not that that they should affect everyone in just the same way.

How might a difference-blind liberal defend this reply? One way to do this would be by drawing an *analogy* between the case of the Ethiopian Zionist Coptic Church and a more familiar kind of case, on which most people are likely to agree. Suppose that a supermarket decides to operate a 'first come, first serve' parking policy. People who

Figure 3.8 No smoking sign, public house, Killarney, Ireland, 2006. Photographed by Adrian Muttitt. Photo: © Adrian Muttitt/Alamy. In 2004, the Republic of Ireland introduced a law forbidding smoking in workplaces. A similar ban was imposed in Scotland in 2006, and in England and Wales in 2007. The ban impacts more heavily on smokers than on non-smokers. Is it unfair?

drive to the supermarket have to park their cars in the available slots, and no slots are put aside for any specific group. Clearly, this policy will not affect everybody in the same way. For example, people who are particularly busy and who can visit the supermarket only at peak times are likely to find that the policy is more inconvenient for them than it is for other people. Nevertheless, I imagine that most people would not think that the policy discriminates unjustly against people who are busy.

If this is right, it suggests a way in which a difference-blind liberal might try to support the claim that it is not unjust to enact laws that have a heavier impact on some cultural groups than on others. The argument would go like this:

> The supermarket's parking policy impacts more heavily on people with busy lives. But that does not make it unfair. In the same way, the fact that the prohibition of cannabis impacts more heavily on members of the Ethiopian Zionist Coptic Church does not mean that the law is unfair. The two cases are *analogous*.

In the next section, we will consider in more detail how this argument is supposed to work, and whether or not it is a good argument.

3.7 ARGUMENTS BY ANALOGY

Lots of arguments in philosophy take the form of an **argument by analogy**. You have already heard Tim Chappell mention arguments by analogy as you listened to 'Plato's *Laches* – a discussion with Tim Chappell'.

An argument by analogy is one that compares two cases – Case A and Case B. We want to decide something about Case B. We know that Case A is just like Case B, so, by analogy, we can conclude that something that is true of Case A is likely to be true of Case B. For example, suppose that I am trying to decide whether it is wrong to break a promise. Breaking a promise, I take it, is similar in important ways to lying – for example, they both involve misleading someone. I already believe that lying is wrong; so, I conclude, breaking a promise is probably wrong too.

Arguments by analogy can be a very useful tool in philosophy: a good analogy can shed fresh light on an issue, suggesting a new and illuminating way of thinking about a problem. But it is also important to understand their limitations. An argument by analogy is not a deductive argument. As you saw in the chapter on Plato's *Laches*, deductive arguments are proofs: if the premises of a deductive argument are true, you can be certain that the conclusion is true. But an argument by analogy is not a proof: even if lying and breaking promises are similar in some important ways, it does not necessarily follow that they are similar in every way. An argument by analogy gives us some reason to accept its conclusion, but it does not establish it for sure.

Most importantly, an argument by analogy is only as good as the analogy it rests on. If there turn out to be some significant dissimilarities between lying and breaking promises, then the analogy between them will break down. Building strong analogies relies on the ability to spot relevant similarities between cases, and to exclude important dissimilarities. This is one way in which philosophy requires imagination and judgement, not just the analytical skills needed to get a deductive argument correct.

Activity Look again at the argument by analogy at the end of the last section. Do you think that the analogy to which the argument appeals is a good one? Can you think of any relevant differences between the two cases?

Discussion There are several good answers that might be given to this question, but here is one possibility:

'No, I don't think that the analogy is a good one, because there's an important dissimilarity between the two cases. People who are busy are busy because of the choices that they make, and it's not unfair to ask them to bear the costs of their choice of lifestyle. But religion and culture are not a matter of choice. And as we saw in Section 3.3, choice is an important consideration in deciding whether or not a case of discrimination is unjust.'

You might notice that this brings us back to one of the general principles we identified earlier. Arguments by analogy are often a powerful way of identifying or highlighting general principles: spotting relevant similarities or dissimilarities between two cases can often help us to see an underlying principle at work.

It might be suggested, then, that the argument by analogy that I presented at the end of Section 3.6 fails, because there is an important dissimilarity between the two cases. A busy lifestyle is a matter of choice, but culture and religion are not. Indeed, it might be thought that there is a much more appropriate analogy that could be drawn – one that compares the members of the Ethiopian Zionist Coptic Church, not with busy shoppers, but with shoppers who have limited mobility. Like busy shoppers, shoppers with limited mobility are likely to find that the supermarket's parking policy makes life particularly difficult for them. Arguably, though, they have rather better grounds for complaining that the supermarket's policy is unfair to them, because limited mobility is not a matter of choice. This suggests that we might be able to construct an alternative argument by analogy – one that supports, rather than undermines, the case for cultural exemptions:

> The supermarket's parking policy impacts more heavily on people with limited mobility. And that makes it unfair. Similarly, the prohibition of cannabis impacts more heavily on members of the Ethiopian Zionist Coptic Church. And so, by analogy, it is also unfair.

But which of these two arguments by analogy (if either) should we accept? Is the situation of the members of the Ethiopian Zionist Coptic Church analogous to that of the busy shoppers? Or is it is analogous to the situation of people with limited mobility? Are culture and religion a matter of choice or of chance? (See Figure 3.9.)

Is it just a matter of chance that it turns out that someone is a member of the Musqueam band, or a Roman Catholic, or a Sikh? Some people will emphasise the way we are thrown into a culture from birth: for example, we have no choice about what language we learn as toddlers. Again, if one's religious beliefs are simply imposed by one's upbringing or education, they do not seem to be chosen. If this is right, there is a reason to think that it is wrong to discriminate on the basis of cultural identity or religious beliefs – it would be like discriminating on the basis of gender or skin colour.

Figure 3.9 Jewish father and son praying together. Photographed by Geoff Manasse. Photo: Geoff Manasse/Getty Images. How far are religious beliefs and practices a matter of choice, and how far are they simply transmitted from one generation to the next?

On the other hand, many religious communities emphasise the need for people to make a conscious choice to join or to stay on as adults. Moreover, as you saw in your work on *Tradition and Dissent*, cultural traditions are not static: they change over time, and they change, in part, as a result of the choices that people make. But if religious beliefs or cultural traditions are more a matter of choice than chance, the situation of cultural minorities seems to be analogous to that of the busy shoppers, who ought to bear the costs of their choice of lifestyle.

These issues are explored further by Bhikhu Parekh and Brian Barry on the Audio CD 'Discussing Cultural Exemptions'.

So, the argument from analogy that I set out at the end of Section 3.6 is inconclusive. This is because it is not clear whether or not the analogy is a good one. To decide this, we would need to think further about the relationships between culture, religion and choice. This is a very complex issue, and it seems unlikely that there will be a simple answer. Rather than pursue this further here, I am going to consider a third attempt to defend the rule and exemption approach.

3.8 AUTONOMY AND CULTURAL RESOURCES

As we saw earlier, liberals value autonomy. We have also seen that it is not possible to defend the rule and exemption approach by making a simple appeal to autonomy. Nevertheless, there is another way of bringing autonomy into the discussion, and I am going to explore that here.

Autonomy means being able to make my own choices, and to live in accordance with those choices. To do that, I need to have certain resources. These might include *physical* resources: if I want to build a house, I need some bricks. They might also include *economic* resources: to buy bricks, I need money. Without these physical and economic resources, I am not free to build a house, but only free to wish that I could.

Some of the things that I might choose do require what we might think of as *cultural* resources. For example, it is reasonable to think that being easily understood by those around you is necessary for you to achieve some of the things you want to do in your life. This means having people who share a language with you. To live among people who are unable to understand you might well make you feel trapped and powerless. This is a point that is made in Shakespeare's play *Richard II* (*c.*1595). Thomas Mowbray, sentenced to lifelong exile, laments the loss of his native tongue:

> The language I have learnt these forty years,
> My native English, now I must forgo,
> And now my tongue's use is to me no more
> Than an unstringèd viol or a harp [...]
> Within my mouth you have enjailed my tongue,
> Doubly portcullised with my teeth and lips [...]
> What is thy sentence then but speechless death,
> Which robs my tongue from breathing native breath?
>
> (Act 1, Scene 3, ll. 153ff.)

Mowbray describes his situation as a kind of imprisonment ('you have engaoled my tongue') – the very opposite of autonomy. In Chapter 4, you will read a short story, 'In Cuba I was a German Shepherd', that further explores the sense of displacement and frustration that can be experienced by people living in an unfamiliar culture.

For reasons of this kind, it has sometimes been suggested that people who value autonomy ought also to value special exemptions for minority cultures. Cultural exemptions help to preserve cultural resources of various kinds, by building strong communities in which people feel at home and can pursue activities that matter to them. In contrast, laws and policies that ignore cultural differences risk destroying cultural resources, leaving members of minority cultures isolated and adrift.

Figure 3.10 Street signs in both English and Bengali, Brick Lane, London. Photographed by Alex Hinds. Photo: © Alex Hinds/Alamy.

Two philosophers, Avishai Margalit and Joseph Raz, have recently argued that it is important to preserve cultural traditions. Margalit and Raz are liberal philosophers, but they reject difference-blind liberalism. This is because they hold that cultural groups should be able to live in accordance with their own principles. They call this 'self-determination'. There is a close connection between self-determination and cultural exemptions, because cultural exemptions make self-determination possible for minority cultural groups.

Activity Work carefully through Reading 3.1, and answer the following questions:

1. In what ways, according to Margalit and Raz, are individuals shaped by their cultural background?
2. How would they respond to the claim made earlier, that membership of a cultural group is a matter of choice?
3. Why is the point about choice important to their argument?
4. What do they suggest is the connection between the well-being of a cultural group and the well-being of the individual members of that group?

Discussion

1. Margalit and Raz suggest that membership of a certain cultural group helps to determine what people want, and what they are able to do with their lives. Cultural background can influence the kinds of work

people are able to do; the kinds of activities they enjoy; the way in which they interact with other people; and the kinds of expectations they have about the way their lives should go.

2. Margalit and Raz allow that people can choose to adopt a new culture, perhaps as a result of moving to another country, but they suggest that the process is 'painful and slow' and rarely complete.
3. Margalit and Raz want to reject the idea that people who lose some aspect of their culture can compensate by simply adopting a new cultural tradition: for most people, they suggest, being born into a particular culture has a profound influence on the kind of person that they are; and so the loss of cultural traditions will almost always have a damaging effect on them.
4. They argue that the well-being of an individual depends on the well-being of their cultural group. People who are taken away from their cultural group, or whose cultural traditions are diminished or destroyed, are less able to live as they choose to live. Since they cannot easily adopt another culture, they are likely to lead frustrated and unfulfilling lives.

If Margalit and Raz are right, their argument ought to be taken seriously by liberals. This is because it turns on the idea that the membership of a flourishing cultural group enhances one's autonomy. This might be taken to suggest that difference-blind liberals are wrong to argue that cultural differences are irrelevant to public policy. Liberals hold that laws and public institutions ought to support people in living autonomous lives. So if cultural resources are needed to secure autonomy, liberals should conclude that cultural differences are relevant to public policy after all.

Are Margalit and Raz right? Pause now and think about your own case. Can you identify one significant way in which your own cultural background influences the way in which you live now? (You might think about the kinds of example suggested by Raz and Margalit.) Now imagine that a law has been enacted that prevents you from taking advantage of this aspect of your own cultural tradition. Would you find it easy to adjust? Or would you find yourself adrift, like Thomas Mowbray without his native tongue?

The claim that cultural exemptions can foster autonomy does seem plausible to me. But do they always have this effect? Consider the case of the fundamentalist Christian parents who wanted to stop their children from encountering what they took to be non-Christian ideas at school. It might be argued that the point of exposing schoolchildren to a broad range of ideas and experiences is to enhance their ability to make choices for themselves. Had the courts allowed the *parents* to exercise their autonomy, the result might have been that the *children* of the community would have been less able to live autonomous lives.

Perhaps the way out of this dilemma is obvious. It is to say, carefully, that *sometimes* cultural exemptions foster and support people's ability to live autonomously, and *sometimes* they thwart autonomy. Some cultural exemptions will enhance the autonomy of some individuals (the parents) and thwart the autonomy of others (their children). You need to look at each case individually, and note the outcome. Often the outcome will depend on the nature of the cultural group which is seeking the exemption. Does the group have a free, equal, and democratic internal regime? Can people join and leave the group easily? Does the group itself value autonomy, as liberals understand it? Note how these questions, though framed in general terms, can only be answered with reference to the actual investigation of particular cases. And notice how the argument is moving overall – from particular cases, to general principles, and then back to the particular cases.

So perhaps what liberals should say is that when cultural exemptions support individual autonomy, they should be put in place, but when they undermine individual autonomy, they should be opposed. We can test the cases out and see which approach does best in enabling people to lead flourishing and autonomous lives.

CONCLUSION

In this chapter we have looked at an issue that arises when a cultural encounter leads to a conflict of values. We have considered how the rule and exemption approach has been developed in order to accommodate the values of minority cultures, and why difference-blind liberals have questioned that approach. This involved thinking quite carefully about what makes it fair to treat different groups of people in different ways. Although we did not give a definition of justice, we did mention two considerations – relevance and choice – that seemed to be important in deciding between fair and unfair cases of discrimination.

We then considered three kinds of argument that appealed to the liberal values of autonomy and equality to support the rule and exemption approach, and so to undermine difference-blind liberalism. The autonomy argument turned out quite quickly not to be an argument against difference-blind liberalism at all. The unequal impact argument introduced the idea that difference-blind rules discriminate unjustly against cultural minorities because cultural identity is not a matter of choice. However, how far culture is a matter of choice, and how far it is a matter of chance, was left an open question.

Finally, the cultural resources argument was shown to challenge the assumption made by difference-blind liberals that cultural differences are irrelevant when it comes to determining public policy. The cultural resources argument aims to show that cultural differences are relevant to public policy because cultural traditions provide resources that people need to live fulfilling lives. But this argument cuts both ways: some cultural exemptions can foster autonomy; others can undermine it. It looks as if we need to think about the practical impact of cultural exemptions – and that is where we need to start looking at the facts of each case.

We began by suggesting that philosophy should lead us to examine and to question assumptions that we might otherwise take for granted. This chapter has highlighted some assumptions that help to shape the debate about cultural exemptions. In particular, the discussion has raised three issues:

- What does it mean to treat different groups of people fairly?
- Is cultural identity a matter of choice or of chance?
- Are there reasons for governments or other public bodies to protect or even to foster diverse cultural traditions?

We have considered these issues against the background of a particular philosophical tradition, liberalism, with its emphasis on the twin values of autonomy and equality. As we have seen, though, when it comes to deciding particular cases, theoretical principles will not yield answers on their own: they need to be combined with a detailed and sensitive understanding of each case. For this reason, I have not drawn any particular conclusions at the end of this discussion, but I hope you have been prompted to think, and think again, about the outcomes of these cultural encounters.

Activity
You should allow about an hour and a half for this activity.

You should end your work on this chapter by listening to the Audio CD 'Discussing Cultural Exemptions'. You should listen to this material in conjunction with the Media notes, which you will find at the end of the Resources section for this chapter.

REFERENCES

Barry, B. (2001) *Culture and Equality*, Cambridge, Polity Press.

Murphy-O'Connor, Cardinal Cormac, Letter, 22 January 2007 [online] http://news.bbc.co.uk/1/hi/uk_politics/6290073.stm (accessed 18 September 2007).

Poulter, S. (1998) *Ethnicity, Law and Human Rights: The English Experience*, Oxford, Oxford University Press.

R. v. Sparrow (1990) 1, SCR, 1075 [online] http://www.musqueam.bc.ca/pdfs/R_v_Sparrow.pdf (accessed 1 October 2007).

Shakespeare, W. (1997 [1597]) *Richard II*. in Greenblatt, S. et al (eds) *The Norton Shakespeare*, London, Norton, pp. 952–1012.

Taylor, C. (1995) 'The politics of recognition' in A. Gutmann (ed.) *Multiculturalism*, Princeton, Princeton University Press, pp. 25–85.

Zook, L. (1993) 'Slow-moving vehicles' in D.B. Kraybill (ed.) *The Amish and the State*, Baltimore, The John Hopkins University Press, pp. 145–60.

RESOURCES

Reading 3.1 National self-determination

[P]eople growing up among members of the group will acquire the group culture, will be marked by its character. Their tastes and their options will be affected by that culture to a significant degree. The types of career open to one, the leisure activities one learned to appreciate and therefore able to choose from, the customs and habits that define and colour relations with strangers and with friends, patterns of expectations and attitude between spouses and among other members of the family, features of lifestyles with which one is capable of empathizing and for which one may therefore develop a taste – all these will be marked by the group culture.

They need not be indelibly marked. People may migrate to other environments, shed their previous culture, and acquire a new one. It is a painful and slow process, success in which is rarely complete. But it is possible [...] The point made is merely the modest one that, given the pervasive nature of the culture of the groups we are seeking to identify, their influence on individuals who grow up in their midst is profound and far-reaching. The point needs to be made in order to connect concern with the prosperity of the group with concern for the well-being of individuals. This tie between the individual and the collective is at the heart of the case for self-determination. [...]

Most people live in groups of these kinds, so that those who belong to none are denied full access to the opportunities that are shaped in part by the group's culture. They are made to feel estranged and their chances to have a rewarding life are seriously damaged.

Source: Avishai Margalit and Joseph Raz (1990) 'National self-determination', *The Journal of Philosophy*, vol. 87, no. 9, pp. 439–61 (extract from p. 444).

Media notes Audio CD: Discussing Cultural Exemptions

Carolyn Price

You should end your work on this chapter by listening to the Audio CD 'Discussing Cultural Exemptions'. Here Jon Pike presents extracts from interviews with two eminent political philosophers: Lord Professor Bikhu Parekh and Professor Brian Barry.

The material is quite dense, and it would be a good idea to listen to it in short sections. One approach would be to take it one track at a time: you might listen to each track once, taking notes; then listen to it again, sitting back to get an overview of what is said. You should spend about an hour and a half working on this material.

We have included some questions and activities below to help you to get the most from the material.

Track 1: Introduction

Jon Pike begins by introducing the material and the interviewees. He mentions that both speakers have held chairs at the 'LSE' – the London School of Economics. He also mentions the controversy over a speech given by the Archbishop of Canterbury in February 2008 concerning 'Sharia law': Sharia law is a body of Islamic religious law, developed over centuries, which applies to a wide range of day-to-day matters, including politics, business and family life.

Track 2: What is a cultural group?

Bikhu Parekh answers this question in some detail. How does he define a cultural group? How does he take a cultural group to differ from a group of model railway enthusiasts?

Jon Pike goes on to put the same question to Brian Barry. (You may notice that he mentions 'Chapter 16'. This is an error: it should be 'Chapter 3'.) Brian Barry's answer to the question is rather shorter. He moves quickly on to the idea that the practices of a cultural group can bring them into conflict with wider society. He mentions 'female genital mutilation': this term refers to a range of practices, found in several parts of the world, which involve the partial or total removal of the female external genitalia, often including removal of the clitoris ('clitorodectomy').

Track 3: Should we be difference-blind liberals?

Brian Barry's initial answer to this question is broadly sympathetic to difference-blind liberalism. He suggests that it is an extension of the 'paradigm' or defining example of liberalism, namely the principle of religious toleration eventually adopted in Western Europe. You might notice, though, that he does not assert that cultural exemptions should *never* be granted.

Bikhu Parekh is much less sympathetic to difference-blind liberalism. His answer is quite complex, and the following activity is designed to help you through it.

Activity

1. Listen carefully to Parekh's answer. What reasons does he give for rejecting the view that the law should treat everyone uniformly?
2. On what point does Parekh agree with difference-blind liberalism? On what point does he disagree?

Discussion

1. Parekh gives three reasons for rejecting the view that the law should treat everyone uniformly:
   (a) If everyone is to be treated uniformly, which practices should be selected as standard? Should the oath that witnesses take in court be one that makes sense to Christians, to Muslims or to atheists? You might contrast what Parekh says here with Barry's assumption that it is possible for the state not to 'instantiate' (that is, to reflect) anybody's particular religious views.

(b) If everyone is treated uniformly, this will sometimes defeat the purpose of the law – for example, if everyone is made to take a secular oath, this will not have the same motivating effect on a Christian or a Muslim, because it does not reflect their values. You might be able to connect what Parekh says here with Margalit and Raz's point about the importance of cultural resources in people's lives.

(c) The law ought to respect people's different identities. Again, you might make a connection with Margalit and Raz's argument.

2 Parekh agrees with difference-blind liberalism that everyone should be treated equally, but he thinks that it is wrong to equate equality with uniformity.

In contrast, Brian Barry argues that there are some cases in which cultural identity is simply unimportant: his example is the law on motorcycle helmets. Why does Barry think that the cultural identity of Sikhs is unimportant in this kind of case? What, according to Barry, is the difference between this case, and the case of a Sikh schoolboy who wants to wear a turban instead of a school cap?

Towards the end of this track, Barry mentions the law in Saudi Arabia forbidding people to 'proselytise': that is, to attempt to convert others to their own religion. He also mentions 'anti-paternalism': that is, opposition to the view that the state should control people's behaviour for their own good.

Track 4: Difference-blind laws and unequal impact

Difference-blind laws impact unequally on different cultural groups. Does this imply that difference-blind laws are unjust?

Jon Pike begins by putting this question to Brian Barry. Why does Barry think that the unequal impact argument is unsuccessful in the case of (a) Sikh motorcyclists, and (b) Amish buggies? Do you find his arguments persuasive?

Jon Pike goes on to raise the issue of unequal impact with Bikhu Parekh, using an argument by analogy. Why does Bikhu Parekh reject the analogy? Do you think that he is right?

Track 5: Which sorts of cultural practices should be the subject of legislation?

In this part of the discussion, Brian Barry and Bikhu Parekh suggest some criteria by which we might distinguish between cultural practices that should be accommodated by the law, and practices that should not. What are the criteria suggested by Brian Barry? What are the criteria suggested by Bikhu Parekh? Are there any points on which Parekh and Barry agree?

In giving his answer, Bikhu Parekh mentions the concept of *laïcité* as it applies to French schools: this is the idea that schools are secular spaces, in which pupils and teachers should refrain from advertising any particular religious affiliation.

You may have noticed that, although Parekh and Barry approach these issues in different ways, there are areas of broad agreement between them; and that their differences are often differences of emphasis, rather than simple clashes of opinion. For example, although Barry is more sympathetic to difference-blind liberalism than Parekh, he allows that cultural exemptions can be defended in some cases; and although Parekh rejects difference-blind liberalism, he does think that there are some considerations that override cultural concerns. The following activity is designed to bring out some points of agreement and disagreement between them.

Activity

Consider the following three cases. What would Bikhu Parekh and Brian Barry say about each of these cases, and why?

1. (An imaginary example.) Members of a religious group seek an exemption from the laws on assault, on the grounds that their religion enjoins them to strike anyone who denies the existence of God.
2. Young Sikhs seek an exemption from a school rule which prescribes that pupils should wear their school cap outdoors.
3. Sikh motorcyclists seek an exemption from a law forbidding anyone to ride a motorcycle without wearing a helmet.

Discussion

1. Parekh and Barry would agree that this exemption should not be granted, and for very similar reasons. Parekh suggests that physically assaulting people for expressing a belief violates a universal moral value; while Barry would argue that it violates a right (the right to free speech) that everyone should have.
2. Parekh and Barry would agree that this exemption should be granted, though for rather different reasons. Barry argues that the exemption should be granted because there's no good reason to insist that pupils should wear a cap instead of a turban: wearing a turban will not undermine the purpose of the school uniform. So, the exemption should be granted because there's nothing very important at stake. In contrast, Parekh would argue that the exemption should be granted because there *is* something very important at stake – namely the significance that wearing a turban has for Sikhs.
3. This is a case on which Parekh and Barry look set to disagree. Barry argues that Sikh motorcyclists should not be exempted from wearing helmets. This is because the law prescribing helmets is justified by considerations of safety that apply to everyone, regardless of culture. In contrast, there seems to be no reason for Parekh to object to the exemption.

What are your own views about these cases? Do you agree with Barry's approach? Or with Parekh's?

Track 6: What contribution can philosophy make to these discussions?

As you listen to this final track, you might consider whether any of the points made by Barry and Parekh reflect your own experience of working through this chapter.

In his remarks on self-respect, Parekh mentions Rawls: John Rawls (1921–2002) was one of the most important political philosophers of the twentieth century.

4 SHORT STORIES

Lynda Prescott

MATERIALS YOU WILL NEED

- *A World of Difference: An Anthology of Short Stories from Five Continents*, ed. L. Prescott (set book). (This is referred to in the chapter as the Anthology, and you will be reading three of the stories in detail: 'The Ultimate Safari', 'Pit Strike', and 'In Cuba I was a German Shepherd.')

AIMS

Building on the work you have done in previous English sections of the course, this chapter will:

- introduce you to the critical reading and understanding of a specific literary genre, in this case, the short story
- provide you with opportunities to reflect on texts from different cultures: here the historical period covered is short and recent, but the geographical and cultural reach is wide
- help you to develop an appropriate critical vocabulary for discussion of prose narratives, including some terms drawn from linguistics.

4.1 'THE ULTIMATE SAFARI'

You will notice when you turn to the first story in your Anthology (*A World of Difference: An Anthology of Short Stories from Five Continents*) that it begins with an epigraph, a quotation from a newspaper. This is fairly unusual for a short story, so before we begin to read the story itself, we will pause for a moment to think about the title and the epigraph. By following the link from the course website, you can check the entry for 'safari' in the online version of the *Oxford English Dictionary*. By clicking the 'etymology' tab, you'll see that it's a Swahili word meaning simply 'journey'. If you have time to look up 'Swahili', too, you'll see that, like 'safari', this word comes from Arabic and relates to East Africa, an area penetrated by Arab culture long before Europeans arrived in Africa. Here we have our first, small example of a theme that will recur throughout this chapter: namely, that language, history and culture are inextricably linked. But what about the rest of the title? What would the *ultimate* safari be?

incapable of being distangled / untied

The travel advertisement, from the British Sunday newspaper the *Observer* (Anthology, p. 5), suggests that this particular safari will be an adventure somehow in the spirit of the past (it's an African adventure that 'lives on'), and that it will be a great challenge ('You can do it!'). We can assume that the advertisement is addressed to people in Britain who want an exciting holiday in Africa, but there is an element of reassurance in this expedition being undertaken with 'leaders who *know* Africa' – as if Africa is a unitary, knowable fact. Perhaps 'the *ultimate* safari' suggests an adventure that is extremely exciting, even exotic, and also (the advertisement seems to hint) gets to the heart of something.

Bearing in mind, then, whatever it was that the title implied for you, I suggest that you now read the story straight through (it is only ten pages long and, even reading at a fairly leisurely pace, you should find that the first reading takes you less than half an hour). As with your work on *Dr Faustus* and *The Faber Book of Beasts*, we will be doing a certain amount of rereading in order to understand our texts better, but first readings are really important, and the more alert you can be as you first read through a new story, the better. It's not important at this stage to know anything about the writer, Nadine Gordimer, but later in this chapter we will refer to the short author-introduction that prefaces the story in your Anthology.

-Written simply
-Grandfather died
-Why villages ransacked?

Activity

Read 'The Ultimate Safari' now, and afterwards take half a minute to jot down a few words about any strong impressions, and maybe questions, you were left with at the end (you will return to these brief notes later).

The narrator's voice

We'll start with just the first two sentences of the story: 'That night our mother went to the shop and she didn't come back. Ever.'

Activity As a very short and simple exercise in creative (re-)writing, I'd like you to imagine you are writing another story beginning with the same situation, and are going to recast the information in one or two sentences of your own. Try writing an alternative version of the opening two sentences of the story.

Discussion Although there are as many possible versions as there are people doing this activity, here's an example of the kind of same-but-different opening that might emerge:

> One day the woman went out shopping, leaving her children at home. They waited for her to come back, but they never saw her again.

It's probably inevitable that any rewriting will suggest some changes: for example, in the version I've just given, the imagined situation shifted, in my mind, to a British context where mothers usually (though not always) go shopping in the daytime. This doesn't matter – the whole purpose of this activity is to draw our attention back to Gordimer's sentences to see what effects she has created through her choice of words and sentence structures.

Perhaps the most significant change between the opening of Gordimer's story and the rewritten version above is that, in the original version, the reader sees the situation from the inside, as it were, because it is one of the children who speaks, using words like 'our', then later 'I' and 'we'. Since the conventional grammatical term for the pronouns 'I' (singular) and 'we' (plural) is 'first person' (the second person being 'you' and third person 'he', 'she', 'it' or 'they'), we can say that this story is being told 'in the *first person*'. In contrast to the **third-person** rewritten version above, there is a much greater sense of immediacy and involvement in the **first-person narrative**. This is the first major thing to notice about Gordimer's choice of how to tell the story.

We know, because we are reading a piece of fiction, that 'I' in this case is not necessarily Gordimer herself, though it is a little while before we discover who the speaker is, and, in fact, we never learn her name – or anyone else's in the story.

We will return later to this point about namelessness, but meanwhile let us stay with the opening, and consider the effect of the second sentence, 'Ever.' It's quite unusual to have a sentence that only consists of a single word, and, in the strictest grammatical sense it could only be a complete sentence if that word were a verb (for example, 'Stop!'), but it is, I think, fairly clear why Gordimer has chosen to put this single word into a sentence on its own, and that is for emphasis. The opening sentence has set a time-frame of a particular night and even though the effect of '*That* night' is immediately more pointed than the flatter sounding '*One* day (or night)' in the rewritten version, our first assumption might be that the mother just failed to return that night. But then we have the startling 'Ever', which suddenly makes the situation more dramatic, and tragic.

Reading on from this very striking opening, we come into closer contact with the narrator, who addresses the reader with a question,

'What happened?' The everyday-sounding answer, 'I don't know', expresses a condition that, we soon realise, will become a feature of the reader's experience as well as the narrator's. Because the story is told entirely from the perspective of the first-person narrator, the reader can only see what the narrator sees, so when it is confirmed for us, a few sentences later, that the narrator is a child, in the midst of devastating circumstances (a civil war), we realise that we will have to read between the lines in order to figure out the meaning and significance of some of the things she tells us. I've already started this task of interpretation by using the phrase 'civil war', which is not one that the child-narrator uses, but which helps me to 'place' the situation described here. Other things we don't know – and won't be able to work out for some time – are where and when this is all happening; we have to be patient and adjust to the limited point of view of the narrator.

Activity Now reread the first seven paragraphs of the story, up to 'they seemed to know where that was better than we did' (p. 7). What do you notice about the narrator's choice of words, and especially the way that she uses the word 'away' towards the end of this section?

Discussion I expect you were struck by the simplicity of the language, in keeping with the vocabulary of a child (we subsequently learn that the narrator, at the supposed time of telling the tale, has 'turned eleven') and the village environment that has so far formed the limits of her experience. The sentence structures are also mostly simple and short, for example: 'We stayed there all day. Waiting for her' (p. 6). However, Gordimer is careful to vary the sentence lengths because too many short sentences together can produce a dulling effect, and limit the subtlety of the telling. So we also have some longer sentences, such as the one that follows those just quoted. This moves beyond the statements of what the children did and into the narrator's mental state; you'll have noticed that 'not knowing' crops up again, twice, in this sentence, reinforcing the negative effects of 'no school, no church any more'. But in contrast to the dire situation the children and their grandparents find themselves in, an alternative arises at the bottom of page 6: 'away'. Very simply, 'away' promises a solution to the problems of hunger, bandits, and the vacuum created in the family by the loss of the children's father and now mother. In the child's account, 'away' becomes not just a direction, but a place in its own right.

The journey

As the next section of the story opens, we have the first mention of a specific place: the Kruger Park, which stands between the refugees (another word that is outside the child-narrator's **lexicon**) and 'away'. Although the narrator does not use the term 'safari', it is clear from her description of this vast game reserve 'where white people come to stay and look at the animals' that here we have the first link with the story's title and epigraph.

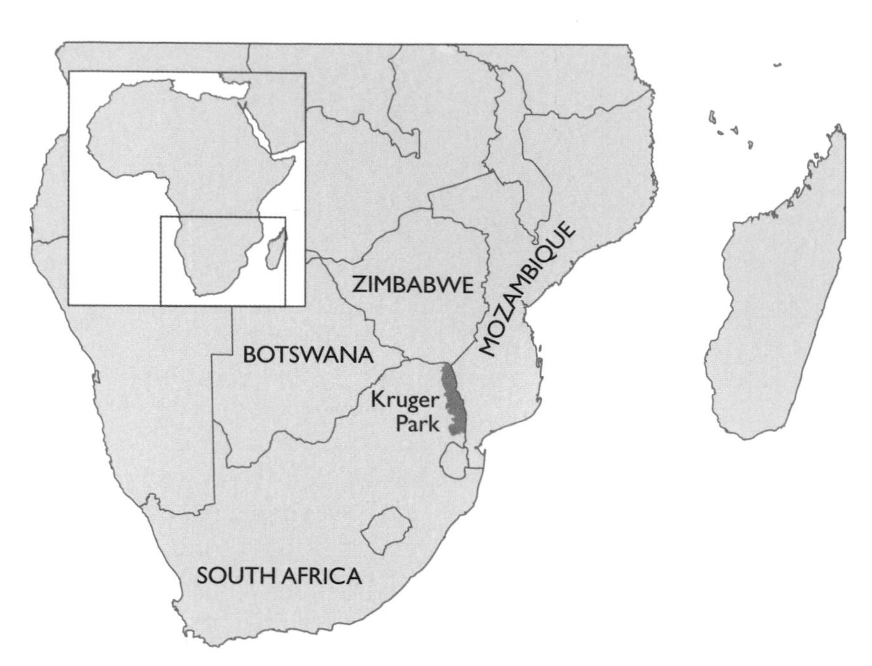

Figure 4.1 The refugees' journey in 'The Ultimate Safari' takes them across the Kruger National Park, South Africa's largest game reserve (which covers over 7,000 square miles), bordering Mozambique.

Activity

Reread the story from 'To get there we had to go through the Kruger Park' (p. 7) to the break before the final section of the story ('We started to go away, again', p. 11), and make some brief notes on the way this journey resembles and differs from what we think of as a safari.

Discussion

The most obvious resemblance, I suppose, is that the narrator and her companions get to see a lot of animals during their trek across the park. As well as the monkeys and birds they are used to at home, there are new sights, one of the most spectacular being the elephants (p. 8). The narrator's account of these new (to her) animals is full of wonderment: 'I was so interested I forgot to be afraid', she says. They also encounter lions, usually sleeping during the heat of the day (p. 8), but just a couple of paragraphs later they hear them nearby, at night. The danger that the refugees find themselves in might be distantly related to the excitement hinted at in the 'African Adventure' of the safari advertisement, but very distantly indeed: terrible fear drives the refugees into a tight bundle of bodies, knowing that they are easy prey for the animals.

Fortunately, like the tourists, the refugees have a leader who knows the game reserve, and who is able to protect them from the lions and other dangers. That is about where the similarities end, I think. The white people in their camps have plenty of food and people to serve them, but the refugees are starving, unable to live off the land because if they light fires they will be discovered and sent back to where they came from. Although their leader tells them they must be like the animals, it is, says the narrator, very hard to do, when they can only eat the baboons' ant-filled figs. Walking day and night, carrying young children, across a game reserve the size of a small country is a far cry from the 'expedition' of the safari-tourist.

We soon realise that the refugees' journey is as much a matter of life and death as was their precarious existence in their war-torn homeland. The narrator's account of the journey culminates in the disappearance of her grandfather and her grandmother's heart-wrenching decision to continue without him. 'Left behind' at the end of this section undercuts any hopefulness in the final statement, 'We started to go away, again' (repeated from p. 7).

The journey's end

The last five pages of the story give us a picture of what 'away' turns out to be. It is a massive refugee tent where two hundred people live among cardboard partitions. We learn at last where the refugees have come from: Mozambique, the former Portuguese colony where civil war broke out after Independence in 1975 and continued, with huge loss of life and displacement of people, until 1992. Mozambique is on the eastern border of the Kruger Park (named after the Boer resistance leader, Paul Kruger). The refugees share a common language with the inhabitants of the territory they have come to, which we can assume is part of South Africa, and a long time ago, says the narrator, 'there was no Kruger Park between them and us, we were the same people under our own king' (p. 13).

Activity Now reread the final section of the story, from 'There's a very big tent', noticing especially the role of the grandmother in this new life. What effects does Gordimer create by concluding the story with the interview between the grandmother and the white woman?

Discussion It is clear that the grandmother, being determined, literate and, above all, 'still strong', is the lynchpin of her surviving family now they are 'away', just as much as she was on the journey. She is the one who has secured them a healthy place against a side of the tent, made the children's sleeping mats, cared for the sick baby, claimed whatever welfare rights are available, earned some extra money so she can buy items that are just above survival requirements, and made it possible for the narrator and her older brother to go to school. As we read this account of life in the refugee camp, we can hardly fail to be impressed by the grandmother's amazing resilience, resourcefulness and selflessness.

Yet we can also see that all this is probably invisible to the white woman who squeezes 'into our space' in order to ask the grandmother questions for a film about the refugees. In this 'cultural encounter', it is not just the need to communicate through an interpreter that gets in the way of mutual understanding. The gulf between the grandmother and the interviewer seems to widen as the white woman persists in asking questions that assume some hope for the future, some belief in the idea of 'home', while the grandmother can only respond in negatives. Any idea of faith in the future rests with her grandchildren: their being able to 'get good jobs and money' is all that will count in a world where 'There is nothing. No home.'

The narrator, however, being only eleven years old, is more optimistic; she still hopes to find her mother and grandfather, still hopes for a return home, and a reuniting. Different perspectives are emerging, and we might note that this is really the only point in the story where the first-person narration shifts into sustained dialogue, giving the grandmother and the interviewer distinct voices. Perhaps in keeping with the simplicity of the narration, the words spoken by other characters are not enclosed within quotation marks – the usual way of signalling direct speech – or even separated from the rest of the narrative with dashes, a technique favoured by Gordimer in other stories. We only spot the introduction of a new voice through paragraph indentation, and this makes for an easy slide back into the narrator's (unspoken) words in the final paragraph, which seem to be in balance with the interview rather than set outside its frame.

So what is the effect of the story's ending? I'd suggest that the interview sequence reinforces the sense of distance between the worlds of the black refugees and their well-meaning white interrogator – a sense of distance that has already been established by ironic reflections on the story's epigraph, and our new understanding of 'the ultimate safari'. The presence of the white woman, squeezing into the tiny space that the narrator's family occupies in the huge tent, is a reminder of the continuing intervention of white outsiders, first European settlers and now the white-owned media, in the lives of black Africans. However, the fact that the last word belongs, rightly, to the young narrator allows Gordimer to poise the buoyancy of youth with the rather bitter experience of age.

Here we might recall the point we noted earlier about none of the characters being named. We certainly develop quite a clear sense of what the main participants in the action are like, but because none of them acquires a name, our sense of their generic characteristics (when we're thinking of 'the first-born brother', 'the grandmother' and so on) remains powerful. So although Gordimer is telling us a story about an individual family, her technique here has affinities with the use of archetypes in traditional tales, implying a wider significance in what she describes. The fact that we are not able to pin the events down to a particular time and place until quite late on in the story also keeps the reader alert to general rather than specific implications.

Now return to the brief notes you made after first reading 'The Ultimate Safari'. I hope that rereading the story in conjunction with this discussion will have helped to clarify your initial responses, and to answer any questions that you were left with after your first reading. If there are reflections you made on the story that have not been touched on, that does not, of course, mean that they are irrelevant; our analysis has certainly not been exhaustive, and you may have noted different points, which there was no space to explore here. The most important thing to take away from this section is not any specific interpretation of 'The Ultimate Safari' but the recognition that the *way* the story is told is crucial to what it tells us.

Figure 4.2 Dorah Ngomane, image of the Kruger Park, 1995, hand-coloured lithograph, from Gordimer, Nadine (1995) *The Ultimate Safari*, limited edition artists book, Johannesburg, The Artists' Press. Photo: The Artists' Press, © Dorah Ngomane. The illustrations for this special edition of Gordimer's story were created and hand-coloured by three Mozambican women who normally work as seasonal farm labourers. They had all made the dangerous trek on foot to South Africa, and participated in a special workshop to learn the lithographic printing process and create images to accompany the story with which they so closely identified.

4.2 THE SHORT STORY AS A GENRE

We have begun this chapter with a discussion of a particular short story in order to give us experience of reading a work in this genre. It's very likely, of course, that you have read other short stories, of various kinds, and some of them might have taken the shape of legends, folktales or fables, perhaps. You'll remember from your work on *The Faber Book of Beasts* that some of the oldest and simplest poem-patterns can be recognised in forms such as nursery rhymes as well as in the work of a poet like William Blake. We can make a similar point about short stories: although the 'modern literary short story' is, as we'll see, a relatively new literary form, with its own distinctive characteristics, 'short stories' in a more general sense have a long history that goes back to antiquity.

Originally, folktales, legends and similar kinds of stories would have been transmitted orally rather than in writing, and something of the intimate relationship between storyteller and listener that belongs to the oral tradition can still be felt in many written short stories. We know that every society has its stories, even if they have not all been written down. Some of these stories belong firmly within a religious framework (the parables of Mahayana Buddhism and Christianity are good examples of short stories used for religious teaching), while others may have roots in mythic tales of creation and salvation. Then there are legends and folktales of heroes and villains, many of whom seem to crop up in similar kinds of stories across the world. I wouldn't want to overplay the connection between ancient tales and the modern short story, but perhaps, in addition to the lingering traces of an oral tradition, there is some residual sense that a short story often has – if not exactly a message – a *point* to which its meaning can be reduced.

Activity Here you might pause to ask whether this expectation of finding a distinct 'point', or maybe even a 'message', formed part of your reading experience of 'The Ultimate Safari'.

While you reflect on this, I'd also like to consider the effects of rereading a text. I was aware the first time I read Gordimer's story that I was being drawn imaginatively into a situation I hadn't tried to imagine before, and I felt moved and, in a small way, changed by what I read. Subsequent readings have left other impressions with me. The political and historical dimensions of the story coloured my second reading; later I was struck by features such as the way the story juxtaposes human and animal worlds, raising painful questions about race and power. No doubt when I return to this story in five, ten, twenty years' time, other 'points' will foreground themselves.

This is rather different from the experience of reading Aesop's fable of the fox and the grapes and taking away from it the moral that 'some men, when they fail through their own incapacity, blame circumstances' (see the section on William Blake in Book 2, Chapter 2). As you have already gathered from your work on *Dr Faustus* and *The Faber Book of Beasts*, it is impossible to boil down literary texts to a clear-cut 'essence' without losing a sense of their literary qualities. What is also likely to be lost in this kind of attempt is the delicate poise, balance or tension between different ideas or viewpoints that a literary text can give play to, in a way that we seldom find in more factual kinds of writing, where what matters is to get something done or convey specific information. So although we may sometimes want to sum up in a phrase or two what a particular text means to us, we're aware that this is no more than convenient shorthand. As we noted earlier, in 'The Ultimate Safari' the manner of the telling is itself part of the story's meaning.

The evolution of the short story

One fundamental point about the way that short stories are told – so basic that we take it for granted – is that the modern short story is written in prose, not verse. With older short stories this was not necessarily the case. One of the oldest collections of short stories in English is Geoffrey Chaucer's *Canterbury Tales* (*c*.1387–1400), written mainly in rhyming couplets, with some prose passages. We can find other, later, examples of this kind of collection, such as *The Earthly Paradise*, a 'Big Book of Stories in Verse', by the nineteenth-century English writer, William Morris. These stories, published in the late 1860s and very popular with Victorian readers, were reshapings of tales from ancient Greek and Norse sources (an interesting combination). However, around the same time as nineteenth-century writers and scholars like Morris were collecting, and sometimes reworking, tales from around the world, an important new strand in the history of the short story was developing. American writers such as Nathaniel Hawthorne and Edgar Allen Poe were publishing remarkable original stories, often labelled as 'sketches' or 'tales', in some of the magazines and journals that were proliferating across the USA, and discussions about the nature of the short story as a literary genre were starting to appear.

It is worth spending a moment on these critical discussions, because they open up for us two different ways of focusing on the special characteristics of short stories. Poe's 1842 review of Hawthorne's *Twice-Told Tales* is the usual starting-point. He placed considerable emphasis on the fact that the short story, unlike most novels, can be read at a single sitting, and can thus achieve a unity of effect comparable to that of a lyric poem (see Hanson, 1985, p. 3). **Lyric poetry** is different from the kind of narrative poetry we find in *The Canterbury Tales* or *The Earthly Paradise* in that it doesn't attempt to tell a story, but is concerned instead with feelings, thoughts and perceptions. So Poe was claiming a fresh connection between short stories and poetry, quite apart from the fact that they can both be vehicles for narrative. However, by contrasting the short story with that much more extended kind of prose fiction, the novel, Poe also initiated a long-running debate about how these two prose narrative forms differ. The novel is, of course, one of the most popular literary genres today, and since the nineteenth century it has also been one of the most prestigious, so perhaps it isn't surprising that literary critics have wanted to discuss the short story's relationship with it. But by the closing decades of the nineteenth century, when the short story began to emerge as a significant genre in its own right, it was the poetic qualities Poe had pointed out that were seen as particularly significant.

What, then, was different about these late nineteenth-century short stories? At this period, in all the arts, including literature, perspectives were shifting as established relationships between the individual and society were called into question, and artists explored new ideas of what it means to be human in a fast-changing and uncertain world. This quest involved experiment, and an increasing self-consciousness about the means and media used by artists. So, in the case of literature, the texture of language itself was foregrounded in literary works that adopted new shapes and addressed their readers in new ways. This is not to say, of course, that everything was suddenly different, and in fact the well-established **realist** base of most prose fiction, through which late nineteenth-century readers identified recognisable people, places and things, still provided a solid foundation for the fiction of this period.

The short story, however, because of its brevity, its narrow cast of characters and its tendency to focus on a single incident, can combine spontaneous-sounding realism with the sort of compression that forces awareness of language up to the surface, as in poetry. So from the late nineteenth century onwards the short story's potential for suggestion, for unobtrusive revelation, and for reverberation in the mind of the reader, has provided many writers with the literary scaffolding they have needed for their artistic purposes.

To try to put some flesh on these generalisations, perhaps, we can turn to Nadine Gordimer again and a famous critical statement she made (not surprisingly, some of the most insightful criticism about short stories comes from writers who use this form) in an international symposium on the short story in 1968:

> Each of us has a thousand lives and a novel gives a character only one. *For the sake of the form*. The novelist may juggle about with chronology and throw narrative overboard; all the time his characters have the reader by the hand, there is a consistency of relationship throughout the experience that cannot and does not convey the quality of human life, where contact is more like the flash of fireflies, in and out, now here, now there, in darkness. Short story writers see by the light of the flash; theirs is the art of the only thing one can be sure of – the present moment. Ideally, they have learned to do without explanation of what went before, and what happens beyond this point.
>
> (Quoted in Hanson, 1985, p. 57)

There is a lot to think about here, but perhaps the key point is the claim that, in the short story, 'the present moment' is of paramount importance.

Activity Pause here to ask yourself how far this statement about 'the present moment' chimes with your experience of reading 'The Ultimate Safari'.

Discussion We saw from our analysis of the story's opening that the reader is drawn immediately into a dramatic and desperate situation (though we may also be able to think of novels that do the same). The child-narrator can only give us a hazy sense of time, but the final section, after the break (when we read short stories we need to take careful note of spaces between paragraphs), takes us into the present tense with 'There's a very big tent'. It is very often true that short stories are structured to propel the reader towards a moment of clarity, of realisation, perhaps of disappointment, at the end, and often, too, the relation of events leading to this moment will have begun as close to the end as possible. This doesn't mean that short stories are incapable of dealing with memory and the past – far from it – but Gordimer's image of the flash of fireflies does, I think, convey something of the vivid intensity we often associate with good short stories.

Having said all this, there is really no critical consensus as to what a good short story ought to be like (or even how long); nor should there be. The genre has always been marked by enormous variety and, since initial publication is often in magazines, the short story has also acquired a reputation for accessibility and popularity. Many of the great fiction writers of the twentieth century, especially in the USA, reached their widest readership through publishing short stories in general-interest magazines; as writers such as F. Scott Fitzgerald and Ernest Hemingway discovered, this was often very profitable, too. Opportunities for magazine publication gradually declined during the second half of the twentieth century, but different outlets for short stories emerged: we are now quite likely to encounter short stories in collections, whether all by the same author, or organised thematically, or to hear them on the radio, or in live storytelling events. The comparative brevity of the short story also makes it a suitable candidate for online publication, and you will find many old and new short stories in online libraries and on websites.

The writer in the story

There is one more general question we might briefly consider before moving on to our next story, and this refers back to the mainly realist base of fictional writing that I mentioned earlier. In contemporary fiction-writing – and I'm thinking here about novels as well as shorter forms – the boundaries between real life and fiction are often hard to draw, raising the question of how far we should be looking for an expression of the writers' personal experiences in the fiction that they write.

Activity Read the brief profile of Nadine Gordimer in your Anthology (pp. 3–4). Are there any elements in her background that seem particularly relevant to an understanding of 'The Ultimate Safari'?

Discussion You have probably already noticed that Gordimer is a white South African, writing about the experience of black characters (from a different, neighbouring country). There are, however, elements of the migrant experience in Gordimer's background, her father having been a Jewish immigrant from Latvia. Do we need to know this in order to understand 'The Ultimate Safari'? My own view is that the story is so completely and successfully imagined that knowing about Gordimer's own transplanted history adds little, if anything, to our reading. (Some of her earlier short stories, however, do relate more directly to the first-generation immigrant experience.) But I think we can see that Gordimer's fictional work must owe a great deal to what she has witnessed throughout her life in southern Africa. Fictional narratives, including short stories, provide a space in which writers' personal experiences and perceptions of the world they live in can be distilled, and at the same time given colour and shape through imagined elements.

4.3 'PIT STRIKE'

The next story we will be reading closely is Alan Sillitoe's 'Pit Strike' (pp. 199–218 in your Anthology), which offers a number of contrasts with Gordimer's story. You'll notice for a start that this story is told by a third-person narrator who allows the characters to speak for themselves. In fact, 'Pit Strike' was made into a television film, and I think you'll easily spot the dramatic possibilities of the text, including the vivid passages of dialogue. The 'cultural encounters' here happen fairly close to home, but issues of culture, language and (in a broad sense) history still loom large, as the central character, Joshua, travels from Nottinghamshire to what for him is another country – southern England. To help us in our analysis of these issues we will be using some terms drawn from linguistics (a field of study closely allied to literature): **dialect** and **register**.

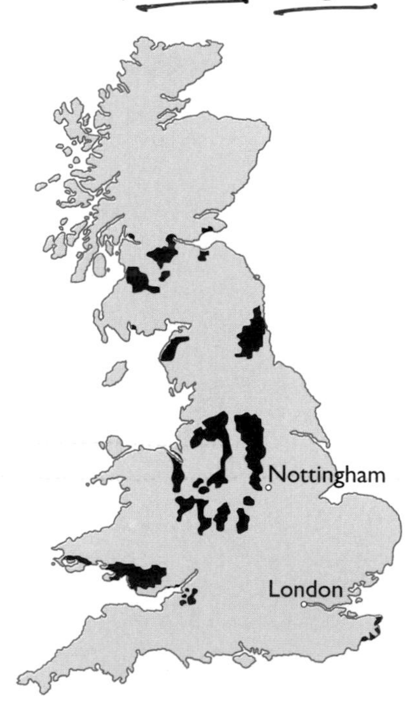

Figure 4.3 Map showing coalfields in the UK. At the time of Sillitoe's story, the British mining industry was still important to the nation's economy, though it had been declining since the Second World War, and pit closures forced miners to move from coalfield to coalfield in search of secure jobs.

Before you begin reading the story, I suggest you look at the introduction to Alan Sillitoe's work on pages 197–8 of the Anthology. You'll see that Sillitoe, who was born in Nottingham, is often regarded as a 'regional' writer, because much of his fiction is set in the English Midlands, and the speech of his characters is sometimes coloured with traces of Nottinghamshire dialect. Dialect can be related to class as much as to locality, and one kind of cultural encounter we will come across in this story is a meeting across the working/middle-class divide, with dialect playing its part in the dramatisation of the issue.

You will also see that the story's title refers not to the year-long British miners' strike of 1984–5, which had such dire national consequences for the mining industry and trades unions, but to a shorter confrontation, in 1972, between the National Union of Mineworkers and the Conservative government led by Edward Heath. This background information, though limited, should be sufficient to make the story fairly comprehensible on first reading, and since this is the kind of story where the narrative drive is strong, you will probably want to read it fairly fast.

Activity Read 'Pit Strike' now.

You'll have noticed that the story opens quite dramatically, in the midst of a skirmish between picketing miners and police at the port gates on the River Medway (we learn the precise details later, when the narrator returns us, on p. 212, to the opening incident). After the first six paragraphs, though, the narrative slips back to provide something of the central character's history, and to acquaint us with the kind of man he is.

Activity Reread the first three sections of the story, up to the point where the miners set off for Kent (to p. 204, 'Heath'll be playin' his organ by candlelight before we've done', an allusion to the Prime Minister's musical pastime, and perhaps, by *double entendre*, to his bachelor status). Make a list of the different 'voices' appearing in the narrative.

Discussion Up to this point there are, by my count, four characters whose words appear in speech marks: the Welsh/Kentish miner; Joshua; his wife, Jessie; and Joshua's fellow-miner, Bill Marriott. You might also have included the third-person narrator's voice in your list; although he (or is it 'she'? I'm inclined to opt for 'he' in this case) is not a participant in the story, it would be appropriate to think of this as a separate, distinctive voice. And you might have identified some other phrases appearing in inverted commas ('false raiment', 'turning the other cheek', 'eye for an eye') as belonging neither to the narrator nor, directly, to any of the characters. You may recognise these as being biblical phrases, and they are associated chiefly with Joshua, who, as well as bearing the name of an Old Testament figure, is also known to his mates as a 'Bible man' (p. 201). Although these phrases don't belong to a separate 'voice', they do belong to a separate text: the 'King James' or Authorised Version of the Bible (1611). Joshua's Bible, both as a material object and as the foundation for his view of the world, will play an important part in the story, and the repeated biblical references alert us to the power of this text for Joshua, outside of any sacred context.

Dialect

Going back now to the passages of direct speech in these first few pages (from the four characters listed above), let us see how Sillitoe establishes his characters' identities through their own words. The Welsh miner is given just one line, calculated in its crudity, but the only non-standard element in it, as far as language goes, is the slang term 'knackers'. It is left to the narrator to tell us that this is a Welsh voice so that with our mind's ear, as it were, we might imagine the rising inflexion of that particular accent. Although accent, or the way that words are pronounced, is one of the first things to strike us when we hear someone speaking, it is extremely difficult to represent it in writing. Sometimes spelling can do the trick, as with Jessie's 'allus' for 'always' on page 203, or Bill Marriott's 'owd' for 'old' on page 204, but Sillitoe is rightly sparing with this kind of deviation from standard English spelling because it can actually slow down the reader considerably if over-used. However, accent is only one component of dialect, the term linguists use to denote a distinctive variety of language shared by people in a particular group, whether that is social or geographical. There are two other components, grammar and vocabulary (or **lexis**, to use the term from linguistics), that are much easier to convey on the page.

> 'It's going to be a long do,' he said. 'They don't want to know. The truth means nothing to them.'
>
> Since it was wickedness to be still, Jessie knitted pullovers, went at the rate of two a year, and had a drawer full upstairs. She was a tall woman, but thin. 'We'll have to manage.'
>
> He made two cigarettes, and put one back into the tin. 'There's plenty more besides us. The young blokes'll feel it most.'
>
> 'They say the country don't need coal any more.'
>
> 'They say a lot o'things. Time'll tell.'
>
> 'It'll be a long while, though.'
>
> He stood up. 'Nobody denies that. They think they've got us where they want us, forcing us into a strike so's they can finish us off. It's the last thing I wanted.'
>
> 'It's early days yet, Josh.'
>
> 'It's tragic, though,' he said. 'It's going to be a whole waste of time, and time's the most valuable thing in the world. There's none of us got that much as we can throw it away.'
>
> 'Ne' mind. Cheer up, love. We've had worse bouts. I'll put the kettle on. I know you allus get thirsty when you get depressed.'
>
> (Prescott, 2008, pp. 202–3)

Activity Look at the dialogue between Joshua and Jessie in the box above and pick out one or two elements in their speeches that suggest they share a 'distinctive variety of language'.

Discussion You probably noticed more frequent elisions, or running together of words, than would be usual, even in the relatively informal voice of the story's third-person narrator. Certainly the narrator uses contracted forms like 'didn't' and 'he'd', but Sillitoe gives us less ordinary elisions in the speeches of Joshua and Jessie, such as 'Time'll tell' and 'Ne' mind'. Sometimes the elision is combined with a grammatical variant on standard English, as, for example, in 'the country don't need coal any more'. These features of dialect could probably be seen as belonging to working-class speech in a way that is not specific to any particular region. It is often vocabulary that gives the distinctively regional mark to a dialect.

The dialogue between Joshua and Jessie is not especially remarkable in terms of lexis, although Joshua's use of the word 'do' (in 'It's going to be a long do') and Jessie's 'bouts' (in 'We've had worse bouts') strike me as belonging more firmly to northern than southern dialects. However, you may have noticed elsewhere in the story that the narrator sometimes uses dialect words: 'welloes' for 'wellington boots' on page 201 is a classic Nottinghamshire term (and this confirms, if we needed confirmation, that the narrative voice is sympathetic to the miners – literally, speaking the same language). If you happened to pick out different features from the dialogue on pages 202–3, perhaps you could spend a moment before reading on to decide which component of dialect they illustrate: accent, grammar or lexis.

So far, then, we've seen how Sillitoe sketches in a sense of community among his Nottinghamshire characters through their shared dialect. What happens when Joshua ventures into the – to him – foreign places south of the Trent?

Activity Reread the rest of 'Pit Strike' now, paying particular attention to the episode at the filling-station (pp. 205–7) and Joshua's first encounter with the Seymour children (p. 209).

Discussion In a dramatised version of the story we would undoubtedly notice the contrast in accents as the action switches to London and the south-east, but on the page Sillitoe does not attempt to characterise the garage owner's speech (p. 205) as anything out of the ordinary. Instead, the reader's attention is directed first to the politics of the encounter, then – and I suspect this is why Sillitoe holds back on the dialect front – to an extraordinary transformation in Joshua's speech as he advances on the garage owner, literally as well as metaphorically waving his Bible at him. We're by now familiar with the written representation of Joshua's dialect, and his first words, 'Nay, lad,' remind us that this is the foundation of the way he speaks, but the words 'Philistine' and 'cubits' alert us to something other than dialect creeping in. These are words with biblical associations and, in the paragraph beginning 'Pharaoh is pursuing us', we find much more of this kind of language. I expect you will have noticed the proper names Pharaoh, Moses and Egypt, as well as phrases such as 'house of bondage' or 'seven plagues', and individual archaic words like 'victuals' or 'verily'. Part of this speech, from 'And Moses said' to 'out from this place', is an exact quotation from the Old Testament (Exodus 13: 3), but Joshua's own words that are wrapped

Figure 4.4 Unknown artist, National Union of Mineworkers Banner for the Nottinghamshire Area, Ollerton Branch, *c.* 1980s. Photo: courtesy of the Nottingham N.U.M. Ex and Retired Mineworkers Association. Miners' banners, some of them very old, are still used at the head of marches and processions (accompanied sometimes by brass bands) to symbolise the mineworkers' pride and solidarity. This modern banner from the Ollerton NUM branch in north Nottinghamshire shows an official picket line of striking miners, over the slogan 'So few, so strong'.

around the quotation have the same kind of 'colouring'. We could thus describe the tone and style of the whole speech as biblical or, to use a term drawn from linguistics, we could say that Joshua is speaking in a biblical 'register', denoted principally by the lexical choices that he makes here.

Register

The concept of register is quite a helpful one for students of literature. It signifies a distinctive use of language, whether in writing or speech, for a particular kind of situation. We have only to dip into a computer manual, a travel brochure, or a legal document to encounter some of the myriad registers available within the bounds of the same language.

Just a few pages back, however, we were also describing 'dialect' as a distinctive variety of language, so it might be useful to make some distinctions between the two terms. We most often think of dialect in connection with spoken forms of language, although it can, as 'Pit Strike' demonstrates, feature in written texts (and in fact, what is usually termed 'standard' written English is based on a dialect of Middle English spoken and written in the prosperous East Midlands in the fourteenth century). All of us, whichever language we speak, speak a dialect of that language or perhaps a hybrid version of different dialects. For example, I was born in County Durham but grew up in London, and my dialect includes northern family words, such as 'bairn' for 'child', even though I have a southern accent now. But I'm aware that my language use also slips in and out of different registers, depending on the situation I'm in, whether the context is formal or informal, whether I'm writing or speaking, and so on.

Linguists have specialised terms for these variables, the most relevant for our purposes being 'mode', meaning the medium of communication, be it speech, writing, or a blend of both. In 'Pit Strike' we have already noted elements of dialect in the characters' speech, but the mode that we're dealing with here is actually writing (in this case, printed writing) designed to be read, not heard.

This limits what can be done in terms of representing dialect; register, though, is mainly a matter of lexis, which can be readily analysed in written texts. When you move on to studying Heaney's *The Burial at Thebes* in Chapter 6, the mode will vary according to whether you are reading the text on the page, or listening to actors speak the words, though here again distinctions are not clear-cut, since the words were written down before being spoken. You will encounter the concept of register again in that chapter, and you may find it useful in your own analysis of other short stories in your Anthology.

We said earlier that register involves a particular kind of language use for a particular kind of situation, and usually when we choose a register, consciously or unconsciously, we are looking for a suitable fit between language, situation and our purposes. Does the biblical register that Joshua slips into during the episode at the filling-station suggest the usual kind of 'fit' between language and situation? I think you'll agree that it doesn't. What we have here is actually a mismatch between register and situation, producing odd effects. The word 'chariot' for Bill's 'owd banger', for example, is surely comical, as is 'victuals' (a rather loose connection being made here between 'food' and 'fuel').

Jokes, satire and pastiche often hinge on a mismatch between register and situation, or inappropriate mixing of registers, and it's not hard for us to see how Sillitoe achieves a comic tone here. But the scene isn't pure comedy. The political argument that opens the episode reveals a genuine conflict between the garage owner and the miners that seems set to spill over into physical violence. Joshua's intervention is both physically and verbally threatening, and I'd suggest that his choice of a biblical register fits his purpose of intimidating the garage owner by asserting difference. The language of the Bible, especially the kind of Old Testament rhetoric that Joshua deploys, is striking and sonorous, standing outside the sounds and rhythms of contemporary speech. He has tapped into a language of power that, regardless of its inappropriateness, carries in itself a majestic weight. No wonder that Joshua's colleagues are 'either dumbfounded or cracking with amusement'.

Activity There is much more we could say about language and power, but our next passage for discussion touches briefly on the issue of language and class (which is, of course, not unrelated to power). As we return to the episode in which the Seymour children meet Joshua (three short paragraphs from 'Pam was getting the children' on p. 209), try rewriting Barney's speeches as if they were spoken by a child from Joshua's home village.

Discussion There are some elements that we could change quite easily, 'Mummy' becoming 'Mam', for example. And, remembering Joshua's later reference to this conversation (p. 211), we might decide to use his word 'collier' in place of 'miner'. I imagine 'horrid' might disappear in our rewritten version, but how do we deal with the breezy assumption of ownership in 'is this our new miner?' and 'we have one as well' when we transpose these speeches into a working-class voice? Even with some dialect change such as 'we've got one an' all', the underlying difficulty remains, and you may well have found this piece of rewriting trickier than changing the opening sentences of 'The Ultimate Safari'. The basis of Joshua's stay at the Seymours' house is supposedly 'solidarity' (Marriott's term on p. 210 belongs to a political register) across class boundaries; but the child, innocent of such principles, reveals the gulf between their worlds in the words that he speaks. To transpose the words into a working-class Nottinghamshire child's voice would mean putting that child into Barney's place, exposing different social assumptions as well as different ways of speaking. The cultural encounter between Joshua and the Seymours is as much to do with class as with geography, and language plays its part in dramatising this.

You may have been wondering, during that last activity, whether we were concerned with dialect or with register. This is a very relevant question to ask, but it's not easy to answer. I made a few suggestions above about words or phrases that might be changed in a way that suggests dialect-transposition, but the social (as opposed to geographical) dimension of dialect does overlap considerably with register. At the risk of making things sound still more confused, I'd like, very briefly, to make a point about the language we're using in order to analyse language. You're probably well aware that definitions of analytical terms can vary according to the academic field within which you are working, and as we noted at the start of this section, linguistics and literature are separate though adjacent disciplines, so when we try to find common ground we can run into questions about the meanings that particular terms are being asked to carry. The word 'register' itself has, of course, a variety of meanings, and it only began to feature as a linguistic term in the mid-twentieth century, drawing perhaps on the musical meaning of 'a range of tones produced by a particular voice or instrument'. It is even more recently that 'register' has begun to feature in literary analysis, and its usage here is influenced by modern cultural theory, especially the concept of 'discourse analysis', which straddles a number of academic areas, looking at language in specific contexts. So we have to approach terminology with a degree of caution, recognising that as academic disciplines develop and sometimes cross-fertilise, their language changes, too, and meanings of terms can shift. However, discussions that are carefully grounded in close textual analysis can keep possible confusion or ambiguity in check.

Discussion of terminology may have taken us a long way from Joshua and the miners' strike, but we know that language certainly matters to Joshua. Watching television on the first day of the strike, he is 'filled with bitter loathing' when news announcers say the miners are 'idle' instead of 'on strike' (p. 202). And in the struggle at the Medway port gates the Welsh miner's voice and 'its foul words' enrage him (p. 199). But principally it is the language of the Bible that influences him. His political opinions are couched in biblical terms ('Caesar' standing for worldly authority; that is, in Joshua's world view, the Conservative government), and his imagination works in terms of Old Testament motifs (in his strenuous act of sabotage he 'knew the strength of the walls of Jericho' (p. 215)). However, Joshua is essentially a man of deeds, and it is fitting that the story reaches its climax with a second-by-second account of his dramatic action on the motorway sliproad. Our sense of 'the present moment' is stretched out almost to breaking-point here, before the narrator steps back to widen the picture in the final, more reflective, section of the story.

4.4 'IN CUBA I WAS A GERMAN SHEPHERD'

Having looked quite closely at narrative technique and language in Sections 4.1 and 4.3, we will now add another dimension to our analysis of short stories by focusing on structure. To a large extent this means looking at how the writer handles time: where do we start, where are we by the end, and how have past events been conveyed to us? We noted earlier, in connection with Gordimer's comment about the short story being the art of the present moment, that this does not rule out memory and the past as key elements in short stories. 'The Ultimate Safari' falls into two unequal sections, with a change of time as well as place between the two: the first section is set in Mozambique and leads to the journey through the Kruger Park; the second is set in the South African refugee camp two years later. In a novel we would usually expect the break between these two sections to coincide with a chapter break, but in a short story we have to observe more muted typographical signals, such as a double space between paragraphs, or a small row of dots, marking the breaks between sections. Our third story uses these divisions much more extensively than the examples we have considered so far.

Activity Read Ana Menendez's story, 'In Cuba I was a German Shepherd' (pp. 19–36 in your Anthology, along with the introduction on pp. 17–18 if you would like some background information on the Cuban–American setting), taking note of the story's timespan.

Time and rhythm

The story was first published in 1999, and it seems to begin in the present-day, that is, the late 1990s, when Bill Clinton was still President of the USA. Then, in the second section, we move back to the period of the Cuban revolution, and we are given the precise date, January 1961, when Máximo left Havana. There are even some references to a time before that – the fifteen years before the revolution during which Máximo and Raúl had lived on the same street, and, more importantly as the story develops, remembered moments in Máximo's earlier life, such as the night he met his wife, Rosa (pp. 26–7), and his recollections of family Christmas Eves (or, in the occasional Spanish of the story, Nochebuenas) when their children were small (p. 30). You will have noticed that the story swings back and forth between the present, with the four old men playing dominoes in a park, and the past, first in Cuba and then among Cuban exiles in Miami.

Figure 4.5 Map showing Cuba and Florida. The distance between Havana and Miami is only 225 miles, but the waters that divide Cuba from the USA are some of the most dangerous in the world.

Activity To home in on the present in more detail, I suggest you skim through the story again, noting events that happen in the 'now' of the story: that is, from the period at which the story begins.

Discussion In comparison with the sections relating to earlier years, it seems that nothing very much happens in the present-day sections. The four men sit in the park with traffic thundering by on the other side of the fence, they play dominoes, they chaff each other, the park gets decorated for Christmas, Antonio brings along a special box of dominoes, tourists come to watch them playing, Máximo loses his temper in a dramatic but futile outburst against the tourist guide. You may have picked out these or other 'events', but most importantly, perhaps, Máximo tells jokes. We learn, in the second paragraph of the story, that Máximo's jokes are a regular feature of the old men's day; they are prepared rather than spontaneous, and they are usually about Castro. The final joke, though, about the little dog Juanito, is not delivered easily; it is about the condition of being exiled, and at the end of the story Máximo is identified with the 'short, insignificant mutt' of his joke, out of place but still trying to hold on to some pride. This is very hard to do, not just because of the contracting lives that the old men lead, but also because – in an uncomfortable and debased kind of 'cultural encounter' – they have become 'a goddamn spectacle' (p. 33) for the tourists in Miami's Little Havana.

The final overlap between the Juanito joke and Máximo's own reduced state brings the story to a touching conclusion, but I think there is also another way in which the jokes relate to the structure of the story. Jokes themselves often have a distinctive rhythm, as illustrated in the Clinton joke with its two warming-up phases before the Castro punchline, and Máximo relishes his control of this structure, loving the moment when 'the men were warming to the joke and he still kept the punchline close to himself like a secret' (p. 20). So, as well as references to stories as memories (see p. 21 and 'the stories that began with "In Cuba I remember"'), we have several acts of storytelling through jokes embedded in the structure of Menéndez's story. And just as Máximo's listeners fall into the rhythm of his jokes, so we, Menéndez's readers, fall into the rhythm of the short story as it oscillates between past and present.

Structure

I don't want to over-state the link between the jokes and the story's rhythm, because the structure of this story is far from formulaic. It appears to flow inconsequentially to and fro, but gradually we perceive its distinctive shape in which the past catches up with the present. The to-and-fro structure of the story also offers scope for rich contrasts of mood and tone, from the everyday world of the domino park to the lyrical evocation of Máximo's dreams. But as well as contrast, the idea of repetition or 'returning' is also a key element in the story's structure.

Activity Reread the last two paragraphs of the story (from 'Antonio began to laugh') and then go back to the story's opening paragraph, noting what the two sections have in common.

Discussion The setting for the beginning and the end of the story – the domino park – is the same, and references to the banyan tree and the wind recur. The opening paragraph alludes to the 'tourist maps' of Miami, and we are very conscious, at the end of the story, of the tourists on the other side of the park's fence watching the old men play dominoes. One of the most memorable phrases of the opening paragraph is the final one about the sound of the wind in the leaves reminding the men of home. This isn't repeated exactly at the story's conclusion, but Máximo is conscious of something behind him, which at one level is simply an observer leaning on the park fence, though at another level we may still be hearing echoes from the very poignant paragraph just before this ('Máximo turned ...', p. 36) and the phrase 'Now he stood with the gulf at his back'. Máximo's memories of 'home', at the end of the story, are coloured by a sense not just of loss, but of failure and shame; hence the wry and affecting '"Tell them, no pictures."'

> Máximo turned so the men would not see his tears. The afternoon traffic crawled eastward. One horn blasted, then another. He remembered holding his daughters days after their birth, thinking how fragile and vulnerable lay his bond to the future. For weeks, he carried them on pillows, like jeweled china. Then, the blank spaces in his life lay before him. Now he stood with the gulf at his back, their ribbony youth aflutter in the past. And what had he salvaged from the years? Already, he was forgetting Rosa's face, the precise shade of her eyes.
>
> (Prescott, 2008, p. 36)

So there are numerous echoes between the beginning and end of the story, as well as a sense of returning to a point in place and time close to where we began. Because of the short story's comparative brevity, we're likely still to have something of the opening images in our reading memory by the time we reach the end of the story (there are analogies here with listening to a piece of music), and certainly, if we follow the impulse to go back immediately to the opening that is often triggered when we come to the end of a rich short story, we will notice these connections afresh.

However, the story has not simply come round full-circle. We are aware of a change in Máximo, and of the complicated depths of emotion that can lie beneath nostalgic memories of 'home'. In fact, the end of the story offers a working-through of the very general point about the Cuban exiles' stories made in the story's third section:

> In Cuba, the stories always began, life was good and pure. But something always happened to them in the end, something withering, malignant. Máximo never understood it. The stories that opened in sun, always narrowed into a dark place.
>
> (Prescott, 2008, pp. 21–2)

The implication at the end of the story is, I think, that Máximo does now understand, in some way, this shift from light to dark, and thus the reader's own sense of the story's 'present moment' is intensified.

Perhaps it is appropriate that the 'shifting shade' of the banyan tree, offering pleasant protection from the morning sun in the story's opening paragraph, has turned to 'shadow' by the end of the story. It is probably only on careful rereading that a change as subtle as this catches our conscious attention, but it is part of the musical principle of repetition-with-variation that we often find at work in short stories, alongside the rhythm of the narrative line. There is much more we could say about Menéndez's story, of course, but I hope the facets we have singled out here demonstrate that a story's structure, just as much as its language and narrative technique, is a vital part of the way that the story is told, and the effects it has on its readers.

Figure 4.6 Javier González Gallosa, *El Palo Guachinango*, 2005, acrylic on canvas, 74 x 110 cm. Indigo Arts Gallery, Philadelphia. Photo: Indigo Arts Gallery, www.indigoarts.com. © Javier González Gallosa. Gallosa was born in 1975 in Cienfuegos, a town in southern Cuba where a number of artists, self-taught like Gallosa himself, have congregated. The religious procession depicted in Gallosa's painting is contemporary and a reminder of earlier cultural encounters in Cuba's past. In the colonial period, African slaves superimposed their own spiritual figures onto Catholic ones and the term 'Palo' refers to this mixing of belief systems. Such practices persist today despite Cuba officially becoming a secular state in 1959.

READING ON ...

We have looked at just three stories in detail, but I hope that when time permits you will be able to enjoy more of the short stories in the Anthology. Reading the general Preface to the Anthology – if you have not already done so – will reinforce and extend your understanding of some of the key points made in this chapter.

REFERENCES

Hanson, C. (1985) *Short Stories and Short Fictions, 1880–1980*, London, Macmillan.

Prescott, L. (ed.) (2008) *A World of Difference: An Anthology of Short Stories from Five Continents*, London, Palgrave Macmillan.

FURTHER READING

Beachcroft, T.O. (1968) *The Modest Art*, London, Oxford University Press.

Hanson, C. (ed.) (1989) *Re-reading the Short Story*, Basingstoke, Macmillan.

May, C.E. (1995) *The Short Story: The Reality of Artifice*, New York, Twayne/Oxford, Maxwell Macmillan International.

O'Connor, F. (2004 [1963]) *The Lonely Voice*, Hoboken, NJ, Melville Publishing House.

Shaw, V. (1983) *The Short Story: A Critical Introduction*, London, Longman.

5 FROM GREECE TO THE MIDDLE EAST TO EUROPE: THE TRANSMISSION OF MEDICAL KNOWLEDGE

Deborah Brunton

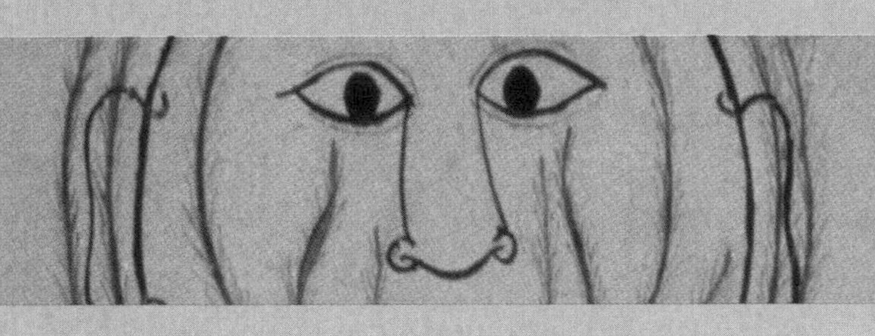

MATERIALS YOU WILL NEED

- Illustration Book
- Podcast – this contains a lecture by Dr Peter Pormann of Warwick University on the background to Islamic medicine; ideally, you should listen to the lecture before working through Section 5.2, 'Greek medicine travels to the Islamic world'. The podcast and transcript can be found on the course website.

AIMS

By the end of this chapter you will have:

- acquired a basic grasp of humoural medicine
- understood some of the problems inherent in translating texts
- realised the importance of context in fostering the translation of medical knowledge.

INTRODUCTION

Stories of medical discoveries appear regularly in newspapers and on television and radio – accounts of the invention of new therapies or new understandings of the causes of disease which may help with previously untreatable conditions. Usually we don't even think about how the information reaches us: how it is published in medical journals; how journalists write up accounts of the discovery, translating the technical language used by scientists into that used by the general public; how the resulting article may then be translated into many different languages before being flashed round the world. Getting news of medical discoveries is a complex business.

But what happened in the past, before television and the internet? How did medical ideas travel then? How did doctors in medieval times learn about new theories or new treatments? You might guess that medical news did not travel very far or very fast. In fact, almost a thousand years ago, a set of ideas about the body and disease made an astonishing journey from Ancient Greece to the Middle East, and then to Europe. The ideas migrated through written texts, which were translated into Arabic from Greek, and then into Latin. In this chapter, we'll trace this journey, exploring how and why these medical texts were translated and how the body of medical knowledge contained in their pages was changed, developed and extended during this time. Through this study you'll be introduced to a new discipline – the study of the history of medicine.

5.1 MEDICINE IN THE GREEK WORLD

Hippocrates Little is known about the man – even the dates of his birth and death are disputed, but we know that he was a medical practitioner living around 460–370 BCE on the island of Kos. We are not even sure which texts he wrote: many of the items in the 'Hippocratic Corpus' – a group of around 60 texts – were probably written by his followers.

Before we can explore how texts changed over time, you need a basic understanding of Greek medical ideas. Between the fifth century BCE and the third century CE, a number of practitioners developed different theories about how the body worked. (Historians use the word 'practitioner' to cover different types of healers – including physicians, surgeons, healers and midwives.) The most influential theory was devised by Hippocrates. His theories were later expanded and revised by many other practitioners, among whom the most important was Galen of Pergamum (129–220 CE). These ideas about the body and disease spread far beyond modern Greece. They travelled east into the lands conquered by Alexander – parts of the modern Middle East including Syria and Egypt and as far as the borders of India. Historians call this the **Hellenistic** world (literally 'Greekish'), reflecting the use of the Greek language and Greek ideas. Greek practitioners took these ideas to Rome (where Galen lived and wrote) and from there across Europe as far as Britain.

The Greek understanding of the body and disease was very different from that we have today. We think of the body as made up of solid bones and organs such as the brain, heart and kidneys. We think of

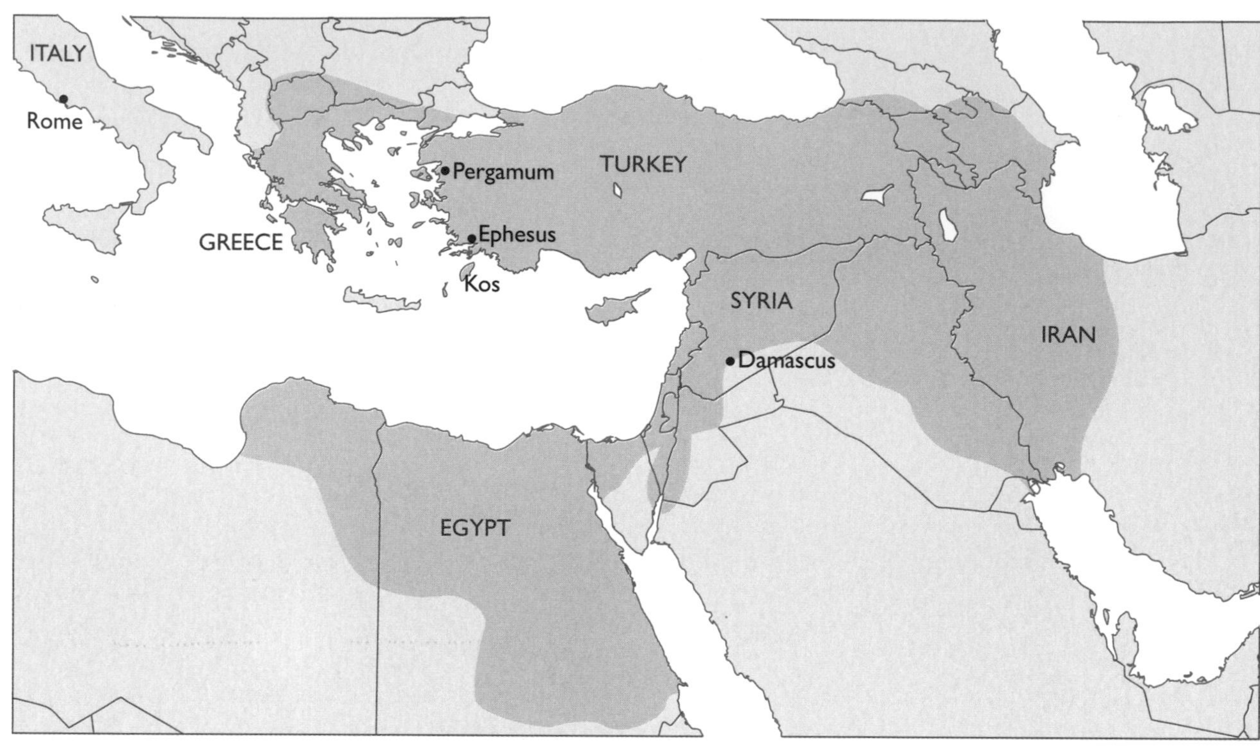

Figure 5.1 Map of Hellenistic world (240 BCE).

disease affecting different parts of the body – we suffer from headaches and heart attacks. But Greek practitioners believed that the most important elements of the body were fluids, or humours.

Hippocratic medicine was based on four humours: blood, yellow bile, black bile and phlegm. At first glance, this theory seems very strange to us. Greek practitioners were not ignorant of human anatomy – they knew about the bones, the organs and even small structures such as nerves and muscles. Their humoural theory was based on reason and observation. Practitioners observed that when we are injured, blood flows out of wounds. Blood is clearly crucial for life – a person who loses a lot of blood may die. Practitioners saw that when we are ill, the body often ejects liquid. Many complaints cause diarrhoea and vomiting, which can include the yellowish fluid which Greek practitioners called yellow bile. Pale, sticky fluids – such as that which runs from your nose when you have a cold or flu – were named phlegm. It's difficult to know what Greek practitioners meant by 'black bile', but it was probably dried or clotted blood. Like every other substance, the humours exhibited four fundamental qualities – they were hot, cold, wet or dry. Blood was hot and wet, whereas phlegm was cold and wet. This in turn related to the four fundamental elements that make up all substances – fire, air, earth and water. Through the humours, qualities and elements, the human body was understood in the same way as the rest of the world, and could be studied in the same manner, through reason and observation.

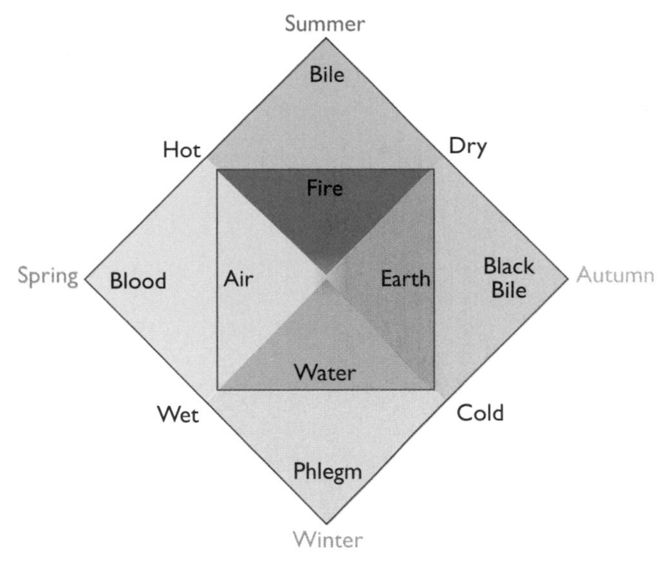

Figure 5.2 Diagram of the Hippocratic humoural system.

A healthy body was one in which the different humours were in balance. One of the Hippocratic texts summed up:

> Health is when these constituents [the humours] are in due proportion to one another with regard to blending, power and quantity, and when they are perfectly mixed. Pain is experienced whenever one of these is deficient or in excess or isolated in the body and is not blended with all the others.
>
> (Quoted in Nutton, 2004, p. 82)

If the balance became seriously disrupted – if there were excessive amounts of one humour or a collection of fluid – then disease would result. For example, fevers were the result of an excess of blood, and diarrhoea was associated with too much bile.

The balance between the different humours could be disrupted by many things: eating too much of certain types of food, drinking too much, taking too much or too little exercise, or overwork. Even strong emotions could cause physical illness. Exposure to excessive heat or cold was believed to be particularly dangerous and the weather was closely linked to disease. According to Hippocrates in *On Airs, Waters, and Places* (*c.*400 BCE):

> if there be rains in autumn; if the winter be mild, neither very tepid nor unseasonably cold, and if in spring the rains be seasonable, and so also in summer, the year is likely to prove healthy. But if the winter be dry and northerly, and the spring showery and southerly, the summer will necessarily be of a febrile [feverish] character, and give rise to ophthalmies [eye diseases] and dysenteries. For when suffocating heat sets in all of a sudden, while the earth is moistened by the vernal showers,

> and by the south wind, the heat is necessarily doubled from the earth, which is thus soaked by rain and heated by a burning sun, while, at the same time [...] the body and its flesh must be loaded with humours, so that very acute fevers will attack all.
>
> (http://etext.library.adelaide.edu.au/h/hippocrates//airs/index.html)

Seasons were linked to particular diseases. Spring weather, for example, caused an increase of blood in the body and predisposed people to suffer from fevers.

Activity To test your understanding of how Greek practitioners thought about disease, think about a time when you had a bad cold or flu. Can Greek medicine explain why you fell ill? Can your symptoms – the signs of disease – be fitted into the humoural system?

Discussion The symptoms of a cold or flu fit very neatly into the humoural system. Initially, you may have felt hot and feverish, or cold and shivery – signs that the balance of humours was upset. Later, you probably had a cough and a runny nose, which would have been interpreted by a Greek practitioner as the body trying to expel excess phlegm. Humoural medicine can also offer an explanation as to why you may have fallen ill. You've probably had colds during the winter – a cold and wet season which was believed to increase the level of phlegm in the body.

Practitioners in ancient Greece believed that when ill, the body would react and try to restore the balance by expelling fluid. It was the job of the medical practitioner to find out what had caused the imbalance. Here is a case history from *On Prognosis* written by Galen of Pergamum:

> I was called in to see a woman who was stated to be sleepless at night and to lie tossing about from one position to another. Finding she had no fever, I made a detailed inquiry into everything that had happened to her, especially considering such factors as we know to cause insomnia. But she either answered little or nothing at all, as if to show that it was useless to question her. Finally, she turned away, hiding herself completely by throwing the bedclothes over her whole body, and laying her head on another small pillow, as if desiring sleep.
>
> After leaving, I came to the conclusion that she was suffering from one of two things: either from a melancholy dependent on black bile, or else trouble about something she was unwilling to confess [...]
>
> After I had diagnosed that there was no bodily trouble, and that the woman was suffering from some mental uneasiness, it happened that, at the very time I was examining her, this was confirmed. Somebody came from the theatre and said he had seen Pylades dancing. Then both her expression and the colour

> of her face changed. Seeing this, I applied my hand to her wrist, and noticed that her pulse had suddenly become extremely irregular. This kind of pulse indicates that the mind is disturbed [...] Thus I found out that the woman was in love with Pylades, and by very careful watch on the succeeding days my discovery was confirmed.
>
> (www.stoa.org/diotima/anthology/wlgr/wlgr-medicine352.shtml)

As Galen's case history shows, the doctor's first task was to observe the patient's symptoms. He would ask how the symptoms started, about the patient's diet and exercise, note the patient's pulse, and record the amount and appearance of urine and faeces. This information would provide insight into the disease processes within the body, so practitioners could discover its underlying cause. Once this was done, the practitioner would prescribe a programme of care which would counteract the humoural imbalance. This could be done in two ways. It could be tackled directly by removing fluids from the patient's body. Many drugs used in the ancient world caused evacuations – vomiting, purging, or the production of urine – which were believed to help rebalance the humours. Bloodletting – cutting open a vein to remove a small amount of blood – was used to directly reduce an excess of that humour. We might dismiss these treatments as useless but they had an immediate and visible effect. When a patient was given a drug which induced vomiting, he or she could feel and see that it caused fluids to be ejected from the body. Today, when we take pills such as antibiotics, there is no immediate effect. We may not feel better for several days, and we keep taking the medicine only because we have faith in our practitioners.

Practitioners also sought to cure their patients by manipulating the qualities of the humours through foodstuffs and drugs which had the opposite qualities. For example, a patient suffering from a cold, where there was an excess of phlegm (a wet, cold substance), should avoid cooling drinks and foods which would make their condition worse. Instead, they should eat foods of a hot, dry quality, such as red meats and spices, and stay in a warm room. On the other hand, patients suffering from a fever caused by an excess of hot blood would be prescribed cold drinks and 'cooling' foods, such as lettuce, cucumber and fruit. Many ancient remedies combined herbal medicines with food. A mixture of warming herbs – hartshorn, pepper, myrrh and wine – was recommended for stomach aches. Lozenges, made from the juice of the herb 'all-heal' combined with honey, were used to treat pneumonia. Remedies could be incredibly complex. Mithridatium – a sort of cure-all and antidote to poisons – contained over sixty ingredients, including poppies, cardamom, frankincense and rose petals.

Figure 5.3 Unknown artist, illustrated page, ink and watercolour on vellum, 37 x 30 cm, from Dioscorides, *Materia Medica*, early sixth century. Österreichische Nationalbibliothek, Vienna, Cod. Med. gr. 1 f. 83r. Photo: ÖNB/Wien. Dioscorides' (c. 40 –90 CE) *Materia Medica* was one of the first pharmacopeias, a comprehensive list of drugs and their uses. His original manuscript had no illustrations: drawings were added, possibly as early as the second century CE. This rare copy of the pharmacopeia, dating from around 515 CE, was made for a Byzantine princess, and contains over 400 paintings. This page contains an illustration of a blackberry plant, showing its characteristic form and shape, while the text (written in Greek script) explains its uses.

Surgery was used in the ancient world but it was known to be dangerous, and was only used as a last resort when other treatments had failed. Practitioners working in the Roman empire (250 BCE to 200 CE) developed a sophisticated range of instruments (some of which are remarkably similar to modern instruments), such as needles, hooks, knives, and even specialised arrow removers. Surgeons could remove tumours and cataracts, deal with varicose veins, and even cut stones out of the bladder.

Theories about the body and disease travelled a long way in the ancient world – from Greece across Europe and into Africa and Asia.

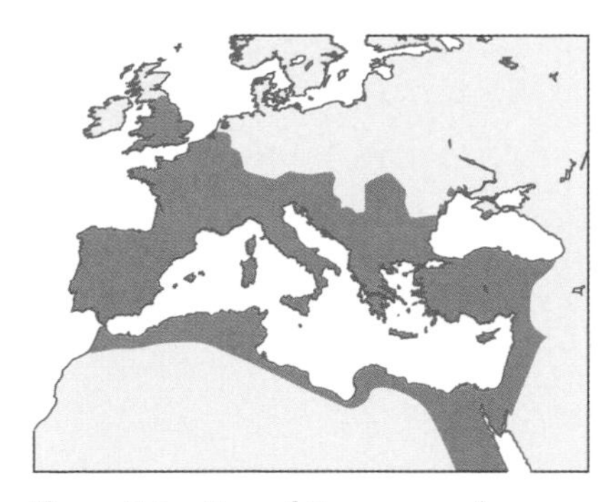

Figure 5.4 Map of Roman empire.

The movement of ideas was quick and easy, because Greek was understood by educated people in all these areas, and ambitious practitioners trained in centres of medical learning such as Alexandria and Constantinople. Ideas moved by word of mouth and through books. Practitioners wrote their ideas in hundreds of texts. Galen, who was a physician to the emperor in Rome, was an incredibly prolific author. By some accounts he produced over 400 books on medicine, each ranging between 50 and 300 pages long. (His productivity was in part the result of something close to plagiarism. He incorporated ideas from other authors within his own works, and did not always acknowledge his sources.) These works were copied by hand, bought, borrowed and sold, like modern printed books. They were also collected in libraries; works by Hippocrates and his followers were gathered in the library at Alexandria, about a hundred years after they were written.

Summary

Ancient Greek medicine, with its focus on the body's fluids, not its solid parts, can seem strange to us today. Its key features were the belief that health reflects a balance of humours which, when disrupted, cause disease. This was treated with drugs, diet and changes in lifestyle. The key characteristics of Greek medicine are that it is *systematic* (humours explain both health and disease, which are determined by following a logical set of rules) and *rational* (most disease has natural, not supernatural causes).

5.2 GREEK MEDICINE TRAVELS TO THE ISLAMIC WORLD

If possible, now listen to the podcast by Peter Pormann on the background to Islamic medicine. The podcast lasts about ten minutes.

From the seventh century CE, humoural medicine spread even further, with its adoption in the Islamic world. A powerful Islamic culture grew from the early seventh century under the prophet Muhammad and his followers. The peoples living in the Arab peninsula (now Saudi Arabia) were unified under Muslim rulers by 680 CE. Syria and Iraq were also conquered in the seventh century; Egypt, north-west Africa, Iran and parts of Spain by the eighth century. This was also a period of economic growth. The Islamic rulers, members of their courts and traders became extremely wealthy and powerful. Towns and cities grew in size. The capital of the Islamic world was shifted from Damascus to the new city of Baghdad, which became a cultural melting-pot, attracting traders and scholars from across the Islamic world.

These military conquests took the Arabic language and the Muslim faith across huge areas of the globe; it also brought Islamic scholars into contact with the Hellenistic world, with the Greek language and Greek ideas. Between the eighth and the eleventh centuries hundreds

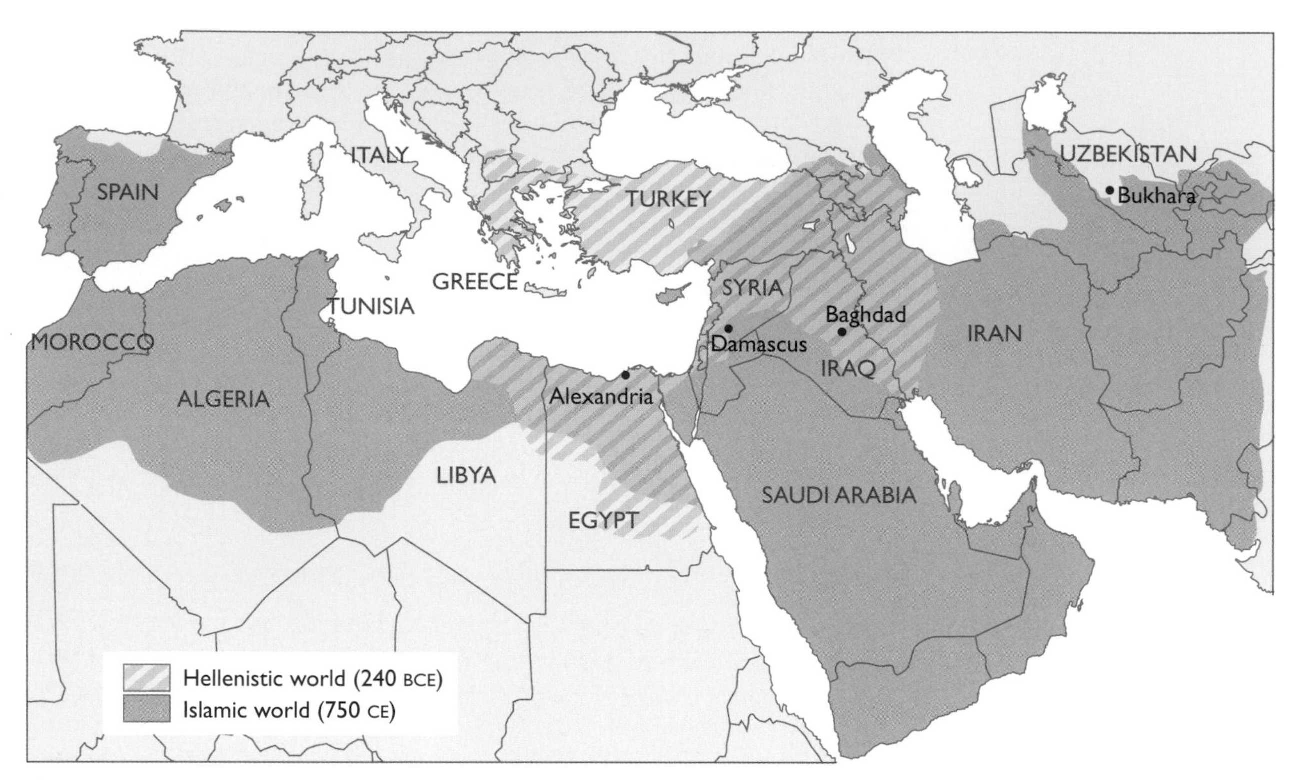

Figure 5.5 Map of Islamic world.

of Greek texts were translated into Arabic – works on mathematics, philosophy and medicine.

Huge numbers of medical manuscripts were translated, especially those of Hippocrates and Galen. Many scholars were engaged in this enterprise, of whom the most famous is Hunayn ibn Ishaq (*c.*808–873 CE), a Christian from southern Iraq. Until recently, historians thought that he led a group of translators who worked together in the *Bayt al Hikma* (House of Wisdom) – a sort of library – but recent research has cast doubt on the existence of such a centre. However, there is no doubt that with his helpers, Hunayn translated well over a hundred works by Galen, as well as texts by other Greek authors including Rufus of Epheseus and Hippocrates. These translations covered every aspect of medical knowledge – on the function of the body, specific diseases, drugs and medical treatment. Important texts were translated several times, as scholars tried to produce better and more accurate versions.

The process of translation

Translating a text from Greek to Arabic was extremely complex. For a start, it could be difficult to find a complete text of a single medical work. Greek works on medicine existed as manuscripts, scattered in libraries across modern-day Syria, Iran and Egypt, which had been copied and recopied by hand for hundreds of years. It took a long time to copy a manuscript, even for specialist scribes and copyists, and practitioners might not want to pay for the copying of a whole text; they might commission a scribe to reproduce only some parts of an original, or they might ask for extracts from several texts to be put together into one book. Pages might go missing or be destroyed. As a result, texts existed in a number of different forms.

Very few people were able to translate between Greek and Arabic. The use of Greek – once the language of scholars throughout the Hellenic and Roman worlds – had declined. The process of translation was dominated by Syriac-speaking Christians because they possessed a very rare combination of language skills. Hunayn and his collaborators had a good knowledge of Greek because they came from a culture where many Greek texts (including the Bible) had been translated into Syriac. The Syriac and Arabic languages are related, so it was then a relatively simple task to translate one into the other. Even so, translators often worked in small groups, pooling their skills and knowledge to produce the best possible translations.

However, they faced another problem. In translating medical texts it is especially important to convey information about diseases and drugs accurately, but in the eighth century there were no Arabic words for many of the diseases and symptoms described in the Greek texts. Translators solved this problem in a number of ways. They created new Arabic words by transliterating Greek words. (**Transliteration** involves translating letters from one alphabet into another – in this case from Greek to Arabic – and thereby produces new and unfamiliar terms. For example, the Greek term 'lethargos' was turned into 'litharghus'.) Some terms were translated by using similar words in the two languages. For example, epilepsy was known to the Greeks as 'the sacred disease' because it was believed to be sent by the gods. It was translated into Arabic as 'al-marad al-ilahi' ('the divine disease'). As well as this, existing words were given new meanings. For example, the Arabic word 'kalab', which meant a reddish-brown colour, began to be used to refer to a skin disease which was characterised by a darkening of the skin, and 'erysipelas', the Greek term for a red inflammation of the skin, was translated as 'humrah', the Arabic word for 'redness'. Although Islamic scholars strove to produce the best possible translations, inevitably errors crept in as unfamiliar terms were repeatedly copied. For example, the Greek 'phrenitis' (probably the disease we call meningitis) was transliterated and became the Arabic word 'faranitis', which eventually became corrupted into 'qaranitis'. However, the Islamic translators developed their skills and became more sophisticated over time.

Very few examples of translations of the same Greek text by more than one Islamic scholar have survived, but there are two translations of Galen's *On the Powers of Simple Drugs*. The first of these versions, written around 800 CE, summarises the sense of the text and makes extensive use of transliteration. The second version, by Hunayn, reproduces very precisely the meaning of the original and makes more use of translation than of transliteration to ensure that the reader will understand the words.

Although scholars took great pains to provide accurate translations, they also consciously and unconsciously altered Greek medicine. They deliberately modified the texts to make them fit into Islamic culture. References to Greek gods were routinely deleted from texts and replaced by Allah. Ascelepius, the Greek god of healing, lost his divine status and was described as a famous healer. Remedies using alcohol, or materials taken from pigs, both of which were forbidden in the Qur'an, were dropped from Islamic pharmacy. Not all Greek texts were translated, thus subtly reshaping the body of Greek medical knowledge. In the Islamic world, Galen became the central authority on medicine, and by the late ninth century all the surviving works of his massive output of medical writings had been translated. By contrast, not all works attributed to Hippocrates were translated, although his ideas were known through summaries made by other writers.

The motives for translation

Why did Islamic scholars expend so much energy on translating Greek medical works? It was not because there was no medicine practised in the Middle East before the eighth century. Although there are very few sources describing this medical care, it seems that a range of remedies were available to treat various common ailments. They had probably been discovered through trial and error, and there was no theoretical framework which explained the causes of a disease and hence why a specific treatment worked. Historians refer to such medicine as 'folk medicine' to distinguish it from more sophisticated systems such as humoural theory. Islamic remedies were based on plants and animal products such as urine and milk. Bloodletting was used, and some practitioners specialised in simple surgical procedures, such as dealing with wounds and lancing boils. Magic was also an important element in their practice. Some diseases were believed to have supernatural causes, and charms and amulets were worn to prevent or cure complaints caused by malicious spirits (called *jinns*) or the evil eye. With the rise of Islam, a religious medicine developed, modelled on the acts and sayings of the prophet Muhammed. This folk, supernatural and religious medical practice was carried on alongside humoural medicine, and sometimes absorbed elements of Greek practice.

The motives for the translation movement have long been debated among historians of medicine. In the following activity, you can compare two accounts of the factors that drove this, one by Lawrence Conrad, and the other by Peter Pormann and Emilie Savage-Smith.

Activity Read the extracts reproduced in Readings 5.1 and 5.2. These are quite long extracts, so don't worry about all the details, but jot down the main factors which the authors identify. Try to classify them – are they medical, social, political, practical or intellectual? Do the accounts contradict one another, or do they provide different explanations? This is a complex exercise, so take a little time over it.

Discussion In Reading 5.1, Lawrence Conrad identifies three factors to explain why Islamic scholars actively sought out and translated classical Greek texts into Arabic. The first he identifies as *social* – the translation of texts was funded by a new, educated elite, based in new cities. I would classify the second factor he identifies as *intellectual*. Conrad argues that Muslim scholars wanted to apply medical ideas to theological debates. Finally, he reminds us of a *practical* point – that Muslim scholars had access to libraries. He makes no claim that the translation movement was driven by a desire for new *medical* knowledge (although he doesn't deny that this might have been a factor).

In Reading 5.2, Peter Pormann and Emilie Savage-Smith focus on *political* factors, suggesting that the translation of Greek texts was a way of connecting the new ruling dynasty with prestigious learning, and pointing to the existing links with the Hellenistic world. They support Conrad's *social* argument on the important role of the elite in funding translations, and criticise another author who suggests that scholars led the translation movement.

The two accounts therefore don't contradict each other, but present a case for different factors helping to drive translators' work.

Islamic medicine

Historians of medicine have debated the contribution made by Islamic scholars to medicine. Until the 1960s, many academics thought of the Islamic translators 'passing on' Greek ideas to later generations, but making few innovations. Historians now disagree with this view. Certainly, no Islamic author attempted to fundamentally revise humoural medicine. Humoural theory explained all aspects of body function in such a systematic way that it is hard to imagine how any part of the theory could be changed without requiring the revision of all other parts. Manfred Ullmann, one of the first historians to work on Islamic medicine, pointed out that for an Arab practitioner

> the literature of the ancients was both example and authority [...] in it, a certain natural truth is laid down which he can only think about, develop and comment on [...] Tradition is for him a treasure chest which he willingly makes use of, and in no way is it possible for him to experience it as a burden that he could or would shake off.
>
> (Ullmann, 1978, p. 24)

However, the translated texts provided the basis for a distinctive Islamic culture of medicine, which continued and developed Greek traditions. Historians usually refer to this as 'Islamic medicine', because medicine was part of a distinctively Islamic culture, although, as we have seen, not all translators and writers were Muslims. Indeed, the most important translators were Christian. Some historians use the term 'Arabic medicine' because the texts were written in the Arabic language, but there are problems with this term too, as some leading practitioners were not Arabs. From the early tenth century, fewer works were translated, but medical scholarship flourished as Islamic scholars turned to writing new books. Thousands of new medical works were produced, all firmly based on humoural theory and using the rational approach so characteristic of Greek medicine. Islamic medical texts adopted the idea of the humours, the role of diet, lifestyle and the environment in causing disease, and the use of drugs, food and exercise to treat illness.

Activity Readings 5.3 and 5.4 contain two examples of texts written by Islamic practitioners. Read the short case history by Abu Bakr Muhammed ibn Zakariya al-Razi (later to become known as Rhazes, *c.*865–925 CE), a distinguished Muslim practitioner. Can you identify the ideas from Greek medical theory and practice used in this case? Then read the entry on 'Asparagus' from *The Book of Simple Drugs* by Ahmad ibn Muhammad al-Ghâfiqî (d. 1165). What do you notice about the sources he uses (and the order in which they appear)? How is the description of asparagus geared to humoural practice?

Discussion In Reading 5.3, every aspect of the case is analysed by al-Razi in terms of humoural medicine. Like Galen, al-Razi takes careful note of symptoms – of heat and pain. The disease is characterised as a 'hot' disease – one of the fundamental qualities. At the end of the case al-Razi analyses the cause of the inflammation as a 'hot (and vicious)' fluid, which had collected in the patient's body. The therapies and the rational choice of treatments are also typically humoural: cooling barley water, cucumber and other herbal treatments to counter the heat, and bloodletting to draw out the bad humour.

In Reading 5.4, al-Ghâfiqî cites Greek and Islamic writers. You can work out that this text was written for practitioners of humoural medicine because the effects of asparagus are described in terms of fluids (it produces purging according to Dioscorides, or is drying according to Galen) and qualities – it is 'hot and moist', it 'heats'. Notice that there is very little agreement between the authors in how they describe the use of asparagus, although they agree that it affects the kidneys. Al-Ghâfiqî gives the Greek sources first – a sign of his respect for their authority.

Islamic translators held Greek learning in such high esteem that the names of plants, animals or minerals not found in Arab-speaking lands were still faithfully translated. In a work on poisons, the translator transliterated the names of snakes, even though no patient of an Islamic physician would suffer from the bite of these Greek snakes and the information on how to treat their bites was quite useless.

As Greek medical theory was adopted across the Islamic world – from Spain to the borders of modern India – Islamic practitioners were able to add new ideas and observations within the established framework. They added new treatments. Practitioners in the Islamic world had a far

Figure 5.6 Unknown artist, illustrated page, colour and ink on paper, from an Arabic translation of Dioscorides' pharmacopeia, *Materia Medica*, 1334. As in the Greek version shown in Figure 5.3, the plant is illustrated (cumin is a spice often used in cooking) beside a text explaining its uses. British Library, Or.3366. Photo: © By permission of The British Library.

greater number of drugs at their disposal. The **pharmacopeia** (a book listing drugs and their uses) written by Dioscorides listed 850 drugs; Islamic pharmacopeias listed over 3,000 items, which included new medicines such as camphor, musk and senna. Drugs were sold and prepared in special shops. New drugs, not used in Greek medicine, were fitted into the humoural system by categorising them by their

Figure 5.7 Unknown artist, 'The Pharmacy: preparing medicine from honey', colour and gilt on paper, 31.4 x 22.9 cm, from Dioscorides, *Materia Medica*, Arabic translation, attributed to Iraq, Baghdad School, 1224. The Metropolitan Museum of Art, New York. Bequest of Cora Timkin Burnett, 1956 (57.51.21). Photo: © The Metropolitan Museum of Art. This picture of an Arabic pharmacist's shop shows two figures preparing medicines. The row of jars along the top is a common feature of such images, suggesting the wide range of drugs available.

qualities – whether hot or cold or drying. From these qualities, practitioners could work out how to use these substances. As well as describing new medicinal substances, Islamic pharmacists developed a number of basic chemical techniques to purify and combine drugs – for example, by distillation and filtration. Texts suggest that where Greek authors stressed the use of diet and changes in lifestyle to treat disease, Islamic practitioners placed a greater emphasis on the use of drugs.

Records of the actual treatment given to patients by al-Razi suggest that he used a small number of tried and tested drugs in most cases.

Islamic practitioners also extended the knowledge of diseases and of treatment. For example, a number of scholars, including the translator Hunayn ibn Ishaq, wrote books on diseases of the eye, identifying a number of conditions not mentioned in any Greek text. Hunayn's work included another innovation – anatomical illustrations showing the structure of the eye.

Al-Razi was the first practitioner to describe the causes, symptoms and treatment of smallpox, and to distinguish it from measles. Although al-Razi's observations and ideas were quite new, they were based on the humoural theory of the body and of disease. He used the idea of humours to explain why people only caught smallpox once. The disease mainly attacked children, causing a high fever and a characteristic rash. Al-Razi claimed that smallpox was caused by impure blood which was present in the bodies of children from birth. He explained that at some point, this bad blood began to ferment. The body would then expel the bad matter, which appeared in spots on the skin. Once this corrupted blood had been expelled, the child could not suffer from smallpox. (Al-Razi was quite right in his observation that people only catch smallpox once in their lives. We explain the same phenomenon by immunity – once a child has been exposed to the smallpox virus, his or her body produces antibodies which prevent future attacks.)

Systemisation

Historians now agree that the greatest achievement of Islamic medical writers was to systematise Greek medicine. Medical texts written in ancient Greece varied widely in their style, context and function. Some texts were made up of simple, short sentences, designed to be easily memorised. Others were complex and their meaning was obscure even to contemporary scholars. Some were written in elegant prose, some were in note form. The subject of texts ranged from accounts of particular diseases, such as epilepsy, to discussions of medical theory, the effects of the environment, and the use of drugs and diet.

Compendia – short compilations of medical knowledge – had been produced in the Hellenistic world, but Islamic authors produced many more. Huge numbers of texts collected, digested and organised medical information, thus presenting a large and complex body of knowledge in a more accessible way. Many of these books followed a pattern established in Greek times and were divided into theory and practice, and included case histories of patients from the authors' own experience to illustrate some aspects of treatment. For example, *Al-Kitab al-mansuri fi l-tibb* (*The Mansurian Book of Medicine*), written by al-Razi in the tenth century, was divided into ten books. The first six dealt with medical theory – diet, hygiene, anatomy, the functioning

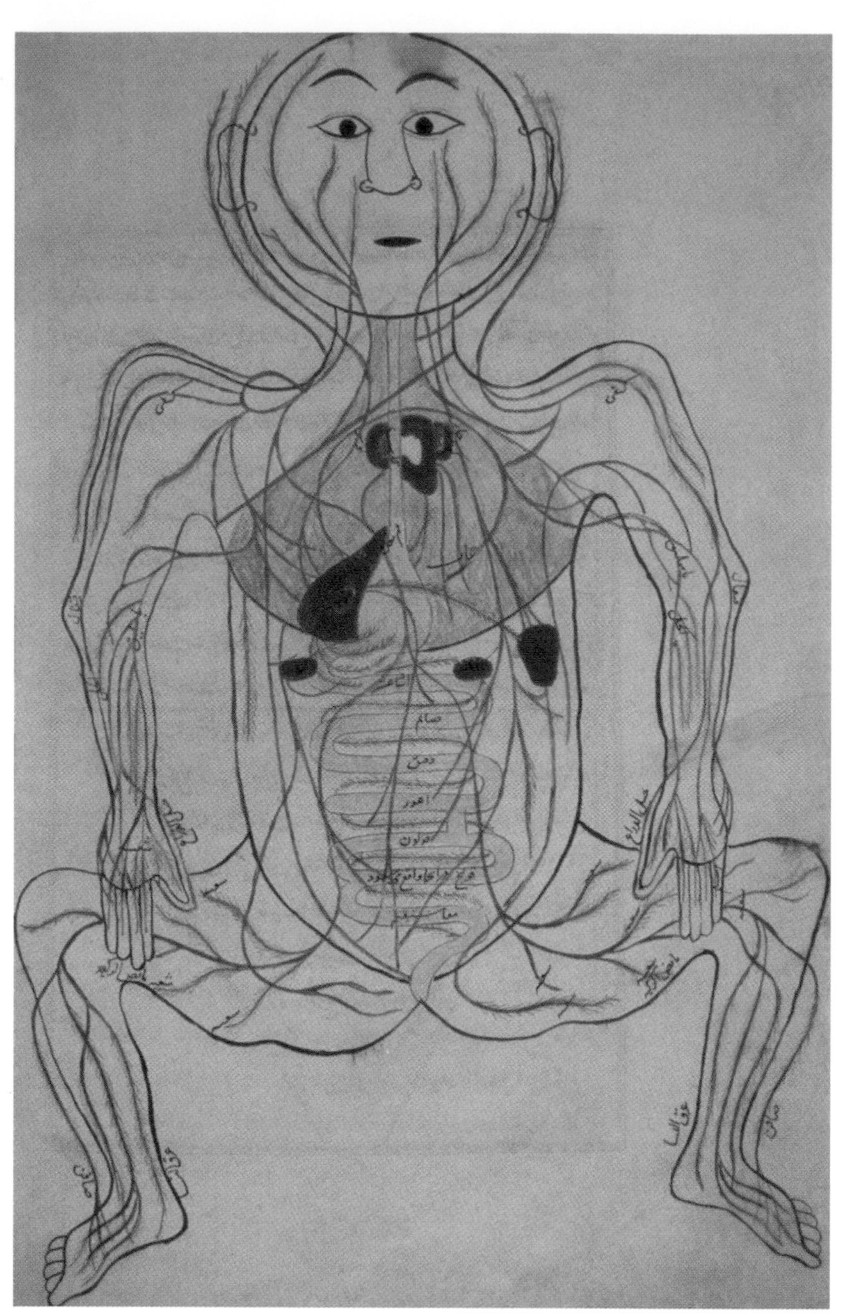

Figure 5.8 Tashri Al-Badan, anatomical figure showing the internal organs and circulatory system, mid-fifteenth century, ink and water colour on vellum. Chester Beatty Library, Dublin. Photo: © The Trustees of the Chester Beatty Library, Dublin/ The Bridgeman Art Library. From the late fourteenth century, Arabic texts on anatomy included illustrations. This slightly later image shows the standard form – a figure facing the viewer, in a squatting position. It shows the main blood vessels and some internal organs, and is one of a series of illustrations showing different anatomical features. The image gives only a sketchy impression of anatomy, reflecting the greater importance placed on the role of humours in health and disease.

of the body and drug treatments. The last four books were more practical, covering diagnosis, therapy, diseases and surgery.

Ibn Sina (more commonly known by his Latin name, Avicenna, 980–1037 CE) was not an Arab, but was born near Bukhara which is in modern Uzbekistan. He was a prolific author, writing poetry as well as books on medicine, law and philosophy.

By far the most famous compilation was Ali ibn Sina's *Al-Qanan fi al-tibb* (*Canon of Medicine*: 'canon' here means an accepted body of ideas which are fundamental to a subject). The *Canon* is a massive text, running to almost a million words in five books (only the first book has been translated into English). The first book gave an account of the knowledge required to practise medicine – medical theory, the causes of disease, hygiene, treatments and surgery. Book 2 dealt with simple drugs – substances that could be used as remedies. Book 3 provided a comprehensive account of diseases, starting with those affecting the head, and going down the body, ending with complaints of the feet. Book 4 dealt with diseases that affected the whole body (such as fever), and Book 5 covered compound drugs. Though very long, the *Canon* was thus a practical and comprehensive reference book. A practitioner faced with a difficult case could immediately see where to find practical help in diagnosing the problem (in Books 3 and 4) or how particular drugs would benefit the patient (Books 2 and 5). If he wanted to better understand the causes of an ailment, he could use Book 1. But it also set practice firmly on a theoretical basis, which allowed practitioners to approach the process of diagnosing and treating patients on a logical footing.

Activity

Read the extract in Reading 5.5 from Ibn Sina's *Canon* on the effects of winds. How does it differ from the passage from Hippocrates' *On Airs, Water, and Places* quoted earlier?

Discussion

Compared with the Hippocratic text, the *Canon* is much more detailed and systematic. Ibn Sina describes the medical effects of each wind direction in turn, describing the diseases that occur when each wind prevails. He even details the effect of the wind at different times of the day.

Huge numbers of medical texts circulated across the Islamic world. Important works like Ibn Sina's *Canon* were read from Spain to the borders of modern India. There was systematic production of manuscript copies of works and in some cases hundreds of copies of particular texts have survived (and probably a much greater number have been destroyed). Libraries in modern Turkey alone hold around 5,000 medical manuscripts in Arabic, including over 1,000 works by 40 authors. This gives the impression that Greek medicine must have been widely practised. Certainly, books on humoural medicine were used by practitioners, and formed the core of teaching. The Islamic emphasis on Galen set the standard by which to judge practitioners: those educated in Galen's writings were seen as having a better understanding of the body and disease. However, such highly educated practitioners worked only among wealthy patients in urban areas. The poorer members of society and those living in the countryside continued to rely on home-made remedies (possibly using a book as guidance) and folk practitioners.

Figure 5.9 Hunayn ibn Ishaq, *Masa'il fi t-tibb* ('Introduction to the Healing Arts'), fourteenth-century copy, ink on oriental paper, 18.6 x 13 cm. Wellcome Library, WMS Arabic 402. Photo: Wellcome Library, London. The *Masa'il fit-tibb* explained medicine through a series of questions and answers, and was probably written for students.

Summary

The translation of Greek medical texts into Arabic occurred in a very specific social and political context. Islamic practitioners adopted Greek humoural theory: health and disease reflected the condition of the body's fluids. However, Islamic writers presented these theories in a more coherent, logical way, drawing on many works to compile comprehensive accounts of body function, disease and treatment. They extended knowledge of diseases and wrote about the use of new drugs.

5.3 GREEK AND ISLAMIC MEDICAL IDEAS IN EUROPE

In the eleventh century, medical ideas went through a second great migration, as works were translated from Arabic and Greek into Latin and spread across Europe. There are many similarities but also some striking differences between these two movements of medical ideas. The first very clear parallel is in the context in which this movement took place. Just as Islamic scholars had come into contact with Greek medicine during the expansion of Islamic rule, the reconquest of parts of Europe by Christian princes brought European scholars into contact with Islamic ideas. From the eleventh century, parts of Spain, southern Italy, Sardinia and Sicily, which had formerly been part of the Islamic world, were conquered. Curiously, the Crusades – campaigns by Christian armies to conquer holy sites in the Middle East – did not have a major impact on the exchange of medical knowledge between Europe and the Middle East.

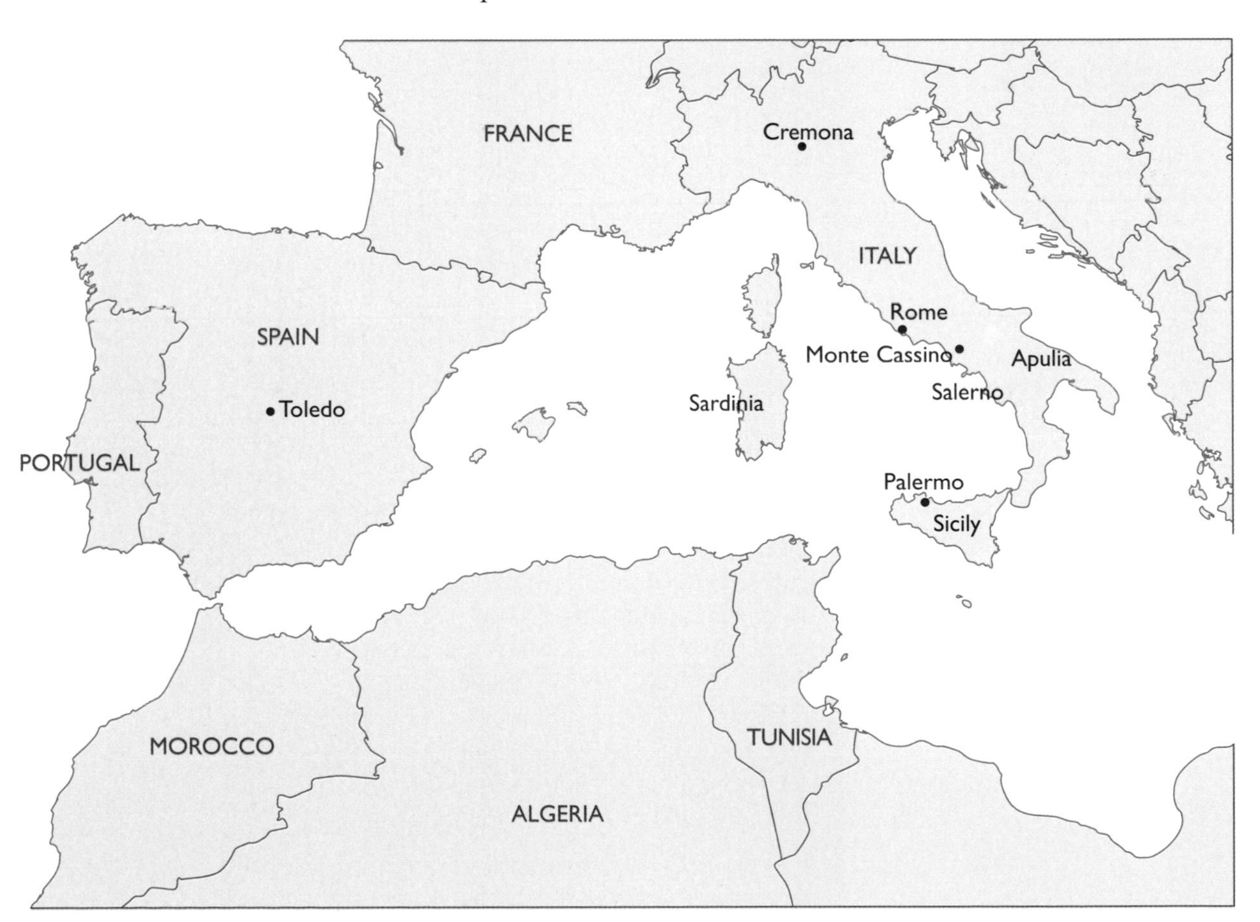

Figure 5.10 Europe showing centres of medieval translation (modern countries are shown for ease of reference).

Translations of books on many subjects were made in these areas of contact between the Islamic east and Christian west, particularly in Toledo in Spain, Apulia (Puglia) in Italy, and Palermo in Sicily. There was a simple practical reason for this. In these areas there was a mix of Muslim and Jewish scholars, who had a good knowledge of Arabic and Hebrew, and Christian scholars, clerics and administrators who used Latin, a language derived from that spoken around Rome, which had become the universal language of scholarship in medieval Europe. Just as in Baghdad centuries earlier, a number of scholars – Muslims, Jews and Christians – pooled their knowledge of languages to produce accurate translations of Arabic texts.

However, as we've seen, having access to texts does not explain why scholars took the time and trouble to translate from Arabic into Latin. The same social and political factors which drove the translation movement in the Middle East were also present in medieval Europe. The region was going through a period of economic growth. The population was increasing, towns and cities grew, and trade flourished. The number of schools grew too, providing skills for a new generation of workers in literate occupations, including medicine. There was a new interest in intellectual matters and a widespread desire to rediscover Greek knowledge and Arabic philosophy and science. In this context, patrons – princes, members of the social elite, clerics and practitioners – had the money to pay for scholars to make translations of Arabic texts on medicine, mathematics and science.

The translation of Arabic texts into Latin

Like the Islamic scholars before them who translated from Greek into Arabic, European translators faced the same problems: often there were no Latin words for Arabic medical terms. They used the same techniques as their Islamic counterparts to deal with this problem. They transliterated Arabic words letter by letter and translated the sense of the terms. For example, the name 'pia mater', one of the membranes covering the brain, was derived from the Arabic 'umm raqiqah' which means 'thin wrapping' (Savage-Smith, 1997, p. 44). In this way, a new medical vocabulary was created. Just as Islamic scholars had taken out references to Greek gods, in Christian Europe references to Allah were removed. A Christian gloss was even added to the understanding of the four humours. As well as relating each fluid to qualities, elements and seasons, authors linked them to the four evangelists – Matthew, Mark, Luke and John – who wrote the Gospels of the New Testament.

Inevitably in the course of translating from Arabic to Latin, and of devising new terms for diseases and drugs, inaccuracies and confusions arose. For example, as previously mentioned, some Arabic texts referred to a disease called 'faranitis', and others called the same condition 'qaranitis'. When this term was transliterated again into Latin in medieval Europe it became 'karabitus'. European practitioners complained that the transliterated names of drugs were quite incomprehensible. Debates sprang up over what plant authors were describing when they wrote of 'rhubarb' (a fairly common remedy) or 'mummy' (a much more exotic one, taken from preserved ancient corpses), and authors compiled glossaries of the various names to try to clarify matters. European practitioners also realised that many of the medicinal plants recommended by Islamic practitioners did not grow in Europe. They could be imported, but this made them very expensive, so they tried to find alternatives or substitutes. Errors also crept in through repeated copying of manuscripts. The illustrations of surgical instruments in Arabic texts originally provided accurate representations of the devices but, over time, copyists who did not understand the function of the tools used the drawings as a basis for decorations to make the manuscripts look attractive. This rendered the drawings quite useless as a record of the instruments (see Figure 5.11).

There are two very striking differences, however, between the translation of medical works into Arabic and those into Latin. First, European scholars had access to a much richer medical tradition than their Islamic counterparts. They translated works written in Arabic, Arabic versions of works by Greek authors (notably Galen), and some texts written in Greek. Second, in the Middle East, scholars seem to have worked steadily at translating from the late eighth century, but in Europe the translation of medical works into Latin took place in a number of phases or stages.

Constantine Africanus (*c.* 1020–1087) One of the most important translators, he was unusual in that he had moved from the Islamic to the Christian world. Born in Tunisia he travelled widely, and studied medicine for a time before becoming a Christian monk.

The first phase occurred in the late eleventh century, and was centred on the monastery of Monte Cassino in southern Italy and the monk Constantine Africanus. He translated works by both Arabic and Greek authors, including a number of texts written by Galen. He also translated *Kitab Kamil al-sina ah al tibbiyah* by Ali ibn al-Abbas al-Majusi. This book – whose title translates into English as *The Complete Book of the Medical Art* – was called the *Pantegni*, in Latin, meaning *The Universal Art*. When Arabic texts were later translated, the names of a number of important Islamic authors were turned into a Latin form. (Both forms are given in this text, as you may encounter them in other materials.) So Ali ibn al-Abbas al-Majusi became Haly Abbas. Constantine also translated works by Ibn al-Jazzar, and by Hunayn ibn Ishaq (whose name was translated into Latin as Joannitius or Johannitius).

Gerard of Cremona (*c.* 1114–1187) Born in Italy, he travelled to Toledo specifically to study Arabic texts. There, under the patronage of the local bishop and working with assistants, he translated a large number of works by Galen and texts by al-Razi and Ibn Sina.

A second wave of translation in the twelfth century is associated with Gerard of Cremona. Constantine's efforts had focused on translating works on medical theory, but Gerard and his assistants in Toledo concentrated on compendia by Islamic authors such as al-Razi's *Al-Kitab al-mansuri fi l-tibb* (*The Mansurian Book of Medicine*), which they translated as *Liber al Almasorem*, while al-Razi became *Rhazes*. The *Canon* by Ibn Sina (whose Latin name is Avicenna) and the surgical sections from Abu al-Qasim's *Al-Tasrif* were also translated in Toledo. Abu al-Qasim (936–1013) was known in Europe as Albucasis, and his manual on surgery as *Chirurgia* (see Figure 5.11 for an

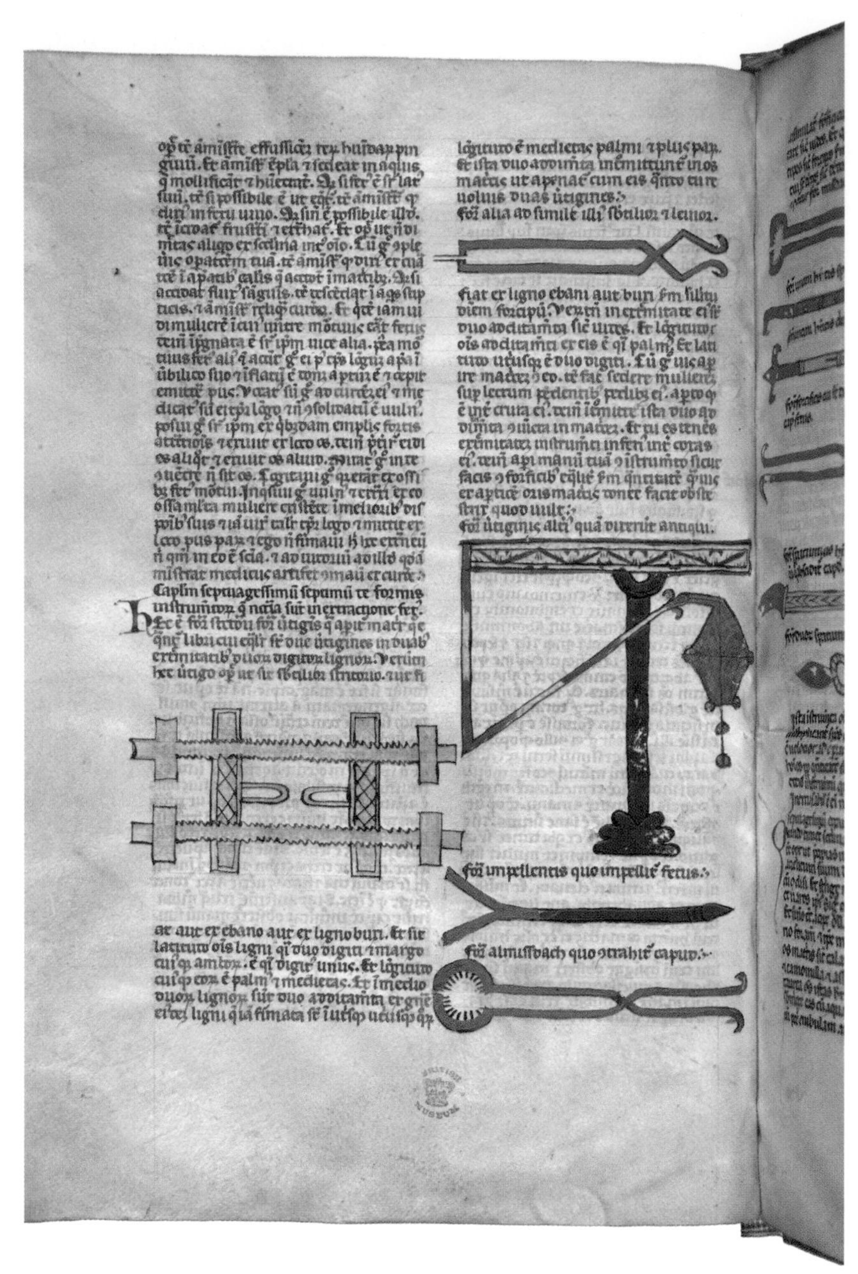

Figure 5.11 Unknown artist, drawing of surgical instruments, ink on vellum, from a copy of Abu al-Qasim's surgical text *Chirurgia,* translated into Latin by Gerard of Cremona, early fourteenth century. British Museum Add. Ms. 36617, f.28v. Photo: Wellcome Library, London. The elaborate decoration on this page is an example of how drawings were transformed over time. The object that looks like a lamp was originally a drawing of a vaginal speculum, but through repeated copying by scribes who knew little of surgery, it has become a decoration.

illustrated page from a Latin translation of this work). A century later, there was a final burst of translations, when the remaining important works by Galen, al-Razi and Ibn Rushd (known as Averroes) were translated from the original Greek and Arabic.

In early medieval Europe, practitioners valued the work of both Greek and Islamic medical authors. We can see this very clearly in the texts taught in the new universities. In the Middle East, students learned medicine by studying books, or by watching and learning from experienced practitioners, and perhaps in formal classes. In thirteenth-century Europe a new institution appeared – the university – to teach the most advanced forms of learning – law and theology – and to issue professional qualifications. Universities were founded across Europe, from Scotland to modern Poland, and Scandinavia to Spain. All subjects were taught from books and the earliest medical teaching was based on a collection of writings known as the *Articella* (*The Little Art of Medicine*; see Figures 5.12 and 5.13), which included works by Islamic scholars such as *Isagoge*, literally 'Introduction', by Johannitius (Hunayn), alongside books by the two great authorities of Greek times – Galen's *Ars Parva* and Hippocrates' *Aphorisms* and *Prognostics*. Later, the *Pantegni* by Haly Abbas (attributed to Constantine) was added to the body of texts, and by the early thirteenth century Ibn Sina's *Canon* had become an established university text.

We can get another glimpse of attitudes to Greek, Arabic and European scholars from the Prologue to Geoffrey Chaucer's *Canterbury Tales*, written between 1387 and 1400.

With vs ther was a doctour of phisyk.	With us there was a Doctor of Medicine.
In al this world ne was ther noon hym lyk	In all this world there was none like him
To speken of phisyk and surgerye. [...]	To speak of medicine and surgery [...]
Wel knew he the oolde Esculapyus	He knew well the old Aesclepius
And Discorides and eek Rufus,	And Dioscorides and also Rufus,
Olde Ypocras, Haly and Galyen,	Old Hippocrates, Haly and Galen,
Serapion, Razis and Avyccn,	Serapion, Rhazes and Avicenna,
Auerroys, Damascien and Constantyn,	Avveroes, Damascene and Constantine,
Bernard and Gatesden and Gilbertyn.	Bernard and Gatisden and Gilbertus.

(Adapted from Chaucer, 1980 [*c.*1387-1400], pp. 48–9)

In Chaucer's text, the learned practitioner knows his Greek medical authorities – Asclepius (the healing god), Dioscorides, Hippocrates and Galen – and the work of Islamic scholars – Rhazes (al-Razi), Avicenna (Ibn Sina), Averroes (Ibn Rushd) and Haly Abbas (Ali ibn al-Abbas al-Majusi). They both rub shoulders with more contemporary scholars – Constantine, the translator; Bernard, a professor of medicine at Montpellier; Gatisden, a physician at Oxford; and Gilbertus, probably the Englishman who wrote a *Medical Compendium* around 1240.

The new translations of Greek and Arabic texts had a rather different impact in Europe from their reception in the Islamic world. There, humoural medicine seems to have been used alongside older folk remedies and religious and supernatural cures. In medieval Europe, some aspects of Greek humoural medicine had lingered on from the time of the Roman empire, but few Greek texts had been translated into Latin. However, some humoural treatments had been incorporated into medical practice. For example, leechbooks – books of remedies, written in English in the early tenth century – included passages based on Greek works. The newly translated Greek and Arabic medical writings therefore provided European scholars with a much more sophisticated form of humoural medicine than was available through existing texts. The new translated texts brought a rational approach to practice, a set of rules by which practitioners could diagnose disease, predict the likely outcome and prescribe a range of treatments adapted to individual patients.

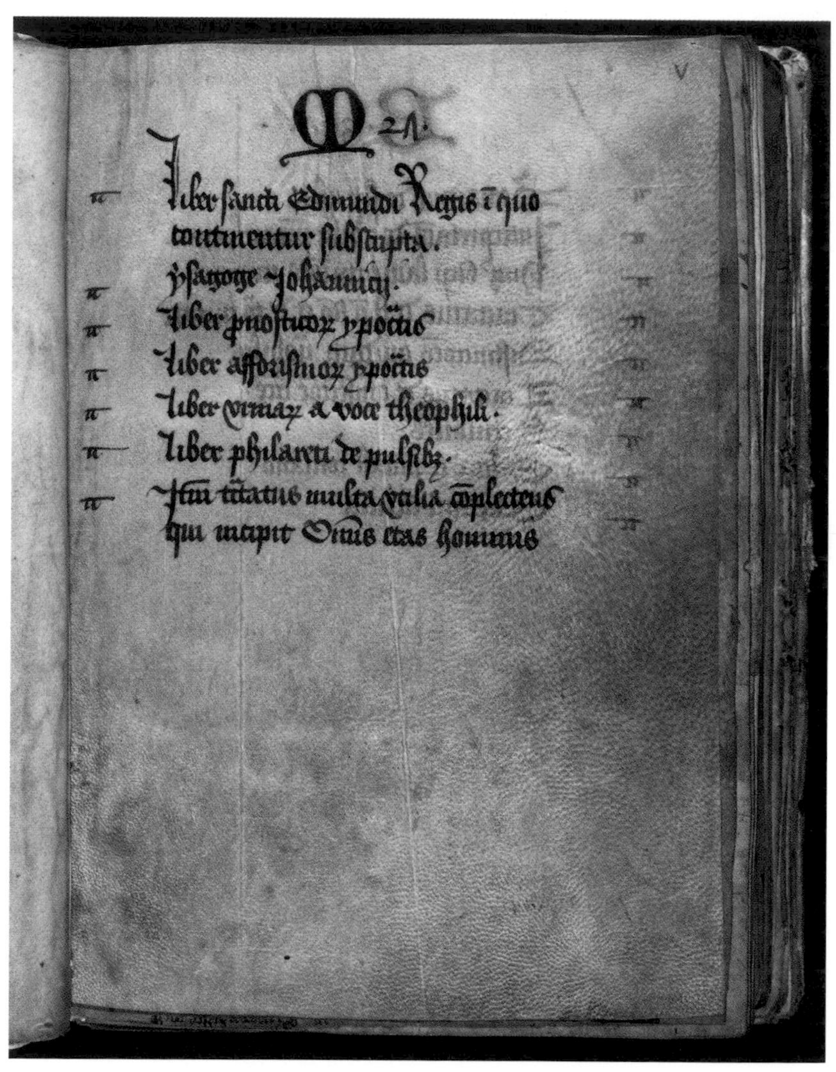

Figure 5.12 Contents page of 'The Bury *Articella*', thirteenth century, ink on vellum, 20 x 14.5 cm. Wellcome Library, WMS & MS801A. Photo: Wellcome Library, London. This is the earliest copy of the *Articella*, produced in Britain at Bury St Edmunds in the thirteenth century. On this title page you can read that the second item is the *Isagoge* of Johannitius (or Hunayn).

Figure 5.13 *Articella* with commentaries, fourteenth century, ink and colour on vellum, 32 x 20.5 cm. Wellcome Library, WMS84. Photo: Wellcome Library, London. In this beautifully written copy, extensive commentaries have been added to the text, written in a smaller script, which discuss particular points.

Activity Read the opening passages of Reading 5.6, the *Isagoge* originally written by Hunayn, and translated into Latin by Constantine. Summarise its content in a few words and then try to think of three or four words to describe the character of this account of medicine and the body. How does the *Isagoge* fit with my description of the approach to medicine introduced to Europe in medieval times?

Discussion You may have used different words, but I simply copied the headings to summarise the content and called the first section 'Principles'. To describe the character of the text I would use the words snappy, rational and logical. I use the word 'snappy' because this text covers all the fundamental principles in just a few sentences. The text is rational and logical: it goes through the principles in a specific order, from the general to the particular. I chose those words to convey the lack of practical medicine in the text – no mention of diseases or patients! Clearly, the *Isagoge* exemplifies the rational approach to medicine.

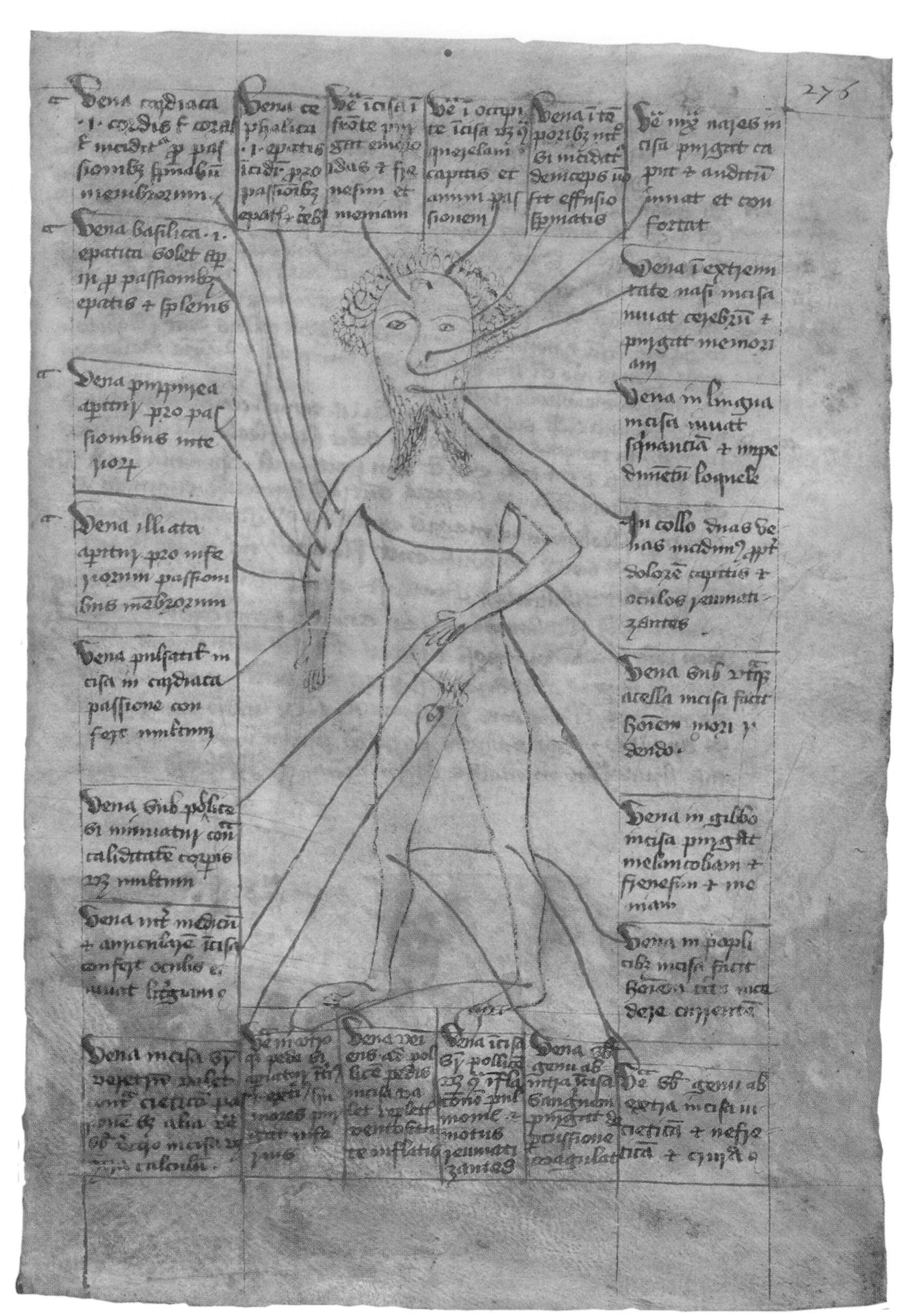

Figure 5.14 Unknown artist, nude figure of a man with parts of the body indicated for bloodletting, pen and wash on vellum, 23 x 14.5 cm, from *Miscellanea Medica XVIII*, early fourteenth century. Wellcome Library, MS.544, p. 276. Photo: Wellcome Library, London. This figure and its accompanying text show the points where blood can be removed from the body and how this can cure various diseases.

Access to Arabic texts also increased the number and sophistication of treatments used by European practitioners. For example, while bloodletting had been practised in Europe in the early medieval period, the Arabic texts provided a much more detailed account of when and how to use the therapy. The use of cautery – a heated metal instrument which was applied to the skin to draw out humours which had become lodged in the body – became more popular following the translation of Abu al-Qasim's manual on surgery. Texts on pharmacy greatly expanded the array of drugs known to European practitioners.

For European authors, like Islamic practitioners, humoural medicine formed a tradition to be preserved and passed on, but which they also sought to extend, adding to the existing body of knowledge provided by Greek and Islamic authors. Hundreds of new medical texts were written. Commentaries on Greek and Islamic texts discussed often very obscure details of medical theory. Many of the new texts took a more practical approach, consisting of case histories, collections of remedies, and books describing the authors' experiences of dealing with diseases.

Activity Reading 5.7 contains an example of such a work. Read 'A Consilium' by Ugo Benzi (Hugh of Siena, 1376–1439), an Italian physician, who learned his medicine from texts at university. A consilium was a written report of an actual case. These reports were sometimes collected and published in book form. As you read, note the similarity between this work and those written hundreds of years earlier by Galen and al-Razi, all of which are underpinned by the same humoural theory, which explains the causes of disease and suggests methods of cure.

Many surgical texts appeared in medieval Europe which had a new emphasis on anatomy. Islamic authors had produced anatomical texts, some with illustrations. In medieval Europe, university teachers revived Galen's advice to study anatomy, and introduced the dissection of animals (or, less frequently, the bodies of executed criminals) as part of their teaching. Authors of surgical texts began to stress the need to study anatomy as the basis for surgical practice. Nevertheless, their texts included few new operations or surgical techniques. This is hardly surprising: without anaesthetics to deal with the pain and with no means of preventing infection, surgery was used only as a last resort. Surgeons were therefore confined to dealing with injuries, chronic conditions arising from infected wounds, the removal of swellings, bloodletting, and a handful of operations, such as the removal of tumours or of cataracts from the eye. Medieval authors did debate the best methods of treatment – for example, whether wounds healed better if they were simply cleaned and bandaged or when ointments were used to promote healing – but any improvements in surgical techniques were minor.

Until the end of the fourteenth century, European practitioners valued the work of both Greek and Islamic medical authors, but in the fifteenth and sixteenth centuries, practitioners began to criticise

Figure 5.15 Unknown artist, nine scenes of medical care, ink and colour on vellum, 23 x 15.5 cm, from Roger Frugardi of Parma, *Chirurgia*, 1300–10. British Library, Sloane 1977, f.6. © By permission of The British Library. The top three images in this illustration from a very expensive and beautifully produced copy of Roger of Parma's book on surgery are biblical scenes. The scenes below show a surgeon (the figure wearing a cap) dealing with a range of injuries to the upper limbs: in the middle row, from left to right, these include resetting a dislocated shoulder, a dislocated wrist and examining a broken or dislocated wrist; bottom row, left to right, examining a damaged finger, diagnosing a dislocated shoulder, and prescribing an ointment or medicine.

Islamic authors and favour Greek texts. The resulting decline of Islamic medicine explains why historians underestimated the contribution of Islamic practitioners until the twentieth century. The criticism of Islamic authors was driven by a wider movement – humanism. Italian scholars argued that human civilisation had reached a peak in classical antiquity, and had declined ever since. To reverse this decline, practitioners should try to recover Greek and Roman ideas by going back to the original Greek texts.

Activity

Reading 5.8 is an extract from Nancy Siraisi's book on the history of Avicenna's (Ibn Sina's) *Canon*. Read the extract now, and then answer the following question:

What aspects of the *Canon* did the European scholars dislike?

Discussion

There are two main points of criticism. First, the authors clearly distrust all Islamic scholars, describing them as 'unreliable'. They don't give any particular reasons for this, but given that humanist scholars saw Greek learning as the best, then everything else was second rate. Second, the authors complain that Ibn Sina had made errors in his translation, and had introduced all sorts of mistakes and misunderstandings in his book. For example, he had 'confused Greek botanical and anatomical terminology'. Notice that Leoniceno and Champier do not criticise the fundamental content of the *Canon* – which was, of course, based on Greek ideas.

Despite these attacks, many practitioners continued to value Ibn Sina's account of Greek medicine: although translation introduced problems, the *Canon* still provided a coherent and systematic account of humoural medicine. As a result, university teachers continued to use it throughout the sixteenth century. Other Arabic authors were also revered as authorities. As late as 1747, an English practitioner, Richard Mead, published a new translation of al-Razi's book on smallpox in an effort to understand why the disease was becoming more prevalent at that time.

The introduction of vernacular languages and printing

In medieval Europe, medical texts went through two more transformations, which I'll cover very briefly. The first was *another* phase of translation – from Latin into vernacular languages. In the medieval world, only the most highly educated people spoke and read Latin. Everyone else spoke vernacular languages (literally, the languages spoken by the native people in a particular area) such as French, English and German. Many more people could read those languages than could read Latin. As a result, practitioners began to translate texts from Latin and to write new texts in these languages, often incorporating knowledge from older Latin texts.

Many (although by no means all) books written in the vernacular were practical, self-help books for non-practitioners. One of the most popular was the *Regimen Sanitatis Salernitanum*. (The title translates

Figure 5.16 Unknown artist, Hippocrates and Avicenna, engraving, vignette detail from title page, Avicenna (1595), *Canon of Medicine*, Venice, Juntas. Wellcome Library, 580/D Vol. I. Photo: Wellcome Library, London. This elaborately decorated title page shows Avicenna (Ibn Sina) standing alongside Hippocrates and Galen, suggesting that he is seen to be their equal. Notice that although Ibn Sina wears a turban, which suggests his Arabic identity, the costume of all the figures echoes contemporary Renaissance dress. The figure on the far right is Aetius (*c.* 502–575 CE), a physician who studied in Alexandria and wrote the *Tetrabiblios*, a compilation of the writings of Hellenistic practitioners. The whole title page is reproduced as Plate 3.5.1 in the Illustration Book.

as *The Regimen of Health of Salerno*. Salerno, a town in Italy, was famous for its medical teaching, so rules of health from Salerno would be considered especially good and effective.) Originally written in Latin verse around the middle of the thirteenth century and later translated into English, the text taught readers how to stay healthy through diet, exercise and hygiene. Here is its very basic outline of anatomy, from a version by Sir John Harington called *The School of Salernum* and published in 1608:

> Now if perhaps some have desire to know,
> The number of our bones, our teeth, our veins,
> This verse ensuing plainly it doth show,
> To him that doth observe, it taketh pains:
> The teeth thrice ten, and two, twice eight a row.

> Eleven score bones save one in us remains:
> For veins, that all may vain in us appear,
> A vein we have for each day in the year:
> All these are like in number and connection.
> The difference grows in bigness and complexion.
>
> (Harington, 1922 [1608], p. 131)

A second transformation came with the invention of printing in 1440, which made the production of books much easier and cheaper. Books began to circulate in much greater numbers, and texts that had been available only in very expensive manuscripts found a new audience in printed form. Ibn Sina's *Canon*, for example, appeared in at least 60 separate editions between 1500 and 1674.

Activity Draw up your own summary of how medical knowledge was changed by its translation into Latin in medieval Europe. Include your thoughts about what remained the same, what was added, and what was revised by European scholars.

EPILOGUE

Greek medicine, enhanced by the work of later generations of Islamic and European scholars, provided the basic understanding of body function, disease and therapy until the eighteenth century. (You may recall from your study in Book 1 of Christopher Marlowe's *Dr Faustus*, written in the late sixteenth century, that the hero studies Galen.) It was not a static set of ideas, but humoural theory provided a flexible tool to explain all aspects of health and disease. When adopted into new cultures, medical learning was repeatedly refreshed and revised by new groups of practitioners.

The predominance of humoural medicine began to decline at the end of the eighteenth century, when it was replaced by a recognisably modern understanding of disease as a set of chemical and biological changes affecting the solid organs and tissues of the body. Only a few echoes of Greek medicine have survived into modern times, but it has left a mark in the English language. Medieval practitioners identified four temperaments reflecting the underlying predominant humour – sanguine, phlegmatic, bilious and melancholic – all words that have survived to the present day, although their meaning has changed. Modern doctors trace their profession back to Greek medicine through the Hippocratic Oath. The original oath dates back to the fourth century BCE (and was probably not written by Hippocrates). It has been altered and updated, but its central promises – for practitioners to serve their patients and to respect their fellow practitioners – remain relevant for today's medical men and women. One last fragment of humoural medicine seems to be finally dying out: until the late twentieth century, many people still believed that you could catch a cold if you went outside with wet hair, or 'catch a chill' if going from a warm to cold atmosphere.

What does the migration of medical ideas from Greece to medieval Europe teach us about the history of medicine? It illustrates two important features. First, although past medical theory and practices may seem strange to us, they need to be understood on their own terms; we need to appreciate why they seemed sensible and effective to contemporary patients and practitioners. Second, medicine needs to be understood in its wider context. It is not a parcel of ideas to be handed on from one generation of practitioners to the next, but is constantly adapted to new social, political, religious and intellectual climates.

REFERENCES

Chaucer, G. (1980 [*c.*1387–1400]) *The Canterbury Tales*, ed. Blake, N.F., London, Edward Arnold.

Galen, *On Prognosis* (trans. A.J. Brock, 1916) [online] http://www.stoa.org/diotima/anthology/wlgr/wlgr-medicine352.shtml (accessed 16 January 2008).

Harington, Sir J. (1922 [1608]) *The School of Salernum: Regimen sanitatis Salernitanum*, London, Oxford University Press.

Hippocrates (400 BCE) *On Airs, Waters, and Places* (trans. F. Adams, 1849) [online] eBooks@Adelaide, http://etext.library.adelaide.edu.au/h/hippocrates//airs/index.html (accessed 16 January 2008).

Nutton, V. (2004) *Ancient Medicine*, London, Routledge.

Savage-Smith, E. (1997) 'Europe and Islam' in Loudon, I. (ed.) *Western Medicine. An Illustrated History*, London, Oxford University Press.

Ullmann, M. (1978) *Islamic Medicine*, Edinburgh, Edinburgh University Press.

RESOURCES

Reading 5.1 Factors behind the translation movement

This revival [of Greek medicine] arose from the confluence of three crucial factors, which explain [...] why it emerged when and where it did [...]. The first was social and economic, the growth of an educated elite with broad interests and the financial resources required to fund scholarship, teaching, and the physical production and maintenance of collections of books. This development was especially pronounced in Iraq, where towns such as Basra and Kufa expanded from primitive garrison camps [...] to become [...] vast thriving cities where cultural influences from places as remote as India and China were felt, and where the resources made available by officials and wealthy merchants and landowners promoted lively and sophisticated scholarship in a broad range of subjects. The founding of Baghdad in 762 led to a further surge of urban growth – within a century the new imperial capital was a focus of incredible wealth and cultural vitality and, with more than a million residents, perhaps the largest city in the world. [...]

Another key precondition was a specific need which a formal medical tradition could fill (excluding the well-being of the general population, with which the early caliphate was not particularly concerned). [...] [T]he developments of this period must be viewed within a context of ubiquitous religious disputation [...]. [T]here was a lively production of [...] literature, with both Christian and Muslim seeking to justify their faith against the other. At the beginning, Muslims were at a disadvantage in these exchanges, for while Christians had for centuries used Greek logic and philosophy to elevate confessional quarrelling to an art, the defenders of Islam had no prior experience in disputation at this level. Not surprisingly, then, they began to turn to the same sources of inspiration which their Christian opponents had long used.

[...]

The extent to which medical works could contribute to the religious concerns of the day was considerable. [...] Galen in particular offered powerful evidence for the ancient and much-used argument from design – if the parts of the body worked together for the benefit of the whole, for example, and accord to some principle of harmony and order, then this necessarily implied a giver of harmony and order, i.e. God. [...]

In summary, in the ninth century both Christians and Muslims stood to benefit from Arabic works which could be used in disputations to defend tenets of their faiths.

The third factor was the existence of a literary corpus to serve as a focus for scholarly work. Here the contribution of the Christian community was crucial, for though books seem to have been scarce in

Byzantine lands, they were more accessible in Egypt, Syria, and Iraq. The main ecclesiastical libraries were large and varied, monasteries kept extensive collections of manuscripts (as they do to this day), and many texts were also in private hands. Whole batteries of scribes could be mobilised to produce copies of required works, and books were often loaned and sent long distances to be read and copied. It also seems that Muslim raiding forces sometimes brought back with them books they had found.

Source: Lawrence I. Conrad (1995) 'The Arab-Islamic medical tradition', in Conrad, L.I, Neve, M., Nutton, V., Porter, R. and Wear, A. *The Western Medical Tradition 800 BC to AD 1800*, Cambridge, Cambridge University Press, pp. 101–4.

Reading 5.2 The emergence of Islamic medicine

The question arises, however, why the ʿAbbāsid elite would want to fund Nestorian Christians to translate Greek texts into Arabic, or, to put it differently, what their political agenda was in doing so. The causes for this phenomenon, as for most momentous historical events, are multiple. [...] [T]he ʿAbbāsids were a dynasty which did not hail from Arab stock, but came from the Persian East. As such, they had an interest in promoting a cultural policy which went beyond the restricted remit of pure Arab heritage to forge a more cosmopolitan identity. Another factor was their wish to portray themselves in some way as successors to the Sasanians, whose medical system [...] was already influenced by Greek ideas. Moreover, the Nestorian milieu in Mesopotamia – especially in the newly founded capital of Baghdad, the 'City of Peace' [...], as it was then called – was itself heavily Hellenised, and this also helped increase the interest in Greek learning. The Greek medical system in the form of humoral pathology had already penetrated and influenced many other cultures. Finally, there was the attraction for elite scholars of the day to Greek thought in its own right. For all these various reasons, it is not surprising that the ʿAbbāsids came under its spell as well.

[...]

[M]isconceptions regarding the translation movement have arisen in scholarly and popular literature. The first concerns the factors which motivated the translation process. Raymond Le Coz has claimed that [...] Nestorian physicians such as Hunayn ibn Isḥāq instigated the translation movement and taught the Greek sciences, and especially medicine, to the Arabs. Dimitri Gutas, on the other hand, has amply demonstrated that the translation movement was the result of intense patronage by ʿAbbāsid rulers who became increasingly interested in Greek science, medicine, philosophy, and astronomy for reasons discussed above. [...] Surely, Nestorian Christians played a crucial role in the transmission of medical knowledge from the Greeks to the Arabs. To call them 'masters of the Arabs', however, as Le Coz does, overlooks the historical and intellectual forces at work in ninth-century

Baghdad, where the ruling elite and their entourage set not only the political, but also the cultural and scientific, agenda.

Source: Peter E. Pormann and Emilie Savage-Smith (2007) *Medieval Islamic Medicine*, Edinburgh, Edinburgh University Press, pp. 26–8 (footnote omitted).

Reading 5.3 A short case history by Abu Bakr Muhammed ibn Zakariya al-Razi

KHĀLID, OF Tabaristān, suffered from a hot (feverish) disease through a fatigue which befell him. I gave him barley-water and the like until (the heat) was extinguished. But this caused him a pain in the region of the flanks and of the abdomen [...]; the doctors thought it to be a colic and intended to administer to him hot electuaries [...] as they supposed that the barley-water had been harmful to him because he had a residue of the feverish disease in his stomach.

I touched the diseased spot and felt it hot and hard. Thereupon I asked him whether he felt a throbbing in it, and he answered 'A rather violent throbbing.' So I supposed that he had a hot swelling (an inflammatory tumour) in that region, made him a venesection in both his armpits [...]. After this I administered to him the juice (or an infusion) of leaves of night-shade [...], endive and cucumber-seeds during several days. He was cured and even to such an extent that his affection was much improved on the day on which I made the venesection.

I supposed that the hot (and vicious) water causing the disease was partly allayed and partly carried to the spot in question, as there had been no perceptible evacuation.

Source: Max Meyerhof (1935) 'Thirty-three clinical observations by Rhazes', *Isis*, vol. 23, pp. 337–8 (footnotes omitted).

Reading 5.4 Hilyawn ASPARAGUS (Asparagus officinalis L.)

It is [...] of two kinds: a cultivated kind with leaves like dill [...] and free of thorns, and a wild kind which is thorny all over like the spinous broom [...]. It is frequent in Spain and is used in medicine.

GALEN [...] – It is detersive and desiccative without heating; it is useful for obstructions of the liver and kidneys, especially the root and flowers. It cures toothache.

DIOSC. [...] [W]hen slightly boiled it purges the bowels and acts as diuretic. It is said that if the horns of a battering ram [...] are cut off and buried in the ground, asparagus grows inside them.

IBN MÂSA – It is hot and moist in the last [...] of the first degree, is diuretic and changes the odour of the urine in the same manner as the action of asa foetida [...]. It is aphrodisiac. If eaten after meals it is more nourishing than if taken before them.

AR-RÂZÎ – It heats the kidneys and bladder, is useful to old men of cold temperaments, good for backache, lumbago, pains in the thighs and lungs, but not good for the stomach; it often provokes nausea, particularly when not boiled.

[...]

Commentary

[...] As to the growing of asparagus on buried ram-horns, it is a misunderstanding of Diosc.'s text. The Greek *Geoponica* [...] writes that the horns of wild rams cut to pieces, buried in the earth and well irrigated, are a good manure for asparagus.

Source: M. Meyerhof and G.P. Sobhy Bey (eds) (1940) *The Abridged Version of 'The Book of Simple Drugs' of Ahmad ibn Muhammad al-Ghâfiqî by Gregorius Abu'l-Farag (Barhebraeus)*, Cairo, Government Press, pp. 542–4 (footnote omitted).

Reading 5.5 Ibn Sina, 'Canon of Medicine'

The North Wind braces and hardens the body; it prevents the flow of visible excretions; it closes the pores, strengthens the digestion, causes constipation, increases the urine, and makes septic pestilential atmosphere healthy. If the south wind precedes the north, the south wind excites mucous discharges, but the following north wind drives these fluids inwardly. A discharge may appear externally. Hence a catarrh [...] may become abundant, and chest troubles are common.

Diseases liable to occur when the north wind prevails: neuritic pains, pains in the side of the chest, in the joints, in the bladder and uterus; difficult micturition; racking cough; shivering attacks.

[...] *The South Wind* is relaxing for the strength; it opens the pores; makes the humours agitated and confused, so that they move from within outwards; the senses become heavy; it induces sleepiness. It is one of the causes of breaking down of ulcers, and makes them itch. It causes diseases to relapse, and debilitates. [...] It excites migraine attacks. It causes fevers to become septic. It does not, however, induce sore throat.

[...] *The East Wind.* – If east winds prevail towards the end of the night, and in the early part of the day, they will have already been modified by the sun, being made more rarefied and less humid. They are, therefore, drier and lighter in nature. But if they occur at the close of the day, and at the beginning of the night, the reverse is the case. On the whole, east winds are more beneficial to health than are westerly ones.

[...]*The West Wind.* – If west winds prevail at the end of the night and in early part of the day, the atmosphere will not have received the heat of the sun, and is therefore denser and more heavy. If they occur at the end of the day and at the beginning of the night, the reverse holds good.

Source: O. Cameron Gruner (1930) *A Treatise on the Canon of Medicine of Avicenna*, London, Luzac & Co., p. 204.

Reading 5.6 Joannitius (Hunayn), *Isagoge*

Medicine is divided into two parts, namely theoretic and practical. And of these two the theoretic is further divided into three, that is to say, the consideration of the naturals, the non-naturals, and the contra naturals. From the consideration of these arises the knowledge of sickness, of health, and of the mean state, and their causes and significations; of when the four humours increase in an abnormal manner, or of what may be the causation [...] or significance of sickness.

OF THE NATURALS

The naturals are seven in number: elements, qualities [...], humours [...], members, energies, operations, and spirits. But some add to these four others: namely, age, colour, figure, and the distinction between male and female.

The Elements

There are four elements: fire, air, water, and earth. Fire is hot and dry; air is hot and moist; water is cold and moist; earth is cold and dry.

The Qualities

There are nine qualities, eight unequal and one equal. Of the unequal, four are simple: namely, hot, cold, moist, and dry. From these arise four compound: namely, hot and moist, hot and dry, cold and moist, cold and dry.

The equal is when the body is so disposed that it is in good condition and in a mean state, when it has a proper amount of all four.

Of the Humours [...]

The humours [...] are four in number: namely, blood, phlegm, reddish bile, and black bile. Blood is hot and moist, phlegm is cold and moist, reddish bile is hot and dry, black bile is cold and dry.

Source: Edward Grant (ed.) (1974) *A Source Book in Medieval Science*, Cambridge, MA, Harvard University Press, p. 705.

Reading 5.7 A Consilium by Ugo Benzi (Hugh of Siena)

The distinguished and noble gentleman, Messer Mariscoto of Nullano (?), about sixty years of age, of a complexion naturally tending to hot and moist, suffers from gout in his whole body and likewise at times from arthritis, whose matter is mixed, although at present, as usual, phlegm predominates. And at intervals he is so free from discomfort that he can easily walk or ride horse-back, although in some of his joints a certain degree of stiffness persists. [...]

(Habitation or 'Air')

First, then, let him occupy a good chamber between two roof-terraces or balconies [...]. The chamber should be warmed in cold weather by a fire of dry wood. And in general he should be amply protected against the cold by clothes, shoes, and other appropriate means.

(Sleep)

And let him sleep seven or eight hours per night, and when that is not sufficient, let him sleep in the morning before tierce, with his head well elevated and his body well covered.

(Regulation of the Bowels)

And let him be sure that he has a movement every day, and if nature does not respond, let him use a clyster.

(Exercise)

And for his exercise let him walk or ride horse-back every day before eating, but not if it gives him much pain; and after eating let him refrain from effort.

(Emotions)

And let him forego sexual intercourse as much as possible.

(Food and Drink)

In regard to his food, he should always incline to moderation, making it a rule to leave the table before his appetite is completely satisfied. Similarly in regard to drink. And let him secure a vessel of seventeen ounces and fill it half full of water of honey, and fill the remaining half with wine, and let him not consume more than the contents of this vessel at lunch or at dinner. His wine should be red, clear, and of moderate strength.

For food let him eat the meat of chickens, partridges, pheasants, larks, and other small birds [...], and similarly kid, veal, and the flesh of young sucklings [...]. He should refrain from waterfowl, domestic pork, lamb and beef [...].

Let him use bread made of good flour, well cooked and well leavened; and let him avoid cheese. Fresh eggs, however, are good [...].

As for vegetables, none are good, but he can make a dish (a salad) of spelt, barley, panic, millet, spinach, blite, borage, bugloss, balm, fennel, anise, parsley, marjoram, and savory herbs, such as sage and thyme, along with bread crumbs and eggs – singly or jointly.

And he should eat but little fish; the less harmful sort are those which are small and scaly, living in clear water and of good odor. Crayfish, however, are not good.

And of fruits the following are suitable: raisins, figs either fresh or dried, almonds, pine-nuts, filberts. And for dessert he can have pears stewed with wine and anise and fennel; but from other moist fruits he had better refrain, such as apples and cherries and peaches and so forth [...].

Source: Edward Grant (ed.) (1974) *A Source Book in Medieval Science*, Cambridge, MA, Harvard University Press, pp. 760–1 (footnote omitted).

Reading 5.8 The *Canon* in the schools and medieval universities

[C]riticism of Avicenna was already an important ingredient in the medical teaching of Nicolò Leoniceno at the University of Ferrara in the last decade of the fifteenth century. [...] [One of his works] contains more than twenty chapters dedicated to exposing specific errors by Avicenna and his 'recent interpreters.' Usually the accusations turn on the allegation that Avicenna has misunderstood or confused Greek botanical and anatomical terminology; however, several chapters also accuse him of providing erroneous terminology for processes of digestion. Leoniceno's chief disciple, Giovanni Manardo, who also taught at Ferrara, broadened the attack in his collection of 'medical epistles' first published in 1521 and widely disseminated in several subsequent enlarged editions. In addition to discussing specific errors by Avicenna, Manardo characterized the *Canon* in general as filled with 'a dense cloud and infinite chaos of obscuritics.' Furthermore, he laid stress on the idea that medieval translations were in general unreliable, and pointed out that Avicenna's work was itself a pastiche based on the writings of other Greek and Arabic medical authors.

[...]

In 1522, [Symphorien] Champier collaborated with [Antonio] Rustico in the publication of a new edition of the *Canon* in which the prefatory matter included both strongly hostile remarks about Islam and a denunciation of Avicenna's philosophical and moral opinions and also a list of scientific issues on which Avicenna erred by differing from Galen and Dioscorides [...]. In 1528, Champier announced that his *Symphonia Galeni ad Hippocratem, Cornelii Celsi ad Avicennam* had been written 'lest Avicenna and Averroes, that impious apostate, deceive Christian physicians through inane and barbarous philosophy.' In the same work, he also stressed the stylistic barbarism of Avicenna, making no distinction between the original and the Latin translation. In another treatise published the same year, he went so far as to pronounce a curse on the doctors of Padua, Salerno, Pavia, and Montpellier who allowed their schools to be occupied by 'Arabs, Persians, Indians, and Mahometans' in a way pernicious for men and calamitous for good letters.

exceedingly harmful

Source: Nancy G. Siraisi (1987) *Avicenna in Renaissance Italy: The* Canon *and Medical Teaching in Italian Universities after 1500*, Princeton, Princeton University Press, pp. 68–9 and 72–3 (footnotes omitted).

6 SEAMUS HEANEY'S *THE BURIAL AT THEBES*

Lorna Hardwick

MATERIALS YOU WILL NEED

- Audio CDs: *The Burial at Thebes* – Part 1; *The Burial at Thebes* – Part 2; *The Burial at Thebes* – Interviews
- Illustration Book
- Seamus Heaney, *The Burial at Thebes* (set book)

AIMS

This chapter aims to:

- introduce you to Heaney's text and to some strategies for analysing it
- help you to understand the conventions of ancient Greek drama
- consider Heaney's version of the play as itself a 'cultural encounter' in the light of other adaptations
- enable you to study and enjoy plays which are new to you.

INTRODUCTION

The main focus of your work in this chapter is to study Seamus Heaney's play *The Burial at Thebes* and to engage with some of the issues that it raises. We chose the play because we thought you would find it enjoyable in its own right and also because it relates closely to the main themes of this book, especially the encounter between different cultures. By this I mean the way in which texts, themes and ideas travel across time, place and language, picking up additional accretions and resonances on the way. Heaney's play is based on the ancient Greek tragedy *Antigone*, created by the Athenian dramatist Sophocles (*c.*496–406 BCE) in the fifth century BCE. We shall spend some time looking at the connections and differences between the two and in thinking about how the play might be staged in a modern theatre environment that is very different from the ancient. I have anticipated a rough division of your work for the week into the equivalent of six two-hour study sessions, and I suggest that you plan your work on the basis that about half of this (approximately three two-hour sessions) will be needed for Section 6.1, which will include your initial reading of the play.

You also have a recording of the play on two Audio CDs and I suggest that you listen to this as often as possible. Theatre is an aural as well as a visual medium, and listening to the CDs will help you to situate yourself in the world of the theatre audience. It will also enable you to respond to the sound and rhythm of the words that you would otherwise read silently on the page. On the second Audio CD, the play is followed by an interview with Seamus Heaney and with the director of the audio production, John Theocharis, and I shall refer you to these interviews later in this chapter.

Heaney's play text is a modern one, created in his own idiom and for a contemporary audience. It was commissioned for first performance at the Abbey Theatre, Dublin, in May 2004 to mark the centenary anniversary of that theatre, which was founded in 1904 by the poet and dramatist W.B. Yeats (1865–1939) and his collaborator Lady Gregory (Augusta Gregory, 1852–1932). Both Yeats and Gregory were cultural nationalists, devoted to the development of a national theatre that would give a stage for drama that was both distinctively Irish and also of international significance (Welch, 1996, Morash, 2002; for a discussion of Yeats's cultural nationalism see also Book 2, Chapter 5). It was natural that Seamus Heaney (b. 1939) should be asked to contribute to the celebratory season because he was Ireland's winner of the Nobel Prize for Literature (1995) and already the author of a version of another tragedy by Sophocles (*The Cure at Troy*, 1990, based on Sophocles' *Philoctetes*).

I expect that you have already developed your own strategies for studying plays as a result of your work earlier in the course on

Marlowe's *Doctor Faustus* (see Book 1, Chapter 2). There you practised close reading of the text and analysis of passages from the play. You were asked to think about genre, about the kind of play that you were reading and about why it might be described as a tragedy (Book 1, Section 2.2). You used your close reading as a basis for drawing out the main themes and issues and you were also introduced to reading the play historically: that is, thinking about some of the connections between the play and the time at which it was written.

In this chapter you will be able to build on that experience and so I shall leave you as much flexibility as possible in organising your work. However, there are some new challenges in that you are now tackling a play that is written in vigorous modern language and with some striking poetry, but is actually based on a play written in ancient Greek over 2,500 years ago for performance in a huge public open-air festival. So I shall offer some fairly detailed help to get you started. In particular I will discuss ways in which Heaney related his play to that of Sophocles.

6.1 READING *THE BURIAL AT THEBES*

Both Heaney's and Sophocles' plays are set in ancient Thebes (the Greek Thebes which is north-west of Athens, not the Egyptian Thebes, which is on the River Nile, near Luxor). The outline of the story, but not the details, is drawn from Greek myth and the action starts very early on a sunny morning.

Activity

You can listen to the opening of the play on track 1 of the Audio CD '*The Burial at Thebes* – Part 1'.

Read the opening sequence of *Burial* (pp. 1–7), in which the encounter between two members of the ruling family, Antigone and her sister Ismene, sets the scene for the action. As you read, make short notes on the ways in which this opening sequence provides the audience with a context for what has already happened and what may happen in the future. What do you think are the most striking aspects of the situation that the two sisters now face?

The following subsections contain relevant background and contextual information on the play. As there are no line numbers in the Heaney text, I shall refer to page numbers as necessary.

The mythological story behind the play

Antigone's opening speech refers to her and Ismene's situation as daughters of Oedipus, and this theme gathers significance throughout the scene. Oedipus was the ruler of Thebes, the man who unwittingly killed his father and married his mother.

An ancient Greek audience would have been familiar with the mythical story of Oedipus and his family, so here Antigone only alludes to it briefly, with the aim of putting the new situation into its context and emphasising the continuity of suffering and catastrophe in the family.

Greek social values

Notice especially how Antigone focuses on the treatment due to the dead (p. 2). The image of leaving a body to rot and to be picked over by wild animals and birds is a standard one in Greek literature, where it is often used as an image of the sufferings of war. The social and religious conventions of funeral rites and practices were elements that bound society together. Women played an important role in these, in contrast to their exclusion from public and political life. You will find supporting evidence for this statement in the images in the Illustration Book, Plates 3.6.1–9, and in the following extract from Thucydides' fifth-century *History of the Peloponnesian War*, Book 2: 34:

> In the same winter [431 BCE] the Athenians gave a funeral at the public cost to those who had first fallen in this war [the war between Athens and Sparta] [...] Any citizen or stranger who pleases joins the procession: and the female relatives are there to wail at the burial.
>
> (Crawley, 1997 [1874], Book 2: 34)

Creon's edict that Polyneices be denied burial not only distinguished between insiders/friends and outsiders/enemies but also subordinated family ties to the interests of the state.

The function of the passage within the play

This opening sequence introduces several issues that will be developed in the rest of the play. The first is the nature of Creon's rule and his attempt to forge unity after civil war ('Whoever isn't for us/Is against us in this case', p. 3). Second, there is the potential conflict between the 'laws of the land' and the 'laws of the gods', which require respect to be shown to the dead. Third, there is a question about whether women should or could take any public action – as Ismene puts it, 'We're weak where they are strong ... We must do as we're told' (p. 5).

The discussion between the two sisters acts as a kind of **Prologue** to the play in that it has the function of orientating the audience and reminding them of the salient aspects of the myth, and Heaney follows Sophocles closely in this respect. However, it is different from the kind of prologue found in other Greek plays, which is usually delivered by a minor character and not by one prominently involved in the action. The Sophocles/Heaney strategy is also different from that used for the Prologue at the beginning of *Doctor Faustus*.

Reading the play: the formal conventions of Greek tragedy

As you read the rest of *The Burial at Thebes* you will spot that it is very carefully structured into sections, each of which uses different kinds of language and rhythms. In this, Heaney follows very closely the formal conventions of Greek tragedy. For a modern reader, both the mythological context and the theatre conventions may at first seem strange; the ancient audiences, of course, expected them to be there. So as your reading progresses I shall identify the most important of the Greek theatrical conventions and ask you to think about why they are important and the effect they have on the modern reader.

Activity You can listen to these passages on tracks 1–3 of the Audio CD 'The Burial at Thebes – Part 1'.

Now read the opening Chorus (pp. 8–9), Creon's first speech (pp. 9–11) and the exchange between Creon and the Chorus (pp. 11–12).

In the ancient context the opening Chorus was called the ***parodos*** (first Choral song, taken from the word for 'entry'). The Chorus in Greek tragedy was a group of fifteen, which sang and danced and also linked ***episodes***, rather like recitative in opera. (This is difficult to transpose to the modern stage where the Chorus is often reduced in number, sometimes speaks rather than sings, and rarely dances.) In Greek drama the Chorus had a major part in the play. It usually combined a number of functions. As well as singing in elevated poetic language the Chorus interacted and discussed with the main characters and offered moral comment. It also usually represented a group affected by the main action of the play but not powerful enough to dominate it – in this case the Theban Elders. So you can see that the Chorus in Sophocles/Heaney is very different from the Chorus you encountered in *Doctor Faustus*.

Activity As you read the *parodos*, think about the language used and how this communicates the feelings of the Chorus on the dawn of the first day after the end of the civil war. Then compare it with the language used by Creon.

Discussion The *parodos* is strongly poetic, both on the page and when heard spoken or sung on your Audio CD. Heaney's diction combines the language of light ('shining guardian', 'dazzle the city', p. 8) with images of metal, which is also shining but vulnerable in its inflexibility ('smashed into shards'). The almost incantatory 'Glory be to brightness, to the gleaming sun' celebrates the new day that marks victory and liberation from civil war. The invocation to Bacchus (god of wine, dance and theatre) provides an almost frenzied climax to the song. This intensifies the contrast with Creon's speech (the technical name in Greek theatre for this kind of solo speech is **rhesis**, linked with the derivation of the English word rhetoric).

The rhythm, tone and language of Creon's speech make an almost shocking contrast with the Chorus (as well as with the exchange between Antigone and Ismene). This is the public speech of a politician and here Heaney uses the iambic beat that you have already met in your study of *Doctor Faustus*.

The sentences are quite long with well-marked beats (blank verse). Note also the metaphor of the 'ship of state', the appeal to the sense of civic identity of the 'crew' ('Solidarity, friends,/Is what we need') and the appeal to duty. This is the context that Creon uses to justify his edict denying burial to Polyneices.

In theatre performance, it would depend on the director's approach whether Creon addresses the Chorus only or whether the speech is delivered to the audience, making them part of the community of citizens in the play. You may have spotted yet another contrast in tone when Creon turns from public pronouncement and speaks directly to the old men in the Chorus, who then take on the role of questioners. At this point Creon becomes much less secure and seems to anticipate opposition from the people of Thebes.

Activity Next, read the first exchange between Creon and the Guard (pp. 12–16) and make short notes on the dramatic function of the scene (how it develops the action of the play and what it tells us about the people involved). Also, take into account the tone, rhythm and vocabulary used by the Guard. What does this add to the perspectives that have already been introduced in the play?

Discussion The effect of the exchange is both to demonstrate the authority of Creon and also to show that Creon's fears were justified. The Guard's prevarication builds up suspense and introduces another register of language – broadening the social scope of the play and giving a different perspective from that of the ruling elite who have figured so far. You will remember from your reading of Sillitoe's story 'Pit Strike' in Chapter 4 that register is one way of marking social and cultural identity. It allows the author to colour the text and shape the response of readers and audiences, and this is particularly important in Heaney's play.

Unlike the Chorus, the Guard speaks here in prose, not verse, and his idiom is colloquial ('I was over a barrel', p. 12). Heaney also makes the idiom that of 'Irish/English' ('Somebody's after attending to it right', p. 13). The Guard's language becomes plainer and penetratingly direct ('Somebody observing all the customs', p. 13). In this respect, the Guard also becomes an observer/commentator, remarking on the absence of tracks. He speaks from the point of view of someone with knowledge of the land ('No rut-marks from a wheel. Nothing but the land, the old hard scrabble', p. 13).

There is a humorous side to this scene but it is not simply a comic interlude. In the course of the scene the Guard moves from the appearance of a working-class stereotype (perhaps even with parodic elements of a 'stage Irishman') to being an authentic voice for truth ('Your conscience is what's doing the disturbing', p. 15; 'the judge/Has misjudged everything', p. 16).

You probably noticed the impact of the short one-line exchanges between Creon and the Guard (p. 15). This is an example of ***stichomythia***, a convention of Greek drama in which brisk one- or two-line exchanges are used to accelerate the pace and point up key issues. You will find some more extended examples of this later in the play. (You can add the term *stichomythia* to Chorus and *rhesis* as examples of the formal conventions of Greek tragedy adopted by Heaney – all these terms are listed in the Glossary at the end of this book.)

The structure of the play

The sequence with the Guard is followed by a Choral Ode (pp. 16–17; track 4 of the first Audio CD). This is based on the famous 'Ode to Man' in Sophocles' play. As you read and listen to it, savour the language and notice how Heaney's use of material first created by Sophocles emphasises some of the aspects which ancient Greek and modern Irish consciousness might have in common, including traditions of agriculture and religious observance. The reference to 'beyond the pale' (p. 17) alludes to the area in and around Dublin that, from the earliest times of Norman and English rule, was associated with the supremacy of urban civic society over the rural hinterland. So the sequence not only develops the contrast between the new laws of the city-state and the persistence of traditional values and practices, but it also metaphorically relates the situation in Thebes to that of the colonially dominated Ireland of the past.

Activity

You should allow 1 hour 45 minutes to listen to the whole play on the Audio CDs.

I would now like you to read the rest of the play and listen to it on the Audio CDs. As you do so, make a short summary of the dramatic turning points and climaxes in the play, and of the ways in which Heaney's language (both poetry and prose) communicates these. A summary is most definitely *not* a retelling of the story. It should include identification of the main features of the structure of the play. These are:

- Prologue (already discussed)
- Chorus (already introduced, but you will need to add notes on its function and poetic and dramatic impact)
- *episodes* (the main 'scenes' in the play)
- ***exodos*** (the closing sequence).

Look carefully at the placing of the Choral Odes and at their tone and content and at the way in which each episode is linked to the next. Heaney has taken over this structure directly from Sophocles. After the first Choral song (*parodos*), the other Odes are called ***stasima*** (singular ***stasimon***). Look for the architectural effect of the successive episodes between Creon and Antigone, Creon and Haemon, and Creon and Tiresias, and comment on what each adds to the action and to the arguments on the central themes of the play. How do these episodes create the transformations of understanding that are so crucial both for the characters within the play and for the audience/ readers?

Add your own notes next to the skeletal outline of the structure of the play in the table below.

Outline structure of the play

	Set book	Audio CDs
Prologue (Antigone and Ismene)	pp. 1–7	Part 1, track 1
Parodos (Chorus)	pp. 7–9	Part 1, track 2
First Episode (Creon, the Guard, the Chorus)	pp. 9–16	Part 1, track 3
First Choral Ode	pp. 16–17	Part 1, track 4
Second Episode (Guard, Antigone, Creon, Ismene)	pp. 17–27	Part 1, track 5
Second Choral Ode	pp. 28–9	Part 1, track 6
Third Episode	pp. 29–36	Part 1, track 7
Third Choral Ode	pp. 36–7	Part 1, track 8
Fourth Episode (Antigone, the Chorus, Creon)	pp. 37–41	Part 1, track 9
Fourth Choral Ode	p. 42	Part 1, track 10
Fifth Episode (Tiresias, Creon, the Chorus)	pp. 42–8	Part 1, track 11
Fifth Choral Ode	pp. 48–9	Part 2, track 1
Exodos (Messenger, Eurydice, Creon, the Chorus)	pp. 49–56	Part 2, track 2

Within each episode you will also find formal features and patterns of language that contribute to the action and to the developing relationships between the characters. For example, you will find further examples of *stichomythia* (e.g. in the fraught encounter between Creon and Antigone, pp. 23–4). You will also notice examples of paired speeches in which opposing characters debate the issues. This feature is called the ***agon*** (Greek for contest) and is a feature of each main episode (you can find another in the episode with Creon and his son Haemon, pp. 29–35).

Notice, too, how the Guard's role is developed (pp. 17–20). In his second intervention he describes in closely observed detail what has happened offstage, so as you read be aware of ways in which this picture is built up. In this aspect, the Guard represents another convention in Greek drama, that of **Messenger speech**. This is used to enable the audience to integrate their observation of what happens on stage with their imaginative re-creation of what takes place offstage. The Messenger speech convention is also used on pages 49–52, especially to describe the awful climax to Creon's action. You will also find examples of the ***kommos*** or lament (notice especially who is doing the lamenting, who is the object of it, and the terms in which the lament is expressed).

I suggest that you mark these formal features on your text, referring to the Glossary as necessary. After a little practice you will find they become as familiar to you as the rooms in your home.

Activity On the basis of your summary, identify the themes that strike you as the most important and comment briefly on *how* the poet/dramatist communicates them. Closely linked with this is the question of the relative dramatic importance of Antigone and Creon. Which of them comes over as the more convincing? Do either (or both) of them attain the status of a tragic figure? Please do not read further in this chapter until you have completed your reading of the play.

In what follows, I want to raise some of the points that you might have noted and to comment on the debate about what Creon and Antigone should do. You can find the passages on the Audio CD by referring to the table above.

The structure of the play is marked both by the theatrical conventions of Greek drama (episodes, Chorus, Messenger, etc.) and by the language that is used within these conventions (the language of the single speech or *rhesis*, the language in the *agon* between paired contesting speeches, the elevated poetic language of the Choral Odes).

The Chorus on the wonders of mankind (first *stasimon*) is the link between the Guard's first encounter with Creon and his return, bringing Antigone after she has been caught 'redhanded' giving burial rites to Polyneices. The closing sequence in this Chorus brings to the fore the issue of the laws of the city (p. 17). The language of the Guard's next speech (p. 19) again uses colloquial idiom ('It was going off'), but his language here also resonates with the imagery of the play, especially the emphasis on light and fire and the contrast with the menacing threat of pollution and plague ('like the sky was/Vomiting black air').

Antigone's arrest leads to her vehement *agon* with Creon about correct conduct and the conflicting demands of loyalty and honour due to the living and to the dead. Notice that Ismene also joins the debate and is more influenced by Antigone than in their earlier discussion.

The Chorus's second *stasimon* (p. 28) strikes a dismal note, lamenting with highly charged imagery the misery of the ruling family ('A surge that hauls black sand up off the bottom') and commenting on the morality of ambition and obsession. The Chorus then introduces Haemon, Creon's son and Antigone's intended husband. The language of this next episode shifts the debate to a more immediately political and pragmatic level. The relationship between father and son is based on the imperative of respect from the young man towards the older. This *agon* is characterised by reason, which Haemon skilfully uses as a means to introduce the views of the ordinary citizens (p. 31), especially their feeling that Antigone has behaved heroically. Haemon takes up the image of the ship of state used earlier by his father. After the initial statements the *agon* becomes sharper with *stichomythia* laying bare the underlying issues: Creon's 'Who's to take charge?' (p. 33), 'Son, you're pathetic. You give in to a woman' (p. 34).

After Haemon leaves, it is the Chorus, in its role of moral interrogator, that influences Creon to spare Ismene, and after Creon exits the short Chorus (third *stasimon*) on 'Love' elaborates the theme of the disruption of Antigone's intended marriage by her forthcoming death (p. 36). Antigone then reflects on this in terms of an approaching marriage with death (p. 37; Acheron was the river of Hades, the place of the dead). You may have noted the references to Niobe (pp. 37–8). Niobe was a mythical figure who became the symbol of bereavement and grief when her daughters and sons were killed by Apollo and Artemis. Niobe wept so copiously that she became a waterfall on Mount Sipylus, the water running down the face of the rock like the tears on her face. You may also know the phrase 'Like Niobe, all tears', which originated in Shakespeare's *Hamlet* but subsequently migrated into the reference frame of the English language. This story from myth would have been familiar to the ancient audiences and it is a feature of Sophocles' play that Heaney chose to retain.

For an image showing the importance of keening in Irish tradition, see Plate 3.6.10.

As death becomes imminent the rhythm of Antigone's short direct statements is the same three-beat line used at the beginning of the play. The scene begins and ends with allusions to the wedding, but by the end the wedding stands for death and Antigone's 'wedding song' becomes a lament for herself. Heaney uses words that link Greek and Irish mourning practices. To 'keen' means to 'lament', the word coming from the Gaelic 'caoineadh', which means to cry or wail. Here it becomes part of the register of lament ('No wedding guests. No wake./No keen', p. 39). Antigone's final exit is marked by her assertion of the primacy of duty to the gods (compare her initial stress on the rites due to her brother). She links duty to gods and brother in terms of religious observance ('practising devotion', p. 41).

The Chorus's fourth *stasimon* provides the link between the episodes, once more linking the events in Thebes to mythological precedent and seemingly looking to the gods to deliver Antigone from her death. The Chorus shifts the terms of the debate away from power and the material world ('Not military power or the power of money', p. 42) and introduces the blind seer Tiresias. He also uses the image of the ship of state but shifts the metaphor completely away from the material to the natural world and the religious omens of the physical contagion represented by the unburied body. This picks up the theme of plague, already seeded in the language of the play by the Guard. Tiresias' arguments to Creon are cosmic, linking Creon's actions with moral as well as physical pollution. Tiresias takes up earlier images, especially the opposition between light and dark, lamentation and conflict, and the representation of the suffering of the world in the actions of the birds. In his invocation of the image of the archer (a characteristic of Sophocles' theatre poetry), Tiresias also stands for truth.

Creon's change of mind about Antigone's entombment is celebrated by an almost manic Chorus (fifth *stasimon*). Even the layout of the printed words (pp. 48–9) points up the contrast with the measured speech of the Messenger as he baldly recounts the dismal events that took place at the tomb (pp. 50–2). The metaphor of the wedding becomes ever more deeply ironic ('blood came spurting/Out of his mouth all over her white cheek ... /That was the kiss he gave his bride-to-be', p. 52). There is a studied sense of inevitability in the brief appearance of Eurydice, wife of Creon, mother of Haemon and of Megareus, already killed in the conflict that preceded the play. After the news of her suicide, Creon alone is left to take responsibility for the events he has set in train. His change of sensibility is reflected in the change in vocabulary, tone and rhythm of his speech in comparison with his earlier politician's rhetoric.

The closing short Chorus, at the end of the *exodos* or final scene, is another convention of Greek tragedy in which the Chorus usually offers a moral comment (often platitudinous). It is also often characterised by language that helps bring the audience back to their own world. It is worth looking closely at how Heaney represents these lines. For once Heaney does not follow the Greek very closely, but uses speech rhythms, images and religious allusions attuned to the cultural framework of *his* potential audience/readers – notice especially the image from agriculture and the biblical allusions underlying it (cf. *Ecclesiastes* 3: 1–8, 'To every thing there is a season'). Use of biblical phrases and echoes is a distinctive feature of Heaney's writing and here these combine to give a specific timbre of Irish tradition and cultural memory to the passage. This is an aspect of his approach that he comments on in the interview on the Audio CD.

We shall be looking at the poetic voice of Heaney in the next section, but before you move on, compare the notes you made in your reading of the play with the points made in my discussion. You may well have selected different points, so think about how your notes add to what I have said and especially see whether you disagree with any of my points or whether you think I have left out material that is important. If so, think about your reasons for disagreeing with me – this will give you the basis for a debate that you might like to pursue in a tutorial.

Antigone and Creon

In thinking about the play you will have developed views on the perennial debate about whether Antigone or Creon is the main tragic figure, or whether they both are. Was Creon a well-intentioned leader who went wrong in trying to restore cohesion after civil war, or was he a tyrant? Is Antigone a fighter for moral values or an obsessive with a death wish? In coming to a judgement about such questions you will need to think about how each character develops in the course of the play. Think especially about the various arguments that they use with different people in order to justify their conduct. Think, too, about how your own views develop in the course of studying the play. How much do you think you are influenced by what goes on in the play, and how much by the views you already hold on such questions because of your own values and life experience?

Needless to say critics are not agreed on these issues, and indeed many people find that the range of perspectives in the play is so rich that it is impossible, and undesirable, to reduce the play to one unequivocal 'meaning'. In the introduction to his edition and commentary to Sophocles' play, Mark Griffith writes:

> *Antigone* may seem to switch back and forth between being a piece of moral or political philosophy, a religious rite, a sociological treatise, an imaginative poem, a stage drama, a political rally, a psychotherapy session, and more [...] this play can be, and should be, all of these things.
>
> (Griffith, 1999, p. 26)

In recent years, Sophocles' play has often been staged and interpreted with Antigone in the role of a protester – either on behalf of women or as a kind of 'freedom fighter' (you may have spotted elements of both in Heaney's approach). Nevertheless, it is worth remembering that, in the Greek context, Antigone was a member of the ruling family in Thebes and her contest with Creon could also be read as one about how the ruling class should act. Furthermore, the values on which she stands are, in ancient Greek terms, quite conservative in their emphasis on religious values and the traditional role of women in funerary and family religious rituals. For evidence from ancient painted pottery, see Plates 3.6.1–9. It is well worth thinking about how and why such 'traditional' values can come to be thought of as 'subversive', not only in the fifth century BCE Athenian context of change from a society dominated by aristocratic families to a citizen democracy, but also in our modern world.

I mentioned earlier the question of how the attitudes of the reader and audience develop and what in the play most influences them. In the next section we shall look more closely at two factors that shape this response: (a) how a writer approaches the creation of a translation or adaptation of a Greek play; (b) how the text is transplanted to the stage. In each case I shall ask you to develop some of your own ideas on how this might be done.

6.2 TRANSLATING SOPHOCLES' *ANTIGONE*

You can see that the published text of *The Burial at Thebes* is described on the title page as 'Sophocles' *Antigone* translated by Seamus Heaney'. In fact, Heaney has described his work as 'not a translation. It's a version. I was looking for meaning, not language' (see Reading 6.1).

There are several reasons why the distinction between 'translation' and 'version' might be made. In the first place, the word 'translation' has normally been used to describe what is produced when the translator knows the language of the original (or 'source') text (in this case Sophocles' of the fifth century BCE) and works closely with it, trying to reproduce its meaning as accurately as possible in the 'target' language (in this case English of the twenty-first century CE). This is, of course, a highly problematic undertaking. However great the translator's knowledge of the source language, decisions have to be made about the intended readership. Does the reader, for example, require a close line-by-line rendering that will help him or her to refer to the source language? In an extreme case, this might require what is called an interlinear translation that places each English word under the Greek to which it refers, but this would read very strangely in English in terms of word order and idiom.

More probably the translator would try to produce a 'readable' translation. This would involve decisions not only about the meaning of the Greek but also about how that might best be communicated to people of another time, place and culture, who would be reading in a language that has different rhythms and patterns. So, even in a translation that aims to be close and scholarly, there is always an interpretative element, involving both the source and target languages. A good example would be the translation of the Greek word *philos* and its derivatives which, according to context, can indicate friend, family member or ally. Sophocles' Greek text plays on the ambivalence of this word and his characters use it in different ways. There is no precise equivalent word for *philos* in English, so the translator has to make a choice in each instance.

Heaney discusses this aspect in the interview on the Audio CD. He did not aim to produce a scholarly translation for (at least) two reasons. The first is that he is not a classical scholar (although he has studied Latin, he does not read Greek). He therefore worked from a number of existing translations, most notably that of the late nineteenth-century Cambridge scholar Professor Richard Jebb. The second reason is that Heaney, like Sophocles, was creating a play for the stage. However distinguished a scholar of Greek may be, it is extremely unlikely that he or she is also a poet, let alone a dramatist. There are, of course, some partial exceptions, such as Louis MacNeice (1907–63), whose work you encountered in Book 2, Chapter 2. MacNeice lectured in Classics at the University of Birmingham and wrote a widely praised translation of Aeschylus' *Agamemnon* (1936). A more recent exception is the poet and dramatist Tony Harrison (b. 1937), who had a classical education and works direct from the ancient texts in order to produce texts for the stage, such as *The Oresteia* of Aeschylus (1981) and Euripides' *Hecuba* (2005). Scholarly translations are comparatively rarely staged in commercial theatres in the English-speaking world, although continental Europe is more confident about doing this, and in presenting avant-garde productions. When a scholarly translation is staged, revisions usually have to be made in the text so that the actors can both speak it easily and move and act. A further complication in terms of the staging is – as we shall see – that the ancient Greek and the modern theatre contexts are also very different; a close scholarly translation will tend to reflect the ancient theatre environment that shaped its language, and this may create problems in modern theatre spaces.

There is also a third factor that influences Heaney's approach. He is a celebrated poet. The works he produces are, and must be seen to be, distinctively his own. So the 'translations' or 'versions' of classical material produced by Heaney and writers like him (Ted Hughes and Frank McGuinness come to mind, as well as Tony Harrison) have to be seen as part of the creative oeuvre of the 'star' writer. This is in contrast to notions that the hand of the translator should be 'invisible' (and consequently even of low status), although, as I mentioned above, there is always an active 'shaping' and interpretative role for the translator. There is, in fact, a long tradition in the UK of poets producing new 'translations' and 'versions' of Greek and Roman material which then became outstanding literary works in their own right: for example, Gavin Douglas's *Eneidos* (an *Aeneid* in Middle Scots, 1553), Alexander Pope's *Iliad* (1715–20), John Dryden's *Aeneid* (1697), Robert Browning's *Agamemnon* (1877) and, most recently, Christopher Logue's *War Music* (which he calls 'Accounts' of Homer and is still in progress).

Activity Now turn to the Resources section and look at the extracts from four translations of Sophocles' *Antigone* into English (Readings 6.2–6.5). All are translations of the opening words spoken by the Guard (lines 245–67 in Sophocles). Think about the words used and the rhythms (it will help if you read the passages aloud). Then see if you can suggest what kinds of readership or audience they were intended for.

There are several different ways in which these translations might be categorised. It is quite easy to tell from the language that Jebb's is the oldest (Reading 6.2). Words like 'the doer' and 'sore wonder' (with its biblical echoes of the shepherds who were 'sore afraid'), abbreviations like 'e'en' and expressions like 'come nigh' and 'we were not privy' differentiate it from late twentieth- or early twenty-first-century diction. Nevertheless, the language is direct and for a late nineteenth- or early twentieth-century readership would have seemed 'literary' rather than unduly archaic. It is worth noting that the Guard is presented as a knowledgeable bumpkin, able to interpret markings and tracks.

Another way of describing Jebb's translation would be to say that it follows Sophocles closely. Even if you do not know any Greek you do not have to take my word for that, for if you were to consult the complete work you would find that the translation was produced as part of Jebb's critical edition with introduction, Greek text, translation and commentary. You can also get a sense of the translator's precision in his choice of words and verbal images.

That precision is also evident in the close translation by the academic Hugh Lloyd-Jones (Reading 6.3). There is a slight formality in the language ('each of us was the doer, but no one manifestly so') and this distances the speech from contemporary idiom or the immediacy of staging. Lloyd-Jones's translation was made for the Loeb series of classical texts which has the Greek or Latin on facing pages to the English translation in order to help readers who wish to follow the ancient language.

The translation in Reading 6.4 is from an edition by David Franklin and John Harrison (no relation to the poet and dramatist Tony Harrison), who are also trained classicists. However, it seems to me that this version might be more 'speakable' in a theatre situation than the previous extracts. The syntax and language are direct and the rhythm is that of the spoken word (you will have discovered this if you read it aloud). It was created for a series that does not include the Greek but does have notes on the text and background information on the facing pages. One of the stated aims of the series to which it belongs (of which John Harrison is joint editor) is to bridge the gap between classical scholarship and modern readers and theatre, and a number of the translations in the series have been successfully staged. As Harrison writes in the Preface:

> The translations are new. Many recent versions of Greek tragedy have been produced by poets and playwrights who do not work from the original Greek. The translators of this series aim to bring readers, actors and directors as close as possible to the playwrights' actual words and intentions: to create translations which are faithful to the original in content and tone; and which are speakable, with all the immediacy of modern English.
>
> (Franklin and Harrison, 2003, p. vi)

The extract from Blake Morrison's translation in Reading 6.5 is from a version created especially for theatre, to be performed by the company Northern Broadsides, directed by Barrie Rutter. In his introduction to the published text (2003), Morrison refers to contemporary stimuli for his work. One was his sense that war in Iraq showed that the struggle between Antigone and Creon was still going on (an aspect that was important for a number of responses to the play at that time, including Heaney's). The other was Morrison's wish to speak to a specific audience:

> Northern Broadsides like to take the classics into communities and parts of the country that theatre doesn't always reach [...] Zeus and Dionysus are present but so are the landscapes of the Yorkshire Dales; and through the lines of blank verse, and the

> lyrics of the Chorus, there's the music of a rough-tongued northern vernacular. Occasionally I depart from Sophocles (in beginning *Antigone* with the choric victory celebrations, for instance), because the performance seemed to demand it. But I've tried to honour the spirit of the original, in a language really spoken by men.
>
> (Morrison, 2003, pp. 4–5)

Morrison's version is the most colloquial and he is the only writer out of the four to have adapted or added to the Sophocles text, partly to emphasise the sense of place and partly to add a rough-and-ready edge to the figure of the Guard. These are aspects that perhaps make it even more appropriate to use the word 'version' rather than 'translation' to describe his play.

We could perhaps draw from these examples that there is no rigid system of definition or classification of what a translation should be (although there is an interesting attempt to do so in Walton, 2006, pp. 182–3, which sets out seven categories, ranging from a literal 'crib' to a cultural relocation). However, a very broad spectrum of approaches might include those summarised below.

Approaches to translation

Translation that attempts above all to be *accurate*, communicating the *letter* of the original. The emphasis is on understanding and communicating the original Greek and assumes that it has a settled meaning which can be transferred into another language.

Translation that concentrates on communicating the *spirit* of the original. This approach recognises that the idioms and cultural frameworks of ancient and modern are not congruent, but works on the basis that the sense and the 'feel' of the source text and context *can* be represented. The translator therefore also has to make judgements about what will be effective in the language of the target audience/readers.

Pragmatic translation, which places particular emphasis on the target language and culture and the purposes for which the translation is made.

You can see that there are overlaps between these approaches but that the emphasis shifts along a line from the primacy of the Greek source language to the primacy of the modern language and its users.

Activity I would now like you to reread the corresponding passage in Heaney's text (pp. 13–14), and then rewrite the Guard's lines as though spoken to and for your own community. Think about how you would make the Guard convey the essential information, how you would mark a sense of place, and what idiom you would make him use. Think also about how you would communicate his attitude towards Creon – fearful? deferential? defiant? (This might also depend on how autocratic and tyrannical you think Creon is.) You might like to compare your version with others in your tutorial group, or discuss it with friends or family. When you reread your own version, think about the extent to which it differs from Heaney's, or whether it follows it closely, as well as the extent to which you have acted as a kind of ventriloquist in deciding what precisely the Guard will say, and how he will express it.

Activity Finally, while you are in a creative mood, here is another practical exercise you might like to do. Imagine that you are to direct Heaney's play in the theatre, that is, *to translate it to the stage*. Make some short notes on how you would want to do this. What kind of setting would you use (ancient? modern? indeterminate?)? What kind of costumes and scenery would you use? How might Antigone and Creon look and behave? How many people would you want to have in the Chorus and how would they speak (in unison? divided parts?)? How would the Chorus represent the 'Elders of Thebes' in sound, dress and movement? What shape and size of theatre space would you want to use? And what kind of audience would you hope to attract?

Keep your notes by you and we shall return to them at the end of the chapter.

6.3 TEXTS AND CONTEXTS: ANCIENT AND MODERN

So far we have concentrated on the text of Heaney's play, with some discussion about different approaches to translating or adapting the ancient text. In this section I look more closely at the context in which Heaney wrote his play and make some comparisons with the context in which Sophocles lived and wrote.

Once we start to identify contexts for the play we move beyond the text and need to use other sources of evidence, as you have done when exploring contexts for other chapters in this book. This does not mean that we lose sight of the text; in fact, when we return to it our understanding should be richer. Nevertheless, there was a very good reason for engaging with the text itself before looking in detail at the various contexts to which it can be related. I think it is very important that in reading the text (or seeing it performed) we feel the freshness of that first experience and base our responses on what is triggered by the form, language and content of the text or performance itself, rather than 'reading into it' aspects that have been suggested by external material.

You can see that in the heading to this section I have used 'contexts' in the plural. There is always more than one context and in your reading for this section you will meet several: the context in which Heaney's play was commissioned; the context and literary traditions in which the author worked; the context in which the ancient play was created; and the performance history of the play. In the time available we cannot explore all these in any detail, but you should be able to get a sense of the ways in which they have all contributed to the play. You should consider the various pieces of evidence critically, and to do so it is useful to keep in mind some basic questions, such as: 'What kind of source or evidence is this? Who created it? Why? For whom? With what purpose?' If you question the evidence in this way, you will be in a better position to decide what weight to give to it. (You have already encountered similar questions in the discussion of primary sources in Book 2, Chapter 4 and elsewhere.)

The commissioning of Heaney's play

I mentioned at the beginning of this chapter that Heaney's play was commissioned by the Abbey Theatre, Dublin to celebrate its centenary anniversary season, and that the theatre was founded in 1904 by W.B. Yeats and Lady Gregory to be an emblem of cultural nationalism. The 2004 season was called 'The Abbey and Europe' and it took place at the time when Ireland held the presidency of the European Union (January–June 2004). This situation was reflected in the articles in the play's programme. During this season, the theatre also hosted debates on the relationship between Irish and European cultural identity and on the role of a national theatre in the artistic life of the nation. In the programme notes, Pat Cox, MEP and President of the European Parliament, praised the theatre for its ability 'to facilitate cultural exchanges across languages, traditions and varied historical experiences'. Other articles in the programme notes also emphasised the importance that European drama had in the repertoire of the Abbey Theatre, as well as its other aims of encouraging new work and providing a national stimulus to 'displace colonial stereotypes of Irishness by encouraging Irish playwrights to produce Irish plays for Irish audiences' (the academic Patrick Mathews in a programme article; see also Mathews, 2003).

But for whom were the programme notes intended? How do they balance cultural and political environments and traditions with the role of the individual dramatist? (You might also question the extent to which audience members really study programme notes in any detail.) || ?

Seamus Heaney's perspective

You should allow about half an hour to listen to the interview with Seamus Heaney on the Audio CD (tracks 12–17, following Part 2 of the play).

You will find Seamus Heaney's own thoughts on his approach to creating the play in the interview following the play on the second Audio CD and if you have not already listened to it, do so before working on this section. Note especially how Heaney relates his work both to his literary and cultural traditions and to the impact of current events. Some of the references Heaney makes in the interview are explained in the Media notes at the end of this chapter.

Activity

Now read Heaney's programme notes, reproduced in Reading 6.6. If you have time, also read his more detailed account in the published article '"Me" as in "Metre": on translating *Antigone*', reproduced in Reading 6.7.

There is some overlap between these items but I have included them both because they were prepared by Heaney for different readerships and the second includes a fuller discussion of his approach to writing Creon's lines.

Figure 6.1 Seamus Heaney, portrait of the poet and writer at the Folkestone Literary Festival, September 1986. Photographed by George Newson. Photo: © George Newson/Lebrecht Music & Arts.

Taken together they convey a striking sense of how Heaney had to grapple with the timescale imposed by the commission.

Heaney also faced the daunting precedent of Yeats, who was not only dominant in the Abbey tradition but had also written versions of Sophocles' *Oedipus* plays, although not a full *Antigone*. (A poem by Yeats based on a Chorus from the play is included in the Resources section as Reading 6.8.)

Heaney's discussions also show his sense of writing within a rich Irish literary context that draws on Gaelic, Anglo-Saxon, Irish/English and European traditions in which translations and adaptations of Greek drama have had a distinctive role. He explains how this background interacted with his decisions about the language and metre given to each of the characters. He also reveals a strong cultural politics, which links his poetic idiom both to issues raised by earlier colonial domination of Ireland by the English and to his perception of contemporary neo-colonialism in the global policies of the USA and its allies.

However, in *The Burial at Thebes* Heaney has to some extent tempered the approach to contemporary politics that he adopted in his earlier version of a Sophocles play, *The Cure at Troy* (1990). This work, based on Sophocles' *Philoctetes*, was also a commission, from the cultural nationalist Field Day Theatre Company of Derry. The play toured extensively in Ireland, England, Scotland and the USA, and is still being revived. As he was to do in *Burial*, Heaney followed Sophocles' text closely in *Cure*, but he added some lines to the Chorus that linked the Sophoclean theme of alienation to the sectarian situation in the north of Ireland. The resonance of Heaney's poetry caught the imagination of politicians, media and public. Some phrases, such as 'When hope and history rhyme', entered public discourse, not just as newspaper headlines at the time of the Good Friday Agreement in 1998, but earlier, too, in speeches by the President of the Irish Republic, Mary Robinson, and the President of the USA, Bill Clinton. Paradoxically, there was aesthetic and political criticism of Heaney for exploiting Sophocles for contemporary ends. He appeared to give equal status to the suffering of both communities in the north of Ireland and so offended both sides of the sectarian divide (Hardwick, 2000, Ch. 5; 2003, Ch. 8). It is noticeable that in *The Burial at Thebes* the Chorus is not given a specifically contemporary political voice, although many critics have found that Creon's stance and speech resonate with those of President George W. Bush. In the Audio CD interview, Heaney discusses the question of whether contemporary allusions are intrusive.

In spite of his two versions of Greek tragedies, however, Heaney's career is primarily that of a poet, not a dramatist, and in exploring the contexts to the writing of *Burial* it is important to look in his poetry for comparisons of subject matter and technique that resonate with his writing for the theatre (think back to Heaney's poems that you read in *Beasts* and especially to the discussion of 'Widgeon' on track 7 of the Audio CD 'What am I? Beasts and Tradition').

The context of ancient Greek theatre

In this section I will outline some aspects of the cultural and political context of Athens in the fifth century BCE within which Sophocles shaped the structure and language on which, as you have seen, Heaney drew so closely in order to make his own play, 2,500 years later. I shall not assume that you have any previous knowledge. You will not be expected to remember the details, but the section provides important information that will help you with the 'multi-tasking' that you have to do when studying a modern text that is a version of a very old one. You can see that there are significant comparisons and contrasts to be made between ancient and modern conditions of performance (think, for example, about how and why the plays came to be written, the physical and cultural environment in which they were performed, who footed the bill, and who saw the performance; how the plays were judged; how a particular play can be situated within the writer's work as a whole; what kinds of life experience the writer had).

For reconstructions of Greek theatre masks, see Plate 3.6.11.

Sophocles wrote his plays for performance in the public dramatic festivals in Athens. In the main festival, the Great Dionysia, which took place annually, there were drama competitions in which three poet-playwrights competed, each with four plays (three tragedies followed by a **satyr play**, which was designed to provide a degree of comic relief after the harrowing experience of watching the tragedies). The playwrights were chosen by a public official (perhaps after a preliminary reading). The expenses of training the Chorus and of costumes were met by a wealthy citizen as a liturgy, a form of taxation

Figure 6.2 Pronomos Painter (attr.), Athenian red figure volute-krater showing the cast of a classical satyr play, late fifth century BCE, earthenware, height 75 cm. Museo Archeologico Nazionale, Naples, inv. 81673. Photo: Courtesy of Ministero per i Beni e le Attività Culturali. For higher quality reproductions of this image, see Plates 3.6.12–15.

that had considerable status as a public service. (The Greek meaning precedes the later association with Church ritual – you can track the derivation in the online *Oxford English Dictionary*.) The *polis* (city-state of Athens) paid the leading actors and the dramatists and the winning writer received a 'crown' of ivy.

The plays were performed in daylight hours in the huge open-air Theatre of Dionysus. Estimates of audience capacity vary (and some researchers are revising these downwards), but probably as many as 14,000 could have attended, including foreign visitors. It is not certain whether women could attend.

For an image of the Theatre of Dionysus in Athens, see Plate 3.6.16.

The plays were part of a festival that was both civic and religious. They included processions, religious sacrifices, libations to the gods, a parade of war orphans and performances of dithyramb (sung poetry) as well as drama. The festivals provided a cultural and political showcase for Athens which, at that time, was leader of an *arche*, an alliance of Greek city-states that had been set up earlier in the fifth century to defend Greece against Persian invasion. However, there was competition for power among the Greek states, and Athens and Sparta became locked in a debilitating war (you will be familiar with this already from the dramatic context of Plato's *Laches*, which you studied in Book 2, Chapter 1). Towards the end of the fifth century, when the Athenian population was depleted, demoralised and impoverished by the war with Sparta, payment for attending the theatre was instituted.

The tragedies and comedies performed at the festivals combined spoken and sung verse. All the actors were male. The Chorus for tragedy consisted initially of twelve and later of fifteen who were trained in singing, dancing and movement. Three actors divided the main parts among themselves. They wore masks that covered the whole face (see Plate 3.6.11), which meant that their gestures and body movements were important as their facial expressions could not be seen. The acting space was called the *orchestra* (initially a rectangular space, but later this became circular) and behind it developed a stage building, the *skene*. The spectators sat on tiered stone seats (see Plate 3.6.16 and Figure 6.3). The judges were appointed from the ten citizen divisions and records were kept of the results (some of which survive, see Figure 6.4). There were smaller theatres in rural centres.

In the fourth century BCE plays continued to be performed and in 338 BCE legislation was introduced to prevent alteration to the texts of the great fifth-century writers. The texts that have survived were transmitted on manuscripts that were copied and recopied over the centuries before the invention of printing. They represent only a small proportion of those written by Sophocles and the other major tragedians Aeschylus and Euripides.

Figure 6.3 Unknown photographer, theatre at Epidaurus, Greece, during a performance of *Philoctetes* by Sophocles in 1991. Photo: R. Sheridan/Ancient Art and Architecture Collection Ltd.

Seven plays survive out of the 120 plus that are attributed to Sophocles. There are also some fragments which are important for reconstructing his work as a whole. Sophocles' career as a dramatist was a long one. *Ajax* and *Women of Trachis* are thought to be his earliest plays. *Oedipus the King* is usually dated to *c*.425, *Electra* to between 415 and 410. *Philoctetes* was produced in 409 and *Oedipus at Colonus* posthumously in 401. *Antigone* is usually dated to 442 on the basis of a story that it was so well regarded that Sophocles was elected to be one of the generals (*strategoi*) for the war against Samos in the following year 441–40.

If this seems an unlikely reason for electing a general, it is worth remembering that Athenians did not draw the kinds of distinction between participation in public and artistic life that we tend to have today. In fact, it is known from inscriptions that Sophocles was active in public life. He held a financial post in the Athenian *arche* in 443–2 in which he managed the annual tribute from the 'allies'. When he was *strategos* in Samos, he had to put down a rebellion in an allied state. In old age Sophocles was one of ten special advisers (*probouloi*) who were appointed to deal with the political crisis that affected Athens towards the end of the war with Sparta and which resulted in the (temporary) change from a democratic to an oligarchic constitution

Figurc 6.4 Inscription on marblc recording victors in the drama competitions at the City Dionysia at Athens, *c.* mid-fourth century. Epigraphical Museum, Athens. Photo: Epigraphical Museum, Athens.

(that is, government by the few instead of by the male citizen body as a whole). I mention Sophocles' public service because it shows that he knew from personal experience about the challenges of decision making in public life, and this is apparent in the situation and language of *Antigone*.

However, it is important to note that Sophocles' *Antigone* does not refer directly to life in Athens. Like all extant tragedies except Aeschylus' *Persians* (472 BCE), which refers to the Greek naval victory over the Persian invaders, Sophocles rewrites a mythical story and *Antigone* is not set in Athens. Tragedians often adapted the myths in different ways: for example, Sophocles' contemporary Euripides is thought to have written an *Antigone* in which Antigone survived and married Haemon. So Athenian spectators who wanted to interpret the plays as being immediately relevant to their own situations had to make an imaginative leap, as we do ourselves.

6.4 HEANEY'S PLAY IN PERFORMANCE ON THE MODERN STAGE

Sophocles' play has an extensive modern performance history, including adaptations in opera from the Renaissance onwards, and in the nineteenth, twentieth and twenty-first centuries it has become a major indicator of the different ways in which Greek drama is perceived in cultural and political life (Macintosh, 1997; Steiner, 1984). On the course website you can follow links to research projects with searchable databases which you can consult for examples (which include translations, versions and adaptations in Africa, the Caribbean and the Americas, often at moments of crisis and change; see, for example, President Nelson Mandela's account in Reading 6.9).

Since it was only staged for the first time in 2004, *The Burial at Thebes* has a short performance history. At the time of writing (September 2007) there have been two major productions in Ireland and Britain – at the Abbey Theatre, Dublin in 2004, and at the Nottingham Playhouse in 2005 – but further productions in London, Oxford and Dublin are imminent. However, the play has also been staged in non-commercial contexts. In 2006 it was used as the basis for a schools' drama workshop on the Welsh Borders and it has also been performed by school students at the Edinburgh Fringe Festival.

Moving a translation or version of a Greek play from the page to the stage involves at least two different processes. First, there is the translation of the ancient work into a new language. As you have seen, this may or may not be done with staging in mind. Then there is the transplantation to the stage (a kind of re-translation) which is brought about by the artistic intervention of theatre practitioners – the director, the set designer, the costume designer, the music director and the actors. Performance is a live and ephemeral art form – you could say that every performance is a new work. This makes it particularly interesting to compare different productions, not just in terms of their quality and aesthetic effect but also in terms of their response to the author's text (and, in the case of an ancient text, in terms of the layers of response between ancient, modern and staging).

Since performance is an ephemeral 'event' we are reliant on a number of different kinds of sources to help us build up a picture of the performance itself. Among these sources are theatrical reviews. Readings 6.10–6.11 are reviews of the productions of *The Burial at Thebes*. When you read them you should bear in mind that reviews such as these are written in a short space of time after a particular performance and are intended for the readership of a particular newspaper or magazine. But, read critically, they do have a role in preserving information and judgements about the set, costume, use of the Chorus, acting styles, music and other aspects of the staging. When using these reviews as sources (or others that you may encounter in the future), bear in mind:

- the propensity of critics (and indeed all audience members) to notice different things and to disagree in their judgements (visual memory can also be fallible, even in the short term);
- the way in which the same text can be staged in very different ways;
- that in making judgements about the impact of the performance, an important element seems to be the compatibility between the acting script/text and the director's concept (from the reviews, this seems to have been more successful in Nottingham 2005 than in Dublin 2004);
- the slight ambivalence (evident in all the extracts) between judging the performance on its own terms as a theatrical event, judging it as a staging of Heaney's text, and judging it as a version of Sophocles' play.

The impact of the director

You should allow about half an hour to listen to the interviews with the director, composer and actors on the Audio CD (tracks 3–11, following Part 2 of the play). You can find the full cast list on the course website, together with further information about the director's work and the way in which he approached this production.

In this chapter much of the emphasis has been on the impact of the author (ancient and modern). But a performance also bears the stamp of the director. If you have not already listened to the interview with the director of the audio performance, John Theocharis, do so now. In it, he discusses the special requirements of oral and aural in performance and tells us how he compensated for the lack of visual triggers to understanding and interpretation.

Following the interview with Theocharis are further short interviews with the composer and actors. Taken together, the interviews indicate how important it is for director, actors and composer to work together to create the performance. (If you were seeing the play in the theatre, you would also need to consider the impact of the visual design: the set, costumes and movement).

Now return to the notes you made on how you would stage the play if you were the director. What difference does it make for your approach whether the play is presented as 'Greek drama', 'Irish drama', or as a play for today? (Look at the images from modern productions and costume design in Figures 6.5 and 6.6 and Plates 3.6.17–18.) How important is it that the director and the writer are thinking along the same lines?

You might find it useful to compare your 'director's notes' with the version of the Guard's speech that you wrote. Taken together, the two might reveal a lot about your own cultural assumptions and about your view of the roles of writer and director, and it would be useful to compare your approach with that of other students in your group. You

Figure 6.5 The Chorus in Frank Bradley's production of Sophocles, *Antigone*, Cairo, 2002. Unknown photographer. Photo: The American University in Cairo.

will be able to adapt your work on this play when thinking about any Greek tragedy that you may read or hear/see in performance.

OVERVIEW

Finally, take a few minutes to review your work on *The Burial at Thebes*. In developing your critical approach to the play we have covered four main areas:

1 close reading of the play text, especially its structure, language and form;

Figure 6.6 Michael Guirguis as Creon, with the Chorus in Frank Bradley's production of Sophocles, *Antigone*, Cairo 2002. Unknown photographer. Photo: The American University in Cairo.

2 consideration of the play's relationship to other texts known to the author or written by him;
3 the contextual richness of the play and the ways in which its influence has migrated via translations and other stagings and rewritings;
4 the play's interaction with the cultural framework and assumptions of a specific reader (yourself) and groups of readers (including your study group and also theatre practitioners, critics and 'live' audiences).

It's worth thinking about which aspects of this work you found most interesting or most difficult, most unexpected or most closely related to approaches you have already encountered on the course. What new ways of studying did you try out – and did they work for you?

REFERENCES

Crawley, R. (tr.) (1997 [1874]) *Thucydides: The History of the Peloponnesian War*, Ware, Wordsworth.

Franklin, D. and Harrison, J. (eds) (2003) *Sophocles: Antigone*, Cambridge, Cambridge University Press.

Griffith, M. (ed.) (1999) *Sophocles: Antigone*, Cambridge, Cambridge University Press.

Hardwick, L. (2000) *Translating Words, Translating Cultures*, London, Duckworth.

Hardwick, L. (2003) *New Surveys in the Classics: Reception Studies*, Oxford, Oxford University Press for the Classical Association.

Harrison, T. (1981) *The Oresteia*, London, Collings.

Harrison, T. (2005) *Hecuba*, London, Faber and Faber.

Heaney, S. (1990) *The Cure at Troy*, London, Faber.

Macintosh, F. (1997) 'Tragedy in performance: nineteenth- and twentieth-century productions' in Easterling, P.E. (ed.) *The Cambridge Companion to Greek Tragedy*, Cambridge, Cambridge University Press, pp. 284–323.

MacNeice, L. (tr.) (1936) *Aeschylus' Agamemnon*, London, Faber.

Mathews, P.J. (2003) *Revival: The Abbey Theatre, Sinn Fein, the Gaelic League and the Co-operative Movement*, Cork, Cork University Press in association with Field Day.

Morash, C. (2002) *History of Irish Theatre, 1601–2000*, Cambridge, Cambridge University Press.

Morrison, B. (2003) *Antigone by Sophocles: a Version by Blake Morrison*, Halifax, Northern Broadsides.

Steiner, G. (1984) *Antigones*, Oxford, Oxford University Press.

Walton, J.M. (2006) *Found in Translation: Greek Drama in English*, Cambridge, Cambridge University Press.

Welch, R. (ed.) (1996) *The Oxford Companion to Irish Literature*, Oxford, Clarendon Press.

RESOURCES

Reading 6.1 A Greek tragedy for our times

A sister defies the law to bury an outlawed brother denied burial by official decree. The king sees no humanity in her act, only betrayal. The chorus, society, looks on, compromised by the need to comply with a ruler intent on revenge.

Sounds familiar? Sounds contemporary? Of course it does: by such ruthlessness is power maintained. Or is it? The story is not a new one. The Greek tragedian Sophocles of Athens, who lived in the fifth century BC, wrote *Antigone*, the first of his Theban plays, as a study of conflict. Antigone mourns her dead brother and breaks the law. King Creon exceeds the dictates of power, a dangerous over-reaching. His son, Haemon, instead of marrying Antigone, must reject his father; he chooses to die with his bride-to-be.

It is a chilling tale and a timeless one. Antigone's dilemma is a fundamental issue of honour. The play remains a foundation text of European theatre. Brecht was drawn to it. As was Anouilh. The French playwright revisited the play for his version, which was performed in 1942 during the German occupation. Initially reacting to the drama as theatre, audiences were to slowly grasp that Creon, a plausible enough characterisation, personified Vichy compromise, while Antigone was none other than France at its most idealistic. The politics of *Antigone* would never be lost on an artist as politically alert as Seamus Heaney, the Nobel laureate in literature.

An autobiographical but never confessional writer, Heaney the poet – who has always remained a teacher in the most honourable and generous sense of the word – is at once direct and complex; his response to the political remains shrewdly subtle.

'I taught *Antigone* to college students in a Belfast teacher-training college in 1963. I talked about it in relation to Aristotle and Greek tragedy. Five years later, in October 1968, I read Conor Cruise O'Brien in the *Listener* using *Antigone* to illuminate the conflict in Northern Ireland – the conflict that is within individuals as well as within the society. Antigone and her sister, Ismene, represent two opposing impulses that often co-exist: the impulse to protect and rebel and the impulse to conform for the sake of a quiet life. From that moment on *Antigone* was more than a piece of the academic syllabus: it was a lens that helped to inspect reality more clearly.'

Incidentally, in the same issue of the *Listener*, Heaney, then an emerging young poet with one collection, *Death Of A Naturalist* (1966), to his credit, contributed 'Old Derry's Walls', an article written in response to an RUC attack on a civil-rights march in Derry.

Antigone is a play that has endured, while Antigone as a character continues to impress and inspire as a heroine of conscience as well as courage. And it is that conscience, even more than the courage, that has inspired other writers to observe her, and the play, again and again. For Heaney, the Abbey's commission to write a new version as part of the theatre's centenary celebrations initially seemed to carry more obligation than inspiration.

'I was a bit wary. Others had been there before me: Tom Paulin, Marianne McDonald (to whom his version is dedicated), Brendan Kennelly, Conall Morrison and Aidan Carl Mathews. I thought to myself, how many more *Antigones* did Irish theatre need?' He laughs, lifts his hands and offers an expression of bewildered amusement. There was also the sense of a return. Like a fellow Irish Nobel laureate, W.B. Yeats, before him, he had already explored the art of Sophocles. In 1990, Heaney, 'not a passionate theatre-goer and no playwright', wrote a version of *Philoctetes*, one of the least performed of the great Athenian's seven surviving works from the 100 plays he wrote during his 90-year life. Inspired by the text, Heaney called his version *The Cure At Troy.*

Drawn to it because he wanted to contribute to Field Day Theatre Company's repertoire, he says, 'The theme of that play is also about the conflict between personal integrity and political expediency.' With a grimace that speaks volumes he adds: 'I liked the title.' The production had its difficulties, and the play had none of the unexpected humour presented by the palace guard, which counters the multiple agonies of *Antigone*.

'First of all the title tells what happens in the play: Philoctetes' poisonous wound is cured. Secondly, that cure is miraculous, and the Irish ear is still ready to detect a miraculous dimension in the word cure. *The Cure At Troy, The Burial at Thebes*, there's a nice balance there, in the shape of the phrases. I think "cure" and "burial" both retain a sacral resonance, and in that way they remind a modern audience, subliminally, of the sacred element in Greek tragedy.'

His initial reluctance to add yet another *Antigone* to the Irish repertoire dissolved with a new sense of the play's relevance after September 11th. 'There was the general worldwide problem where considerations of state security posed serious threats to individual freedom and human rights. Then there was the obvious parallel between George W. Bush and Creon.'

The issue of describing Heaney's treatment of the play as a translation, adaptation or simple version is quickly settled.

'It's not a translation. I worked off the existing 19th-century translation by (R.C.) Jebb and the Loeb (Classical Library) standard one. You could say: he knows no Greek. I know it says "translated by" on the cover. But it's not a translation. It's a version. I was looking for meaning, not language.'

'Jebb, for example, and E.F. Watling, who did the old Penguin translations of *The Theban Plays*, were under an obligation to render the Greek correctly. They had a scholarly discipline to obey. I, on the other hand, did want to give the substance of the meaning, but my first consideration was speakability. I also wanted different registers, in the musical sense, for different characters and movements in the play. You could say mine is a parallel text. I hope I haven't hijacked it.'

He hasn't. It is an atmospheric version that gains much energy and dramatic fire from the characterisation. Above all the text acquires further physicality through Heaney's instinctively graceful and earthy feel for the right word.

Tone holds the key to texture. He refers to searching for tone, 'this looking for the music of the thing'. He says: 'You only have to look at the Greek text in the Loeb edition to see that there are different metres, different line lengths. Obviously, the choruses are elaborate, lyric speech. Creon has a steady, regular form of utterance. Antigone's pleas are in a shorter, more intense register. I just wanted to give equivalent variations in my own English.'

This search led him to the three distinct verse tunes heard in his text. There is also, of course, the central vernacular prose daringly spat out by the indignant palace guard who supplies the unexpected humour upon which the play spins. Falsely accused of burying Polyneices, Antigone's brother, who has been denounced as a traitor, the guard who merely reported the illegal burial instead speaks back to Creon, suggesting: 'Your conscience is what's doing the disturbing.' The guard has a Shakespearean, quasi-comic candour. On capturing Antigone, he rises to verse and is quick to remind the king of his 'tongue-lashing'.

In many ways the guard is a secondary teller of truths who prepares the way for the play's main truth-teller, Tiresias, at his most Beckett-like in Heaney's version. In Sophocles himself lies the essential conflict between Creon and Antigone.

'Sophocles was a member of the Athenian elite,' says Heaney. 'He held public office and obviously sympathised with Creon's sense of order, but he had an artist's instinctive solidarity with the individual sense of honour.'

Why have so many of Ireland's leading writers been drawn to reworking versions of classic works? It seems churlish to ask this of Heaney, whose majestic rendition of *Beowulf* caught the essential quasi-pagan, quasi-Christian grandeur of the great Anglo-Saxon epic, and brought it beyond the universities to a wider reading public. But he smiles as he replies, 'because classics endure'. Then he takes us to a deeper level.

'Because of a situation in this country over the past few decades we have all been driven back to first principles: the relationship between men and women, the problem of justice for the victims, the problem of establishing a commonly agreed system of government. All these fundamental issues are plied with total clear-sightedness for the first time in the Greek classics. But that does not mean that the last word has been spoken.'

Source: Eileen Battersby (2004) 'A Greek tragedy for our times', *The Irish Times*, 3 April (City Edition; Weekend), p. 55.

Reading 6.2 Jebb's translation of *Antigone*

GU. Well, this is it. – The corpse – some one hath just given it burial, and gone away, – after sprinkling thirsty dust on the flesh, and such other rites as piety enjoins.

CR. What sayest thou? What living man hath dared this deed?

GU. I know not; no stroke of pickaxe was seen there, no earth thrown up by mattock; the ground was hard and dry, unbroken, without track of wheels; the doer was one who had left no trace. And when the first day-watchman showed it to us, sore wonder fell on all. The dead man was veiled from us; not shut within a tomb, but lightly strewn with dust, as by the hand of one who shunned a curse. And no sign met the eye as though any beast of prey or any dog had come nigh to him, or torn him.

Then evil words flew fast and loud among us, guard accusing guard; and it would e'en have come to blows at last, nor was there any to hinder. Every man was the culprit, and no one was convicted, but all disclaimed knowledge of the deed. And we were ready to take red-hot iron in our hands; – to walk through fire; – to make oath by the gods that we had not done the deed, – that we were not privy to the planning or the doing.

Source: R.C. Jebb (2004 [1900]) *Sophocles: Plays*, *Antigone*, London, Bristol Classical Press, pp. 57–61 (Sophocles text, lines 245–67).

Reading 6.3 Lloyd-Jones's translation of *Antigone*

GUARD Well, I will tell you! Someone has just gone off after burying the body, sprinkling its flesh with thirsty dust and performing the necessary rites.

CREON What are you saying? What man has dared to do this?

GUARD I do not know; there was no mark of an axe, no earth turned up by a mattock; the earth was hard and dry, unbroken and with no tracks of wheels; the doer left no mark. And when the first daytime watcher showed us, it was a disagreeable surprise for all. He had vanished, not buried in a tomb, but covered with a light dust, as though put there by someone to avoid pollution; and there were no signs of any wild beast or any dog that had come and torn the body. Hard words were bandied between us, one guard questioning another, and it might have ended with a blow, and no one was there to stop it; for each of us was the doer, but no one manifestly so, but he escaped detection. And we were ready to lift lumps of molten lead and to go through fire and to swear by the gods that we had not done the deed and did not know who had planned it or who had done it.

Source: Hugh Lloyd-Jones (ed.) (2002 [1994]) *Sophocles: Antigone, The Women of Trachis, Philoctetes, Oedipus at Colonus*, Cambridge, MA, and London, Harvard University Press, pp. 27–9 (Sophocles text, lines 245–67).

Reading 6.4 Franklin and Harrison's translation of *Antigone*

SENTRY Well, I will tell you. Someone has just buried the body
and left; he sprinkled dry dust on the flesh, and gave it the
proper rites.

CREON What? What man dared to do this?

SENTRY I don't know. There was no mark of a pickaxe, no earth
turned over with a spade. The ground was hard and dry,
unbroken by wheel-tracks; the workman left no trace.
When the first day-watchman showed it to us, it seemed to us
all like a miracle – but ominous for us. For he had disappeared,
not in a grave, but just under a thin layer of dust, as though
someone were trying to avoid a divine curse. There was no sign
that any wild animal or dog had come near, and the body did
not look torn.

Then harsh words flew between us, guard blaming guard, and
it would have ended in blows, with no-one there to stop it.
Each man in turn was the one who had done it, no-one was
proven guilty, and everybody pleaded ignorance. We were
ready to take red-hot iron in our hands, and walk through fire,
and swear by the gods that we had not done it, that we were
not in league with those who planned or carried out the deed.

Source: David Franklin and John Harrison (eds and trs) (2003) *Sophocles: Antigone*, Cambridge, Cambridge University Press, p. 21, lines 228–47 (Sophocles text, lines 245–67).

Reading 6.5 Morrison's version of *Antigone*

GUARD Carrying bad news is like having the squitters –
you don't want people to know, you hold it in
as long as you can.

CREON Enough! Just tell your story.

GUARD The corpse. Somebody has buried the corpse.
Not a proper burial, six foot under –
just a skim of earth over the body
to do right by the soul that passed away.
Then whoever did it vanished in thin air.

CREON Buried? *Buried?* Who'd dare to break my law?

GUARD How would I know? It's not like they left a spade
with their name on it. The ground's so rock-hard
you can't sink a shovel or pickaxe in,
and if a cart were used it left no wheel-ruts.
Not a trace – it's like virgin soil up there.
The security guard couldn't credit it
when he took us to the corpse at sun-up.
As for us lot, we were stunned – we thought
the body had gone at first till we spied
a mound of white flesh, sprinkled with dirt,
like a new potato lying in the earth.
We poked about to see how it had got there:
had a gun-dog buried it like a bone?
But the culprit weren't no creature, that was clear,
so we began laying the blame on each other,
every man among us effing and blinding
till we were all in a rage at being accused.

Source: Blake Morrison (2003) *Antigone by Sophocles: a Version by Blake Morrison*, Halifax, Northern Broadsides, p. 75. (Based on the Sophocles text, lines 245–67.)

Reading 6.6 A note by Seamus Heaney

The invitation to translate *Antigone* for the Abbey's centenary programme was an honour, but at first I wasn't sure whether to accept. How many *Antigones* could Irish theatre put up with? There had been Tom Paulin's *The Riot Act*, done for Field Day in the 1980s, and then last year a version by Conall Morrison that set the action in the Middle East. In between, Marianne McDonald, Brendan Kennelly and Aidan Carl Mathews had also reworked the tragedy, so why take it up again?

One person who had not done a version was W.B. Yeats. Yeats had indeed made prose translations of Sophocles' other two Theban plays for performance at the Abbey, but he had not put his trade mark upon this one. So to that extent at least the road was open. But what gave me the poetic go-ahead was the sudden discovery of a note that connected the distressed heroine of Sophocles' tragedy in the fourth century BC and the author of the great eighteenth century lament we know by its Irish title, *Caoineadh Airt Uí Laoghaire*.

Meanwhile, there was a third, more general consideration. Early in 2003, the situation that pertains in Sophocles' play was being re-enacted in our own world. Just as Creon forced the citizens of Thebes into an either/or situation in relation to Antigone, the Bush administration in the White House was using the same tactic to forward its argument for war in Iraq. Creon puts it to the Chorus in these terms: either you are a patriot, a loyal citizen and regard Antigone as an enemy of the state because she does honour to her traitor brother, or else you yourselves are traitorous because you stand up for a woman who has broken the law and defied my authority. And Bush was using a similar strategy, asking, in effect: are you in favour of state security or are you not? If you don't support the eradication of this tyrant in Iraq and the threat he poses to the free world, you are on the wrong side in 'the war of terror'.

Creon, of course, has a point, and a responsibility. His tragedy, as the Chorus and others repeatedly point out, has to do with his overbearing rather than his basic position. In fact, the tragedy as a whole arises from the passion and extremity of the two main protagonists. Modern audiences are more sympathetic to Antigone's defiant embrace of the law of the gods, her instinctive affirmation of what we might now call a human right against the law and order requirements of the state, but in the dramatic balance that Sophocles achieves, Creon's sufferings weigh heavily and evenly in the scales.

Still, although there was a meaningful political context for a new translation, what was missing was an immediate writerly urge. And then all of a sudden it arrived. Theme and tune coalesced. I remembered the opening lines of Eibhlín Dhubh Ni Chonaill's lament, an outburst of grief and anger from a woman whose husband had been cut down and left bleeding on the roadside in Co. Cork, in much the same way as Polyneices was left outside the walls of Thebes, unburied, desecrated, picked at by the crows. But it was the drive and pitch of the Irish verse that clinched it: in the three-beat line of Eibhlín Dhubh's keen I heard a note that the stricken Antigone might sound in the speedy, haunted opening movement of the play:

> Mo ghrá go daingean thú!
> Lá da bhfaca thú
> Ag ceann ti an mhargaidh,
> Thug mo shúil aire dhuit,
> Thug mo chroí taitneamh duit,
> D'éalaíos óm chairaid leat
> I bhfad ó bhaile leat.

In Frank O'Connor's translation this goes:

> My love and my delight,
> The day I saw you first
> Beside the markethouse

> I had eyes for nothing else
> And love for none but you.
>
> I left my father's house
> And ran away with you,
> And that was no bad choice ...

Gradually then, this voice of a woman in mourning becomes the voice of a woman outraged, as she finds the body of her beloved lying beside a little furze bush, dead, without the last rites, without anyone close except 'an old, old woman/And her cloak about you.'

Because of the pitch of that voice, however, I made a connection between the wife traumatized by the death of her husband at the hands of the English soldiery in Carriganimma and the sister driven wild by the edict of a tyrant in Thebes; and through that connection I found the metre for the first dialogue between Antigone and Ismene:

> Ismene, quick, come here!
> What's to become of us?

Admittedly, there's nothing very distinct about this speech, but the three-beat lines established a tune. And with a first tune established, it was then easy enough to play variations, making the Chorus, for example, speak a version of the four-beat, alliterating, Old English line:

> Glory be to brightness, to the gleaming sun
> Shining guardian of our seven gates
> Burn away the darkness, dawn on Thebes,
> Dazzle the city you have saved from destruction.

This was an echo of the metre that Anglo-Saxon poets used for their grim old pagan wisdom and their new Christian hymns of praise, and it therefore seemed right for a Chorus whose function involves both the utterance of proverbial wisdom and the invocation of gods. Just as the traditional iambic pentameter, with its conventional *tee-tum, tee-tum, tee-tum* seemed right for Creon, who needs to hold the line in every sense, 'to honour patriots in life and death'.

Greek tragedy is as much musical score as it is dramatic script. I wanted to do a translation that actors could speak as plainly or intensely as the occasion demanded, but one that still kept faith with the ritual formality of the original. I was glad, therefore, to find corroboration for this effort in Yeats's sonnet 'At the Abbey Theatre', where he expressed the conflicting demands placed upon his theatre as follows:

> When we are high and airy hundreds say
> That if we hold that flight they'll leave the place,

While those same hundreds mock another day
Because we have made our art of common things.

Source: Seamus Heaney (2004) Programme note for the Abbey Theatre production of *The Burial at Thebes*, 2004.

Reading 6.7 'Me' as in 'Metre': on translating *Antigone*

Verse translation is not all that different from original composition. In order to get a project under way, there has to be a note to which the lines, and especially the first lines, can be tuned. Until this register is established, your words may well constitute a satisfactory semantic equivalent but they cannot induce that blessed sensation of being on the right track, musically and rhythmically.

Readers recognise this rightness immediately. We share vicariously in the promise of openings such as 'It is an ancient mariner/And he stoppeth one of three', or 'I will arise and go now and go to Innisfree' or 'Gile na, gile do chonnaic ar slí an uaignis'. We know intuitively that when the poets wrote those lines they were feeling what D.H. Lawrence felt at the start of his 'Song of a Man who has Come Through': 'Not I, not I, but the wind that blows through me ...' Or, to put it another way – and to quote a different poet – the gift of the right opening line helps the poet and the translator of poetry to escape from what Robert Lowell called 'the glassy bowing and scraping' of the will into a 'maze of composition' led by an 'incomparable wandering voice'.

When he wrote in those terms, Lowell was thinking of Racine, a 'man of craft' who was helped beyond craft when he found a voice for the ancient Greek heroine of his seventeenth-century tragedy, *Phèdre*. Racine may not have been translating but even so, writing lines for a character in a play still requires some displacement of the dramatist's own voice. The two jobs have at least that much in common.

I discovered this for myself recently when I was trying to get started on a translation of *Antigone*. The invitation to do this job came from Ben Barnes at the Abbey Theatre. In 2004 the Abbey was celebrating its centenary and the artistic director wanted to have at least one classical tragedy in the centennial repertoire. I was honoured to be asked, and was attracted to the commission, not least because W.B. Yeats had done versions of Sophocles' two other Theban plays for the theatre, but I still wasn't sure how to respond. How many *Antigones* could Irish theatre put up with? Round about the time the idea was floated, Conall Morrison was touring his adaptation, setting the action in a Middle Eastern context; and a couple of years previously I had read in manuscript Marianne McDonald's unflashy and illuminating translation, where the introduction and footnotes revealed how usefully her scholar's knowledge had paid into her theatrical instincts. And if that were not enough, there was also Marianne McDonald's essay on '*Antigones*' to remind me that Brendan Kennelly, Tom Paulin and Aidan Carl Mathews had already been down the road to Thebes, so why start down it yet again?

One consideration weighed heavily in favour of a new start. Early in 2003 we were watching a leader, a Creon figure if ever there was one, a law-and-order bossman trying to boss the nations of the world into uncritical agreement with his edicts in much the same way as Creon tries to boss the Chorus of compliant Thebans into conformity with his. With the White House and the Pentagon in cahoots, determined to bring the rest of us into line over Iraq, the disposition and passion of an Antigone were all of a sudden as vital as oxygen masks, so I soon found myself doing a version of the 'wonders chorus' and publishing it as a sort of open letter to George Bush:

> let him once
> Overbear or overstep
>
> What the city allows, treat law
> As something he can decide for himself –
> Then let this wonder of the world remember:
> When he comes begging we will turn our backs.

By the time I had reached that part of the work, however, I was already at the keeping-going stage. Getting started was the problem that had to be solved first.

I was to see Ben Barnes on a Monday afternoon in January and on the Sunday night I still wasn't sure what I should say to him. Even though there was an urgent political context, there was no writerly urge. I was reading desultorily about the play in various essays and Introductions and glazing over as again and again the old familiar topics came swimming up: individual conscience versus civil power, men versus women, the domestic versus the public sphere, the relevance of the action in times of crisis, in France, in Russia, in Poland, in Northern Ireland – of course, of course, of course. But why do it again? Indeed, how do it again, if there wasn't a tuning fork?

And then I heard it, and inside seconds I had a pen in my hand and had done the three opening lines. Theme and tune coalesced. Purchase on a language, a confidence amounting almost to a carelessness, a found pitch – all arrived in a breath. 'Not I, not I,' I could have exclaimed, 'but the wind that blows through me.' What had got me going was not my study of the text of the play or the criticism surrounding it, but the words and rhythms of another work entirely. I suddenly remembered the opening lines of Eibhlín Dhubh Ní Chonaill's 'Caoineadh Airt Uí Laoghaire' (Lament for Art O'Leary), lines that are both a feat of rhetoric and a spontaneous outburst of grief, the lament of an eighteenth-century woman whose husband has been cut down and left bleeding, much as Polyneices was left outside the walls of Thebes, unattended, desecrated, picked at by the crows.

> Mo ghrá go daingean thú!
> Lá dá bhfaca thú
> Ag ceann tí an mhargaidh,
> Thug mo shúil aire dhuit,
> Thug mo chroí taitneamh duit,
> D'éalaíos óm chairaid leat
> I bhfad ó bhaile leat.
>
> Is domhsa nárbh aithreach:
> Chuiris parlús á ghealadh dhom,
> Rúmanna á mbreacadh dhom,
> Bácús á dheargadh dhom.

In Frank O'Connor's translation this goes:

> My love and my delight,
> The day I saw you first
> Beside the markethouse
> I had eyes for nothing else
> And love for none but you.
>
> I left my father's house
> And ran away with you,
> And that was no bad choice;
> You gave me everything.
> There were parlours whitened for me,
> Bedrooms palmed for me,
> Ovens reddened for me.

As the poem proceeds, this cadence of lamentation heightens and gathers, an indeflectible outpouring of rage and grief. It is the voice of woman as mourner and woman as avenging fury, a woman fierce in her devotion to a beloved whom she eventually finds lying beside a little furze bush, dead without the last rites, nobody close except

> an old, old woman
> And her cloak about you.

In a flash I saw refracted in Eibhlín Dhubh the figure of the stricken Antigone, and heard in the three-beat line of her keen the note that Antigone might strike at the start of the proposed translation. There was no distinction at that moment between the excitement I felt at the discovery of the trimeter as the right metre for the opening and the analogies I could sense between the predicaments of a sister affronted by a tyrant in Thebes and a wife bereft by English soldiery in Carriganimma in County Cork. Just then, much that I had read in the commentaries was, as Wordsworth might have put it, 'felt along the blood': the contrast between the language of feeling that is spoken by Antigone and her sister Ismene and the language of power used by Creon, the furious compulsion to give the dead their due that overrides every thought of self-preservation, the imperatives of family and religion over the impositions of state authority – all of these things were momentarily palpable and in prospect because of the note I had just heard.

Inside a few minutes I had sample lines to show to the artistic director

> Ismene, quick, come here!
> What's to become of us?
> Why are we always the ones?

Nothing spectacular, admittedly, but the three-beat lines generated a desire to do more of them. And in my excitement I decided there and then that the obvious metre for the Chorus was the four-beat, Old English alliterative line, the line of the veteran Anglo-Saxons, gnomic and grim, but capable also of a certain clangour and glamour. So before I rose from the desk, I had a sample of the first stasimon to bring to the Abbey the next day as well:

> Glory be to brightness, to the gleaming sun,
> Shining guardian of our seven gates.
> Burn away the darkness, dawn on Thebes,
> Dazzle the city you have saved from destruction.

For Creon I didn't even bother with a trial run: blank verse it had to be, iambic pentameter, the obvious medium 'to honour patriots in life and death'. From then on all I had to do was to keep going, which meant getting started again and again in the course of the next three months. To help me with the sense, I kept to hand three earlier translations, those by Jebb, by Hugh Lloyd-Jones (in the Loeb edition) and E.F. Watling (in the old Penguin Classics), but without that first power surge coming through me ('me' as in 'metre') not even those authorities would have been of any use.

Source: Seamus Heaney (2005) '"Me" as in "Metre": on translating *Antigone*', in John Dillon and S.E. Wilmer (eds) *Rebel Women: Staging Ancient Greek Drama Today*, London, Methuen, pp. 169–73.

Reading 6.8 From the 'Antigone'

OVERCOME – O bitter sweetness,
Inhabitant of the soft cheek of a girl –
The rich man and his affairs,
The fat flocks and the fields' fatness,
Mariners, rough harvesters;
Overcome Gods upon Parnassus;

Overcome the Empyrean; hurl
Heaven and Earth out of their places,

That in the same calamity
Brother and brother, friend and friend,
Family and family,
City and city may contend,
By that great glory driven wild.

Pray I will and sing I must,
And yet I weep – Oedipus' child
Descends into the loveless dust.

Source: W.B. Yeats (1963 [1933]) 'From the "Antigone"', in *The Collected Poems of W.B. Yeats*, London, Macmillan, p. 315.

Reading 6.9 Beginning to hope

Our amateur drama society made its yearly offering at Christmas. My thespian career, which had lain dormant since I played John Wilkes Booth while at Fort Hare, had a modest revival on Robben Island. Our productions were what might now be called minimalist: no stage, no scenery, no costumes. All we had was the text of the play.

I performed in only a few dramas, but I had one memorable role: that of Creon, the king of Thebes, in Sophocles' *Antigone*. I had read some of the classic Greek plays in prison, and found them enormously elevating. What I took out of them was that character was measured by facing up to difficult situations and that a hero was a man who would not break down even under the most trying circumstances.

When *Antigone* was chosen as the play I volunteered my services, and was asked to play Creon, an elderly king fighting a civil war over the throne of his beloved city-state. At the outset, Creon is sincere and patriotic, and there is wisdom in his early speeches when he suggests that experience is the foundation of leadership and that obligations to the people take precedence over loyalty to an individual.

> Of course you cannot know a man completely, his character, his principles, sense of judgement, not till he's shown his colours, ruling the people, making laws. Experience, there's the test.

But Creon deals with his enemies mercilessly. He has decreed that the body of Polynices, Antigone's brother, who had rebelled against the city, does not deserve a proper burial. Antigone rebels, on the grounds that there is a higher law than that of the state. Creon will not listen to Antigone, neither does he listen to anyone but his own inner demons. His inflexibility and blindness ill become a leader, for a leader must temper justice with mercy. It was Antigone who symbolized our struggle; she was, in her own way, a freedom fighter, for she defied the law on the ground that it was unjust.

Source: Nelson Mandela (1994) *Long Walk to Freedom: The Autobiography of Nelson Mandela*, London, Abacus, pp. 540–1.

Reading 6.10 *The Burial at Thebes*, The Abbey Theatre, Dublin

SEAMUS HEANEY'S new translation of Antigone has set every possible contemporary vibration of Sophocles' classical tragedy humming.

'He that is not with me is against me,' is how King Creon sees anyone who would side with Antigone, or would help in any way her struggle for justice. And while pedants might point out that it is Matthew's Gospel, rather than George W. Bush, that takes credit for coining the phrase, when Heaney blends the phrase into his translation, it seems unlikely that he is referring simply to the Good Book.

The poet whose political attitude was once defined as 'whatever you say, say nothing' now appears to be saying that he stands against the tyranny of Bush and those who fail to speak against it. But don't expect the Nobel Laureate to start chucking rocks. Instead, Heaney has endowed the drama with smooth Irish linguistic figures and given it a terrible, frighteningly global import.

The Canadian director Lorraine Pintal provides a new staging (with elements of dance theatre) that usefully enhances Heaney's contemporary urgency without sacrificing a deeply sophisticated sense of timeless rage. The designer Carl Fillion aids the campaign with a set of soaring 'concrete' walls, at the bunker-like foot of which we find the people of Thebes.

Source: Luke Clancy (2004) review of 'The Burial at Thebes', *The Times*, 7 April, p. 15.

Reading 6.11 *The Burial at Thebes*, Playhouse, Nottingham

Sophocles was over 50 when Antigone, his second surviving play, triumphed at the Festival of Dionysus. In its uncompromising view of the immutable laws of gods and men, it belongs to an early age of tragedy, a[n] era in which irreconcilable positions clash and all human parties fall victim.

Surprisingly, the gods are absent; there is no prologue, no initial homily. In Seamus Heaney's new translation, *The Burial at Thebes*, penned for the Dublin Abbey Theatre centenary last year and here receiving its British premiere, we are pitched straight into the warring sisters: Ismene, who holds that 'In the land of the living the laws of the land obtain', and Antigone, loyal not to human edicts, but to 'the power that sees all'.

Jessica Curtis's set, 'a mirror image of a Greek theatre, the action taking place on a semi-circular orchestra (dance floor)', supplies a spare, subdued stone-grey background, against which the cast don grey chorus cloaks to speak, sing and dance, then shed chorus garb one by one to assume principal roles. The characters seem almost elemental, as if hewn out of the rocky background; especially effective when Murray Melvin's blind Tiresias confronts Michael Byrne's posturing Creon and dents his breezy self-confidence near the play's close.

The power of Lucy Pitman-Wallace's beautifully crafted production rests in the way she lets Sophocles' lines speak for themselves. Characters, notably Daniel Rigby's doomed Haemon, facing up to his frosty father, do a ritual prowl to introduce themselves before launching in. But action is reined in to a minimum.

Mick Sands' chorus music feels elemental too, superbly sung or intoned by the cast, with lute or solo flute accompaniment. Heaney's chorus metres work wondrously well; some spare three-part chanting, and even in one instance a feel of Irish folksong.

Jodie McNee's Antigone and Michelle Terry's Ismene imposingly lay down the ground rules for this political set-to. Joan Moon's brief blossoming as Eurydice, Creon's hapless spouse, brings added agony to the denouement.

But it's Byrne's smug Creon who unleashes this flood of mishaps. At the outset, he positively preens, basking in the crowd accolades like some dreary demagogue, sputtering doom-laden decrees. Draped in dogma, he looks increasingly like a shipwrecked mariner. What makes Sophocles' version so searingly tragic is that Creon changes his mind. He gives in. But by then, it's too late.

Source: Roderic Dunnett (2005) review of 'The Burial at Thebes', *Independent*, 21 November, p. 48.

Media notes

Glossary for the Audio CD

Bernadette Devlin a young Irish nationalist civil rights leader in the protests of the 1960s. She was subsequently elected to the Westminster Parliament.

Robert Henryson (d. *c.*1508) an important Middle Scots poet and a member of the group sometimes later referred to as the Scottish Chaucerians. His best-known poem is *The Testament of Cresseid* (a variation on Chaucer's *Troilus and Criseyde*). Other works included *The Morall Fabillis of Esope the Phrygian* and *Orpheus and Eurydice* as well as didactic religious allegories. He may have been a schoolmaster and was knowledgeable about the works of the Early Church Fathers.

Lament for Art O'Leary the English translation of the title of Eibhlín Dhubh Ní Chonaill's eighteenth-century Irish poem 'Caoineadh Airt Uí Laoghaire'. It is a lament by a wife for her husband, who was shot and left by the road because he refused to sell his swift horse to Abraham Morris, the High Sheriff of Cork. The keen expresses both the love of the widow for her husband and her desire for revenge against the authorities. It starts as an eulogy and moves to a call for justice.

AFTERWORD

Richard Danson Brown

Book 3 has taken you through a series of cultural encounters, moving across huge periods of time and differing places. You've considered Seamus Heaney's 2004 CE translation of Sophocles' *Antigone*, first performed as long ago as 442 BCE; the transmission of ancient medical knowledge from Greece to the Islamic world and back again to Europe; the conquest of Benin in the late nineteenth century and the changing ways in which the art of Benin has been displayed. In the chapters on 'Cultural Exemptions' and 'Short Stories', you've seen that the modern world is shaped and represented by shifting, dynamic philosophical traditions such as liberalism, and by literary forms, the origins of which stretch back into the remote past. The study of the Arts entails long historical and broad geographical perspectives. We don't expect you to hold all these perspectives in your mind at once, but you might think about the similarities and differences between these chapters, and the extent to which they differ from the work you've done on Books 1 and 2.

As you have been engaging in these debates, you have also been developing a comparably broad range of skills. The chapters on Benin and *The Burial at Thebes* have involved you in interdisciplinary study; through your work on this material, you will have begun to appreciate some of the advantages as well as the challenges of working in this way. At the same time, you have begun to write longer essays, choosing topics that reflect the subjects you enjoy most. Such choices will become more important in Book 4, *Place and Leisure*. This course has been designed to give you a taster of all the different Arts disciplines, and you should now start thinking about which future courses look attractive to you and why.

For now, you might wish to start this work by making notes about your impressions of interdisciplinary study. You'll have the opportunity for further interdisciplinary work when you turn to 'The Seaside' in Book 4.

GLOSSARY

aesthetic pertaining to the appreciation or criticism of the beautiful as distinct from the study of the good (ethics) or the true (the rational or human sciences). Here, it is being used to mean a concern with the form or appearance of art rather than any religious or political purpose which a work of art may fulfil.

agon pair of opposing speeches by two main characters.

anthropology a branch of natural sciences concerned with the study of mankind through a close analysis of human society and through comparisons between cultures over time.

aquamanile a vessel for pouring water, for example in ritual ceremonies.

argument by analogy an argument by analogy starts from the premise that two cases are alike. It is then claimed that something that is true of one must therefore be true of the other. Arguments by analogy are not deductive arguments.

autonomy self-rule. I act autonomously if I act in the way that I choose to act.

compendia a collection of texts or extracts from texts, brought together into a single manuscript or printed book.

craniometry the study and measurement of the skull.

cultural exemption an exemption to a law or public policy granted to members of a particular cultural group in order to protect their cultural identity or religious practices.

dialect a distinctive variety of language shared by people in a particular group, usually regional, but sometimes related to social class.

difference-blind liberalism a specific version of liberalism that centres on the claim that laws and public policies should treat everyone in the same way, regardless of gender, ethnicity, culture or religion.

episode a substantial scene, usually preceded and followed by Choral Odes.

ethnography a method of anthropology. The term is also used to refer to the end product of this study such as a text or a museum display. In the nineteenth century the term was often used to refer to the study of the thoughts and customs of societies through objects, artefacts and observation. Ethnographers studied objects and actions in the context of their purpose and function in forming comparative judgements on the nature of human societies.

exodos closing scene.

factor a trading agent or representative.

fetish the word in its West African origin means 'an amulet or means of enchantment', which (in contrast to an idol) 'is worshipped in its own character, not as an image, symbol, or occasional residence of a deity' (*Oxford English Dictionary*). The term was often used by Europeans to describe all West African religions and their associated ceremonies.

first-person narrative a story told from the point of view of a participant or witness, who uses 'I' when referring to her/himself.

Guinea traditional name given to the region of West Africa which stretches along the Gulf of Guinea.

Hellenistic literally, 'Greekish'. Includes areas beyond Greece where Greek ideas and the Greek language dominated in the post-classical period and in late antiquity.

humours the four fluids believed to determine health and disease. **Humoural medicine** is the system of medical theory and practice built on the idea of humours.

Juju according to the *Oxford English Dictionary*, a juju is 'an object of any kind venerated by West African native peoples, and used as a charm, amulet, or means of protection'.

kommos a lament.

lexis the total word-stock of a particular language (adjective: lexical). **Lexicon** is the more limited word-stock of a particular speaker, region, activity, etc.

liberalism a philosophical tradition that stresses the rights of the individual, the value of personal freedom or autonomy, and the idea that every human being is of equal moral worth.

lyric poetry unlike narrative or dramatic poetry, lyric poetry is concerned less with events or action, and more with moods, perceptions and feelings.

Messenger speech vivid description of action which has taken place off-stage.

Oba the title given to the ruler of Benin.

parodos entry of the Chorus singing their first song.

pharmacopeia a book listing drugs and their uses. Also known as books of *materia medica*.

phrenology a nineteenth-century pseudo-science which set out to study the shape of the cranium as a supposed measure of character and ability.

prologue opening scene.

realist writing that represents human life, experience and the world generally in an accurate, recognisable way.

register a distinctive use of language, written or spoken, for a particular situation.

rhesis main speech delivered by one character.

rule and exemption approach an approach to cultural diversity based on the following principle: while, in general, laws and public policies should apply to all, cultural exemptions may sometimes be granted to members of minority cultural groups in order to protect their cultural identity or religious practices.

Sapi the name given by Portuguese traders to the inhabitants of Sierra Leone.

satyr play the fourth and final play in the sequence presented each day of the ancient drama festivals. The actors represented satyrs, wild followers of Dionysus who had the ears and tails of horses, snub noses and unkempt hair. Hardly any evidence survives about the content of these plays (except for Euripides' *Cyclops*) but they probably involved a carnivalesque humour and release from the tensions of the preceding tragedies.

stasimon (plural ***stasima***) a structured Choral Ode in verse (in Greek theatre this was sung, with dance).

stichomythia short exchange (usually one or two lines between main characters).

third-person narrative a story told 'from the outside', using a narrator who is not part of the action of the story.

transliteration involves translating letters from one alphabet into another – for example from Greek to Arabic – and thereby produces new and unfamiliar terms.

ACKNOWLEDGEMENTS

Grateful acknowledgement is made to the following sources for permission to reproduce material in this book.

Chapter 1

de Pina, R. *Chronicles del Tey Dom Joao II*. Translated in Blake (1942). By permission of Oxford University Press.

Ryder, A.F.C. (1969) *Benin and the Europeans 1485–1897*. Copyright © 1969 Pearson Education Limited. Reproduced by permission.

Chapter 6

Battersby, E. 'A Greek tragedy for our times', *The Irish Times*, 3 April 2004.

'A note by Seamus Heaney', *Antigone: The Abbey Theatre Programme*, 2004. Used by permission of the author.

Heaney, S. (2005) '"Me" as in "Metre": On Translating *Antigone*', in Dillon, J. and Wilmer, S.E. (eds) *Rebel Women: Staging Ancient Greek Drama Today*, Methuen. Copyright © 2005 John Dillon and S. E. Wilmer. Used with permission of Methuen Drama, an imprint of A&C Black Publishers.

Clancy, L. 'The Burial at Thebes', *The Times*, 7 April 2004, p. 15. Copyright © Clancy, L./NI Syndication Limited, 2004.

Dunnett, R. 'Theatre: The Burial at Thebes; Playhouse Nottingham', *The Independent*, 21 November 2005, p. 48. Copyright © 2005 The Independent.

Every effort has been made to contact copyright holders. If any have been inadvertently overlooked the publishers will be pleased to make the necessary arrangements at the first opportunity.

INDEX

Page numbers in **bold** refer to figures.